D1215462

INTRODUCTION TO LATTICE THEORY WITH COMPUTER SCIENCE APPLICATIONS

INTRODUCTION TO LATTICE THEORY WITH COMPUTER SCIENCE APPLICATIONS

VIJAY K. GARG
Department of Electrical and Computer Engineering
The University of Texas at Austin

Published by John Wiley & Sons, Inc., Hoboken, New Jersey
Published simultaneously in Canada

For general information on our other products and services or for technical support, please contact our Customer Care Department within the United States at (800) 762-2974, outside the United States at (317) 572-3993 or fax (317) 572-4002.

Wiley also publishes its books in a variety of electronic formats. Some content that appears in print may not be available in electronic formats. For more information about Wiley products, visit our web site at www.wiley.com.

Library of Congress Cataloging-in-Publication Data:

Garg, Vijay K. (Vijay Kumar), 1963-
  Introduction to lattice theory with computer science applications / Vijay K. Garg.
      pages cm
  Includes bibliographical references and index.
  ISBN 978-1-118-91437-3 (cloth)
  1. Computer science–Mathematics. 2. Engineering mathematics. 3. Lattice theory. I. Title.
  QA76.9.L38G37 2015
  004.01′51–dc23
                                                                                2015003602

Printed in the United States of America

10 9 8 7 6 5 4 3 2 1

1   2015

To my family

CONTENTS

LIST OF FIGURES

NOMENCLATURE

$\perp$	Bottom element of the lattice
$J(P)$	Set of join-irreducible elements of a poset P
L_I	Lattice of ideals
L_{DM}	Lattice of normal cuts
L_{MA}	Lattice of maximal antichains
L_{WA}	Lattice of width antichains
$M(P)$	Set of meet-irreducible elements of a poset P
$\sqcap$	Meet
$\sqcup$	Join
$\top$	Top element of the lattice
$\underline{n}$	A poset consisting of a single chain of length n
$a \sim_P b$	a is comparable to b in P
A^l	Set of lower bounds of A
A^u	Set of upper bounds of A
$D(x)$	Set of elements less than x
$D[x]$	Set of elements less than or equal to x
$DM(P)$	Dedekind–MacNeille Completion of P
P^d	Dual poset of P
$U(x)$	Set of elements greater than x
$U[x]$	Set of elements greater than or equal to x

PREFACE

As many books exist on lattice theory, I must justify writing another book on the subject. This book is written from the perspective of a computer scientist rather than a mathematician. In many instances, a mathematician may be satisfied with a nonconstructive existential proof, but a computer scientist is interested not only in construction but also in the computational complexity of the construction. I have attempted to give "algorithmic" proofs of theorems whenever possible.

This book is also written for the sake of students rather than a practicing mathematician. In many instances, a student needs to learn the heuristics that guide the proof, besides the proof itself. It is not sufficient just to learn an important theorem. One must also learn ways to extend and analyze a theorem. I have also made an effort to include exercises with each chapter. A mathematical subject can only be learned by solving problems related to that subject.

I would like to thank the students at the University of Texas at Austin, who took my course on lattice theory. I also thank my co-authors for various papers related to lattice theory and applications in distributed computing: Anurag Agarwal, Arindam Chakraborty, Yen-Jung Chang, Craig Chase, Himanshu Chauhan, Selma Ikiz, Ratnesh Kumar, Neeraj Mittal, Sujatha Kashyap, Vinit Ogale, Alper Sen, Alexander Tomlinson, and Brian Waldecker. I owe special thanks to Bharath Balasubramanina, Vinit Ogale, Omer Shakil, Alper Sen, and Roopsha Samanta who reviewed parts of the book.

I thank the Department of Electrical and Computer Engineering at The University of Texas at Austin, where I was given the opportunity to develop and teach a course on lattice theory.

I have also been supported in part by many grants from the National Science Foundation. This book would not have been possible without that support.

Finally, I thank my parents, wife, and children. Without their love and support, this book would not have been even conceived.

The list of known errors and the supplementary material for the book will be maintained on my homepage:

`http://www.ece.utexas.edu/~garg`

VIJAY K. GARG
AUSTIN, TEXAS.

1

INTRODUCTION

1.1 INTRODUCTION

Partial order and lattice theory play an important role in many disciplines of computer science and engineering. For example, they have applications in distributed computing (vector clocks and global predicate detection), concurrency theory (pomsets and occurrence nets), programming language semantics (fixed-point semantics), and data mining (concept analysis). They are also useful in other disciplines of mathematics such as combinatorics, number theory, and group theory.

This book differs from earlier books written on the subject in two aspects. First, this book takes a computational perspective—the emphasis is on algorithms and their complexity. While mathematicians generally identify necessary and sufficient conditions to characterize a property, this book focuses on efficient algorithms to test the property. As a result of this bias, much of the book concerns itself only with finite sets. Second, existing books do not dwell on applications of lattice theory. This book treats applications at par with the theory. In particular, I have given applications of lattice theory to distributed computing and combinatorics.

This chapter covers the basic definitions of partial orders.

Introduction to Lattice Theory with Computer Science Applications, First Edition. Vijay K. Garg.
© 2015 John Wiley & Sons, Inc. Published 2015 by John Wiley & Sons, Inc.

1.2   RELATIONS

A partial order is simply a relation with certain properties. A **relation** R over any set X is a subset of $X \times X$. For example, let

$$X = \{a, b, c\}.$$

Then, one possible relation is

$$R = \{(a, c), (a, a), (b, c), (c, a)\}.$$

It is sometimes useful to visualize a relation as a graph on the vertex set X such that there is a directed edge from x to y iff $(x, y) \in R$. The graph corresponding to the relation R in the previous example is shown in Figure 1.1.

A relation is **reflexive** if for each $x \in X$, $(x, x) \in R$, i.e., each element of X is related to itself. In terms of a graph, this means that there is a self-loop on each node. If X is the set of natural numbers, $\mathcal{N}$, then "x *divides* y" is a reflexive relation. R is **irreflexive** if for each $x \in X$, $(x, x) \notin R$. In terms of a graph, this means that there are no self-loops. An example on the set of natural numbers, $\mathcal{N}$, is the relation "x *less than* y." Note that a relation may be neither reflexive nor irreflexive.

A relation R is **symmetric** if for all $x, y \in X$, $(x, y) \in R$ implies $(y, x) \in R$. An example of a symmetric relation on $\mathcal{N}$ is

$$R = \{(x, y) \mid x \bmod 5 = y \bmod 5\}. \tag{1.1}$$

A symmetric relation can be represented using an undirected graph. R is **antisymmetric** if for all $x, y \in X$, $(x, y) \in R$ and $(y, x) \in R$ implies $x = y$. For example, the relation *less than or equal to* defined on $\mathcal{N}$ is anti-symmetric. A relation R is **asymmetric** if for all $x, y \in X$, $(x, y) \in R$ implies $(y, x) \notin R$. The relation *less than* on $\mathcal{N}$ is asymmetric. Note that an asymmetric relation is always irreflexive.

A relation R is **transitive** if for all $x, y, z \in X$, $(x, y) \in R$ and $(y, z) \in R$ implies $(x, z) \in R$. The relations *less than* and *equal to* on $\mathcal{N}$ are transitive.

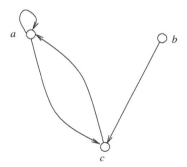

Figure 1.1   The graph of a relation.

A relation R is an **equivalence** relation if it is reflexive, symmetric, and transitive. When R is an equivalence relation, we use $x \equiv_R y$ (or simply $x \equiv y$ when R is clear from the context) to denote that $(x, y) \in R$. Furthermore, for each $x \in X$, we use $[x]_R$, called the **equivalence class of** x, to denote the set of all $y \in X$ such that $y \equiv_R x$. It can be seen that the set of all such equivalence classes forms a **partition** of X. The relation on $\mathcal{N}$ defined in (1.1) is an example of an equivalence relation. It partitions the set of natural numbers into five equivalence classes.

Given any relation R on a set X, we define its **irreflexive transitive closure**, denoted by R^+, as follows. For all $x, y \in X : (x, y) \in R^+$ iff there exists a sequence $x_0, x_1, ..., x_j, j \geq 1$ with $x_0 = x$ and $x_j = y$ such that

$$\forall i : 0 \leq i < j : (x_i, x_{i+1}) \in R.$$

Thus $(x, y) \in R^+$, iff there is a nonempty path from x to y in the graph of the relation R. We define the **reflexive transitive closure**, denoted by R^*, as

$$R^* = R^+ \cup \{(x, x) \mid x \in X\}.$$

Thus $(x, y) \in R^*$ iff y is reachable from x by taking a path with zero or more edges in the graph of the relation R.

1.3 PARTIAL ORDERS

A relation R is a **reflexive partial order** (or, a **nonstrict partial order**) if it is reflexive, antisymmetric, and transitive. The *divides* relation on the set of natural numbers is a reflexive partial order. A relation R is an **irreflexive partial order**, or a **strict partial order** if it is irreflexive and transitive. The *less than* relation on the set of natural numbers is an irreflexive partial order. When R is a reflexive partial order, we use $x \leq_R y$ (or simply $x \leq y$ when R is clear from the context) to denote that $(x, y) \in R$. A reflexive partially ordered set, **poset** for short, is denoted by $(X, \leq)$. When R is an irreflexive partial order, we use $x <_R y$ (or simply $x < y$ when R is clear from the context) to denote that $(x, y) \in R$. The set X together with the partial order is denoted by $(X, <)$. We use $P = (X, <)$ to denote a irreflexive poset defined on X.

The two versions of partial orders—reflexive and irreflexive—are essentially the same. Given an irreflexive partial order, we can define $x \leq y$ as $x < y$ or $x = y$, which gives us a reflexive partial order. Similarly, given a reflexive partial order $(X, \leq)$, we can define an irreflexive partial order $(X, <)$ by defining $x < y$ as $x \leq y$ and $x \neq y$.

A relation is a **total order** if R is a partial order and for all distinct $x, y \in X$, either $(x, y) \in R$ or $(y, x) \in R$. The natural order on the set of integers is a total order, but the *divides* relation is only a partial order.

Finite posets are often depicted graphically using **Hasse diagrams**. To define Hasse diagrams, we first define a relation **covers** as follows. For any two elements $x, y \in X$, y covers x if $x < y$ and $\forall z \in X : x \leq z < y$ implies $z = x$. In other words, if y covers x then there should not be any element z with $x < z < y$. We use $x <_c y$ to

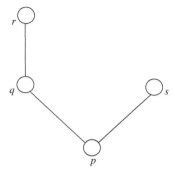

Figure 1.2   Hasse diagram.

denote that y covers x (or x is covered by y). We also say that y is an **upper cover** of x and x is a **lower cover** of y. A Hasse diagram of a poset is a graph with the property that there is an edge from x to y iff $x <_c y$. Furthermore, when drawing the graph on a Euclidean plane, x is drawn lower than y when y covers x. This allows us to suppress the directional arrows in the edges. For example, consider the following poset $(X, \leq)$,

$$X \stackrel{\text{def}}{=} \{p, q, r, s\}; \quad \leq \stackrel{\text{def}}{=} \{(p, q), (q, r), (p, r), (p, s)\}. \tag{1.2}$$

The corresponding Hasse diagram is shown in Figure 1.2. Note that we will sometimes use directed edges in Hasse diagrams if the context demands it. In general, in this book, we switch between the directed graph and undirected graph representations of Hasse diagrams.

Given a poset $(X, \leq_X)$ a **subposet** is simply a poset $(Y, \leq_Y)$, where $Y \subseteq X$, and

$$\forall x, y \in Y : x \leq_Y y \stackrel{\text{def}}{=} x \leq_X y.$$

Let $x, y \in X$ with $x \neq y$. If either $x < y$ or $y < x$, we say x and y are **comparable**. On the other hand, if neither $x < y$ nor $x > y$, then we say x and y are incomparable and write $x||y$. A poset $(Y, \leq)$ (or a subposet $(Y, \leq)$ of $(X, \leq)$) is called a **chain** if every distinct pair of elements from Y is comparable. Similarly, we call a poset an **antichain** if every distinct pair of elements from Y is incomparable. For example, for the poset represented in Figure 1.2, $\{p, q, r\}$ is a chain, and $\{q, s\}$ is an antichain.

A chain C of a poset $(X, \leq)$ is a **longest chain** if no other chain contains more elements than C. We use a similar definition for the **largest antichain**. The **height** of the poset is the number of elements in a longest chain, and the **width** of the poset is the number of elements in a largest antichain. For example, the poset in Figure 1.2 has height equal to 3 (the longest chain is $\{p, q, r\}$) and width equal to 2 (a largest antichain is $\{q, s\}$).

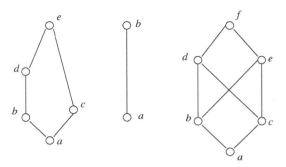

Figure 1.3   Only the first two posets are lattices.

Generalizing the notation for intervals on the real-line, we define an **interval** $[x, y]$ in a poset $(X, \leq)$ as

$$\{z \mid x \leq z \leq y\}.$$

The meanings of (x, y), $[x, y)$ and $(x, y]$ are similar. A poset is **locally finite** if all intervals are finite. Most posets in this book will be locally finite if not finite.

A poset is **well-founded** iff it has no infinite decreasing chain. The set of natural numbers under the usual $\leq$ relation is well-founded but the set of integers is not well-founded.

Poset $Q = (X, \leq_Q)$ **extends** the poset $P = (X, \leq_P)$ if

$$\forall x, y \in X : x \leq_P y \Rightarrow x \leq_Q y.$$

If Q is a total order, then we call Q a **linear extension** of P. For example, for the poset $P = (X, \leq)$ defined in Figure 1.2, a possible linear extension Q is

$$X \stackrel{\text{def}}{=} \{p, q, r, s\}; \quad \leq_Q \stackrel{\text{def}}{=} \{(p, q), (q, r), (p, r), (p, s), (q, s), (r, s)\}.$$

We now give some special posets that will be used as examples in the book.

- $\underline{n}$ denotes a poset which is a chain of length n. The second poset in Figure 1.3 is $\underline{2}$.
- We use A_n to denote the poset of n incomparable elements.

1.4   JOIN AND MEET OPERATIONS

We now define two operators on subsets of the set X—**meet** and **join**. The operator meet is also called **infimum** (or **inf**). Similarly, the operator join is also called **supremum** (or **sup**).

Let $Y \subseteq X$, where $(X, \leq)$ is a poset. For any $m \in X$, we say that $m = \inf Y$ iff

1. $\forall y \in Y : m \leq y$ and
2. $\forall m' \in X : (\forall y \in Y : m' \leq y) \Rightarrow m' \leq m$.

The condition (1) says that m is a lower bound of the set Y. The condition (2) says that if m' is any lower bound of Y, then it is less than or equal to m. For this reason, m is also called the **greatest lower bound** (*glb*) of the set Y. It is easy to check that the infimum of Y is unique whenever it exists. Observe that m is not required to be an element of Y.

The definition of sup is similar. For any $s \in X$, we say that $s = \sup Y$ iff

1. $\forall y \in Y : y \leq s$ and
2. $\forall s' \in X : (\forall y \in Y : y \leq s') \Rightarrow s \leq s'$.

Again, s is also called the **least upper bound** (*lub*) of the set Y. We denote the **glb** of $\{a, b\}$ by $a \sqcap b$ and **lub** of $\{a, b\}$ by $a \sqcup b$. In the set of natural numbers ordered by the *divides* relation, the *glb* corresponds to finding the greatest common divisor (gcd) and the *lub* corresponds to finding the least common multiple (lcm) of two natural numbers. The glb or the lub may not always exist. In Figure 1.2, the set $\{q, s\}$ does not have any upper bound. In the third poset in Figure 1.3, the set $\{b, c\}$ does not have any least upper bound (although both d and e are upper bounds).

The following lemma relates $\leq$ to the meet and join operators.

Lemma 1.1 (Connecting Lemma) *For all elements x, y of a poset,*

1. $x \leq y \equiv (x \sqcup y) = y$ *and*
2. $x \leq y \equiv (x \sqcap y) = x$.

Proof: For the first part, note that $x \leq y$ implies that y is an upper bound on $\{x, y\}$. It is also the lub because any upper bound of $\{x, y\}$ is greater than both x and y. Therefore, $(x \sqcup y) = y$. Conversely, $(x \sqcup y) = y$ means y is an upper bound on $\{x, y\}$. Therefore, $x \leq y$.

The proof for the second part is the dual of this proof.

∎

Lattices, which are special kinds of posets, can be defined using the join and meet operators as shown in the following discussion.

Definition 1.2 (Lattice) *A poset $(X, \leq)$ is a **lattice** iff $\forall x, y \in X : x \sqcup y$ and $x \sqcap y$ exist.*

The first two posets in Figure 1.3 are lattices, whereas the third one is not.

If $\forall x, y \in X : x \sqcup y$ exists, then we call it a *sup semilattice*. If $\forall x, y \in X : x \sqcap y$ exists, then we call it an *inf semilattice*.

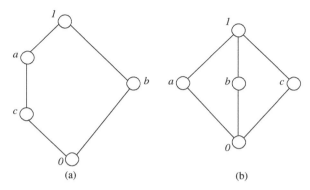

Figure 1.4 (a) Pentagon(N_5) and (b) diamond(M_3).

In our definition of lattice, we have required existence of *lub*'s and *glb*'s for sets of size two. This is equivalent to the requirement of existence of *lub*'s and *glb*'s for sets of finite size by using induction. A poset may be a lattice, but it may have sets of infinite size for which lub/glb may not exist. A simple example is that of the set of natural numbers. There is no lub of set of even numbers, even though glb and lub exist as min and max for any finite set. Another example is the set of rational numbers. For a finite subset of rational numbers, we can easily determine lubs(and glbs). However, consider the set $\{x \mid x \leq \sqrt{2}\}$. The lub of this set is $\sqrt{2}$, which is not a rational number. A lattice for which any set has lub and glb defined is called a *complete lattice*. An example of a complete lattice is the set of real numbers extended with $+\infty$ and $-\infty$.

Definition 1.3 (Distributive Lattice) *A lattice L is* **distributive** *if*

$$\forall a, b, c \in L : a \sqcap (b \sqcup c) = (a \sqcap b) \sqcup (a \sqcap c).$$

It is easy to verify that the above-mentioned condition is equivalent to

$$\forall a, b, c \in L : a \sqcup (b \sqcap c) = (a \sqcup b) \sqcap (a \sqcup c).$$

Thus, in a distributive lattice, $\sqcup$ and $\sqcap$ operators distribute over each other.

Any power-set lattice is distributive. The lattice of natural numbers with $\leq$ defined as the relation *divides* is also distributive. Some examples of nondistributive lattices are diamond (M_3) and pentagon (N_5) shown in Figure 1.4.

1.5 OPERATIONS ON POSETS

Given any set of structures, it is useful to consider ways of composing them to obtain new structures.

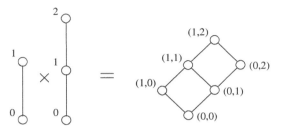

Figure 1.5   Cross product of posets.

Definition 1.4 (Disjoint Sum) *Given two posets P and Q, their* **disjoint sum,** *denoted by P + Q, is defined as follows. Given any two elements x and y in P + Q, $x \leq y$ iff*

(1) both x and y belong to P and $x \leq y$ in P or
(2) both x and y belong to Q and $x \leq y$ in Q.

The Hasse diagram of the disjoint sum of P and Q can be computed by simply placing the Hasse diagram of P next to Q.

Definition 1.5 (Cross Product of Posets) *Given two posets P and Q, the cross product denoted by $P \times Q$ is defined as*

$$(P \times Q, \leq_{P \times Q})$$

where

$$(p_1, q_1) \leq (p_2, q_2) \overset{\text{def}}{=} (p_1 \leq_P p_2) \wedge (q_1 \leq_Q q_2).$$

See Figure 1.5 for an example. The definition can be extended to an arbitrary indexing set.

Definition 1.6 (Linear Sum) *Given two posets P and Q, the* **linear sum** *(or ordinal sum) denoted by $P \oplus Q$ is defined as*

$$x \leq_{P \oplus Q} y \text{ iff } (x \leq_P y) \vee (x \leq_Q y) \vee [(x \in P) \wedge (y \in Q)].$$

1.6   IDEALS AND FILTERS

Let $(X, \leq)$ be any poset. We call a subset $Y \subseteq X$ a **down-set** if

$$\forall y, z \in X : z \in Y \wedge y \leq z \Rightarrow y \in Y.$$

Down-sets are also called **order ideals**. It is easy to see that for any x, $D[x]$ defined below is an order ideal. Such order ideals are called **principal order ideals,**

$$D[x] = \{y \in X \mid y \leq x\}.$$

For example, in Figure 1.2, $D[r] = \{p, q, r\}$. Similarly, we call $Y \subseteq X$ an **up-set** if

$$y \in Y \wedge y \leq z \Rightarrow z \in Y.$$

Up-sets are also called **order filters**. We also use the notation below to denote **principal order filters**

$$U[x] = \{y \in X | x \leq y\}.$$

In Figure 1.2, $U[p] = \{p, q, r, s\}$.

The following lemma provides a convenient relationship between principal order filters and other operators defined earlier.

Lemma 1.7   *1. $x \leq y \equiv U[y] \subseteq U[x]$*
      2. $x = \sup Y \equiv U[x] = \cap_{y \in Y} U[y]$.

Proof: Left as an exercise.

■

In some applications, the following notation is also useful:

$$U(x) = \{y \in X | x < y\}$$
$$D(x) = \{y \in X | y < x\}.$$

We will call $U(x)$ the **upper-holdings** of x, and $D(x)$, the **lower-holdings** of x. We can extend the definitions of $D[x], D(x), U[x], U(x)$ to sets of elements, A. For example,

$$U[A] = \{y \in X | \exists x \in A : x \leq y\}.$$

1.7   SPECIAL ELEMENTS IN POSETS

We define some special elements of posets such as bottom and top elements, and minimal and maximal elements.

Definition 1.8 (Bottom Element) *An element x is a* **bottom element** *or a* **minimum** *element of a poset P if $x \in P$, and*

$$\forall y \in P : x \leq y.$$

For example, 0 is the bottom element in the poset of whole numbers and Ø is the bottom element in the poset of all subsets of a given set W. Similarly, an element x is a **top element**, or a **maximum** element of a poset P if $x \in P$, and

$$\forall y \in P : y \leq x.$$

A bottom element of the poset is denoted by $\bot$ and the top element by $\top$. It is easy to verify that if bottom and top elements exist, they are unique.

Definition 1.9 (Minimal and Maximal Elements) *An element x is a* **minimal** *element of a poset P if*

$$\forall y \in P : y \not< x.$$

The minimum element is also a minimal element. However, a poset may have more than one minimal element. Similarly, an element x is a **maximal** *element of a poset P if*

$$\forall y \in P : y \not> x.$$

1.8   IRREDUCIBLE ELEMENTS

Definition 1.10 (Join-irreducible) *An element x is* **join-irreducible** *in P if it cannot be expressed as a join of other elements of P. Formally, x is join-irreducible if*

$$\forall Y \subseteq P : x = \sup Y \Rightarrow x \in Y.$$

Note that if a poset has $\bot$, then $\bot$ is not join-irreducible because when $Y = \{\}$, $\sup Y$ is $\bot$. The set of join-irreducible elements of a poset P will be denoted by $J(P)$. The first poset in Figure 1.3 has b,c and d as join-irreducible. The element e is not join-irreducible in the first poset because $e = b \sqcup c$. The second poset has b, and the third poset has b, c, d, and e as join-irreducible. It is easy to verify that $x \notin J(P)$ is equivalent to $x = \sup D(x)$. In a chain, all elements other than the bottom are join-irreducible.

By duality, we can define **meet-irreducible** elements of a poset, denoted by $M(P)$.

Loosely speaking, the set of (join)-irreducible elements forms a basis of the poset because all elements can be expressed using these elements. More formally,

Theorem 1.11 *Let P be a finite poset. Then, for any $x \in P$*

$$x = \sup(D[x] \cap J(P)).$$

Proof: Left as an exercise.

∎

An equivalent characterization of join-irreducible elements is as follows.

Theorem 1.12 *For a finite poset P, $x \in J(P)$ iff $\exists y \in P : x \in minimal(P - D[y])$.*

Proof: First assume that $x \in J(P)$.

Let $LC(x)$ be the set of elements covered by x. If $LC(x)$ is singleton, then choose that element as y. It is clear that $x \in minimal(P - D[y])$.

Now consider the case when $LC(x)$ is not singleton (it is empty or has more than one element). Let Q be the set of upper bounds for $LC(x)$. Q is not empty because $x \in Q$. Further, x is not the minimum element in Q because x is join-irreducible. Pick any element $y \in Q$ that is incomparable to x. Since $D[y]$ includes $LC(x)$ and not x, we get that x is minimal in $P - D[y]$.

The converse is left as an exercise.

∎

1.9 DISSECTOR ELEMENTS

We now define a subset of irreducibles called dissectors.

Definition 1.13 (Upper Dissector) *For a poset P, $x \in P$ is an* **upper dissector** *if there exists $y \in P$ such that*

$$P - U[x] = D[y].$$

In the above-mentioned definition, y is called a **lower dissector**. We will use dissectors to mean upper dissectors.

A dissector x decomposes the poset into two parts $U[x]$ and $D[y]$ for some y. In the first poset in Figure 1.3, b is an upper dissector because $P - U[b] = P - \{b, d, e\} = \{a, c\} = D[c]$. However, d is not an upper dissector because $P - U[d] = \{a, b, c\}$, which is not a principal ideal.

The following result is an easy implication of Theorem 1.12.

Theorem 1.14 *x is a dissector implies that x is join-irreducible.*

Proof: If x is an upper dissector, then there exists y such that x is minimum in $P - D[y]$. This implies that x is minimal in $P - D[y]$.

∎

1.10 APPLICATIONS: DISTRIBUTED COMPUTATIONS

As mentioned earlier, posets have a wide range of applications. In this book, we will focus on applications to distributed computing and combinatorics.

Partial order play an important role in distributed computing because a distributed computation is most profitably modeled as a partially ordered set of events. A distributed program consists of two or more processes running on different processors and communicating via messages. We will be concerned with a single computation of such a distributed program. Each process P_i in that computation generates a sequence of *events*. There are three types of events—*internal*, *send*, and *receive*. It is clear how to order events within a single process. If event e occurred before f in the process, then e is ordered before f. How do we order events across processes? If e is the send event of a message and f is the receive event of the same message, then we can order e before f. Combining these two ideas, we obtain the following definition.

Definition 1.15 (Happened-Before Relation) *The* **happened-before** *relation ($\rightarrow$) on a set of events E is the smallest relation on E that satisfies*

1. *If event e occurred before event f in the same process, then $e \rightarrow f$,*
2. *If e is the send event of a message and f is the receive event of the same message, then $e \rightarrow f$, and*
3. *If there exists an event g such that ($e \rightarrow g$) and ($g \rightarrow f$), then ($e \rightarrow f$).*

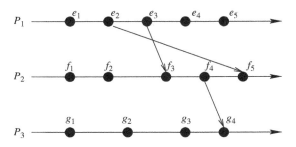

Figure 1.6   A computation in the happened-before model.

Formally, a *computation* in the happened-before model is defined as a tuple $(E, \rightarrow)$, where E is the set of all events and $\rightarrow$ is a partial order on events in E. Figure 1.6 illustrates a computation where $e_2 \rightarrow e_4$, $e_3 \rightarrow f_3$, and $e_1 \rightarrow g_4$.

Since a computation is a poset, all the concepts that we have defined for posets are applicable to distributed computations. For example, in distributed computing, the notion of a consistent global state is defined as follows.

Definition 1.16 *A **consistent global state** of a distributed computation $(E, \rightarrow)$ is any subset $G \subseteq E$ such that*

$$\forall e, f \in E : (f \in G) \wedge (e \rightarrow f) \Rightarrow (e \in G)$$

As the reader can verify, there is one-to-one correspondence between consistent global states and down-sets of a poset. Therefore, many results in lattice theory carry over to distributed computing. For example, the set of all down-sets of a poset forms a distributive lattice implies that the set of all consistent global states forms a distributive lattice.

1.11   APPLICATIONS: COMBINATORICS

We now discuss an example from combinatorics. Integer partitions have been studied in combinatorics for centuries. We show how we can use lattices to model sets of integer partitions.

Definition 1.17 (Partition) *An integer sequence $\lambda = (\lambda_1, ..., \lambda_k)$ is a **partition** of the integer n if*

 1. $\forall i \in [1, k-1] : \lambda_i \geq \lambda_{i+1}$
 2. $\sum_{i=1}^{k} \lambda_i = n$
 3. $\forall i : \lambda_i \geq 1$.

For example, $(5, 2, 2)$ and $(4, 3, 2)$ are two of the partitions of 9. Integer partitions are conveniently visualized using Ferrer's diagrams.

Figure 1.7   Ferrer's diagram for $(4, 3, 2)$ shown to contain $(2, 2, 2)$.

Definition 1.18 (Ferrer's Diagram) *A* **Ferrer's diagram** *for an integer partition* $\lambda = (\lambda_1, ..., \lambda_k)$ *of integer* n *is a matrix of dots where the ith row contains* λ_i *dots. Thus, row i represents the ith part and the number of rows represents the number of parts in the partition.*

We define an order on the partitions as follows: Given two partitions $\lambda = (\lambda_1, \lambda_2, ..., \lambda_m), \delta = (\delta_1, \delta_2, ..., \delta_n)$, we say that $\lambda \geq \delta$ iff $m \geq n$ and $\forall i : 1 \leq i \leq n, \lambda_i \geq \delta_i$. This can also be viewed in terms of containment in the Ferrer's diagram, i.e. $\lambda \geq \delta$ if the Ferrer's diagram for δ is contained in the Ferrer's diagram of λ. For example, consider the partitions $(4, 3, 2)$ and $(2, 2, 2)$. The Ferrer's diagram for $(2, 2, 2)$ is contained in the Ferrer's diagram for $(4, 3, 2)$ as shown in Figure 1.7. Hence, $(4, 3, 2) \geq (2, 2, 2)$.

Definition 1.19 (Young's Lattice) *Given a partition* λ, **Young's lattice** Y_λ *is the poset of all partitions that are less than or equal to* λ.

The Young's lattice for $(3, 3, 3)$ is shown in Figure 1.8. Note that partitions less than a given partition are not necessarily partitions of the same integer.

Again, it follows easily from lattice theory that the Young's lattice is distributive. Furthermore, assume that we are interested in only those partitions in Y_λ which have distinct parts. The notion of slicing posets (explained in Chapter 10 can be used to analyze such subsets of integer partitions.

1.12   NOTATION AND PROOF FORMAT

We use the following notation for quantified expressions:

$$(op \text{ free-var-list} : \text{range-of-free-vars} : \text{expression})$$

where *op* is a universal or an existential quantifier, free-var-list is the list of variables over which the quantification is made, and the range-of-free-vars is the range of the variables. For example, $(\forall i : 0 \leq i \leq 10 : i^2 \leq 100)$ means that for all i such that $0 \leq i \leq 10$, $i^2 \leq 100$ holds. If the range of the variables is clear from the context, then we simply use

$$(op \text{ free-var-list} : \text{expression}).$$

For example, if it is clear that i and j are integers, then we may write

$$\forall i : (\exists j : j > i).$$

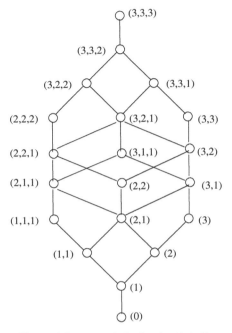

Figure 1.8   Young's lattice for $(3, 3, 3)$.

We use a calculational style of proofs for many of our theorems. For example, a proof that $[A \equiv C]$ is rendered in our format as

$$A$$
$\equiv$ { hint why $[A \equiv B]$ }
$$B$$
$\equiv$ { hint why $[B \equiv C]$ }
$$C.$$

We use implication ($\Rightarrow$) instead of equivalence when proving $A \Rightarrow C$.

A predicate with free variables is assumed to be universally quantified for all possible values of free variables. We use the usual convention for binding powers of operators. In order of increasing binding powers, the operators are as follows:

$\equiv$
$\Rightarrow$
$\vee, \wedge$
$\neg$
$=, \neq, <, \leq$, and other relational operators over integers and sets,
arithmetic operators, and
function applications.

Operators that appear on the same line have the same binding power, and we use parentheses to show the order of application. We sometimes omit parentheses in expressions when they use operators from different lines. Thus

$$x \leq y \wedge y \leq z \Rightarrow x \leq z$$

is equivalent to

$$\forall x, y, z : (((x \leq y) \wedge (y \leq z)) \Rightarrow (x \leq z)).$$

1.13 PROBLEMS

1.1. Give an example of a nonempty binary relation that is symmetric and transitive but not reflexive.

1.2. The *transitive closure* of a relation R on a finite set can also be defined as the smallest transitive relation on S that contains R. Show that the transitive closure is uniquely defined. We use "smaller" in the sense that R_1 is smaller than R_2 if $|R_1| < |R_2|$.

1.3. Show that if P and Q are posets defined on set X, then so is $P \cap Q$.

1.4. Draw the Hasse diagram of all natural numbers less than 10 ordered by the relation *divides*.

1.5. Show that if C_1 and C_2 are down-sets for any poset $(E, <)$, then so is $C_1 \cap C_2$.

1.6. Show the following properties of $\sqcup$ and $\sqcap$.

$(L1)$	$a \sqcup (b \sqcup c) = (a \sqcup b) \sqcup c$	(associativity)
$(L1)^\delta$	$a \sqcap (b \sqcap c) = (a \sqcap b) \sqcap c$	
$(L2)$	$a \sqcup b = b \sqcup a$	(commutativity)
$(L2)^\delta$	$a \sqcap b = b \sqcap a$	
$(L3)$	$a \sqcup (a \sqcap b) = a$	(absorption)
$(L3)^\delta$	$a \sqcap (a \sqcup b) = a$	

1.7. Prove Lemma 1.7.

1.8. Prove Theorem 1.11.

1.9. Complete the proof of Theorem 1.12.

1.14 BIBLIOGRAPHIC REMARKS

The first book on lattice theory was written by Garrett Birkhoff [Bir40, Bir48, Bir67]. The reader will find a discussion of the origins of lattice theory and an extensive bibliography in the book by Gratzer [Grä71, Grä03]. The book by Davey and Priestley

[DP90] provides an easily accessible account of the field. Some other recent books on lattice theory or ordered sets include books by Caspard, Leclerc, and Monjardet [CLM12], and Roman [Rom08]. The happened-before relation on the set of events in a distributed computation is due to Lamport [Lam78]. Reading [Rea02] gives a detailed discussion of dissectors and their properties. The proof format adopted for many theorems in this book is taken from Dijkstra and Scholten [DS90].

2

REPRESENTING POSETS

2.1 INTRODUCTION

We now look at some possible representations for efficient queries and operations on posets. For this purpose, we first examine some of the common operations that are generally performed on posets. Given a poset P, the following operations on elements $x, y \in P$ are frequently performed:

1. Check if $x \leq y$. We denote this operation by $leq(x, y)$.
2. Check if x covers y.
3. Compute $x \sqcap y$ ($meet(x, y)$) and $x \sqcup y$ ($join(x, y)$).

In all such representations, we first need to number the elements of the poset. A useful way of doing this is discussed in Section 2.2. In the following sections, we consider some representations for posets and compare their complexity for the set of operations mentioned earlier.

2.2 LABELING ELEMENTS OF THE POSET

Assume that a finite poset with n elements is given to us as a directed graph (Hasse diagram), where nodes represent the elements in the poset and the edges represent the cover relation on the elements. We number the nodes, i.e., provide a label to each node from $\{1..n\}$ such that if $x < y$ then $label(x) < label(y)$. This way we can answer

Introduction to Lattice Theory with Computer Science Applications, First Edition. Vijay K. Garg.
© 2015 John Wiley & Sons, Inc. Published 2015 by John Wiley & Sons, Inc.

some queries of the form "Is $x < y$?" directly without actually looking at the lists of edges of the elements x and y. For example, if $label(x)$ equals 5 and $label(y)$ equals 3 then we know that x is not less than y. Note that $label(x) < label(y)$ does not necessarily imply that $x < y$. It only means that $x \not> y$. One straightforward way of generating such a labeling would be :

1. Choose a node x with in-degree 0 and assign the lowest available label to x.
2. Delete x and all outgoing edges from x.
3. Repeat steps 1 and 2 until there are no nodes left in the graph.

The above-mentioned procedure is called **topological sort** and it is easy to show that it produces a linear extension of the poset. The procedure also shows that every finite poset has a linear extension. The following result due to Szpilrajn shows that this is true for all posets, even the infinite ones.

Theorem 2.1 *([Szp37]) Every partial order P has a linear extension.*

Proof: Let $\mathcal{W}$ be the set of all posets that extend P. Define a poset Q to be less than or equal to R if the relation corresponding to Q is included in the relation R. Consider a maximal element Z of the set $\mathcal{W}^1$. If Z is totally ordered, then we are done as Z is the linear extension. Otherwise, assume that x and y are incomparable in Z. By adding the tuple (x, y) to Z and computing its transitive closure, we get another poset in $\mathcal{W}$ that is bigger than Z contradicting maximality of Z.   ■

2.3   ADJACENCY LIST REPRESENTATION

Since a poset is a graph, we can use an adjacency list representation for a graph. In an adjacency list representation, we have a linked list for each element of the poset. We can maintain two relationships through an adjacency list :

1. Cover relation $(e_{<_c})$: The linked list for element $x \in P = \{y | y \in P, x <_c y\}$
2. Poset relation $(e_{\leq})$: The linked list for element $x \in P = \{y | y \in P, x \leq y\}$.

Figure 2.1 shows an example of a poset with its adjacency list representation for both the relations. Choosing between the two relations for creating an adjacency list involves a trade-off. Representing $e_{<_c}$ requires less space, while most operations are faster with the $e_{\leq}$ representation. For example, representing a chain of n elements using $e_{<_c}$ requires $O(n)$ space as compared to $O(n^2)$ space using $e_{\leq}$. On the other hand, checking $x \leq y$ for some elements $x, y \in P$ requires time proportional to the size of the linked list of x using $e_{\leq}$ as compared to $O(n + |e_{<_c}|)$ time using $e_{<_c}$.

For very large graphs, one can also keep all adjacent elements of a node in a (balanced) tree instead of a linked list. This can cut down the worst case complexity

---

[1]This step requires Zorn's lemma, which is equivalent to the axiom of choice

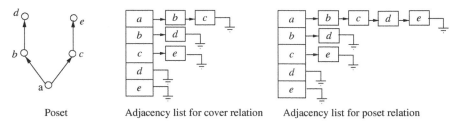

Poset   Adjacency list for cover relation   Adjacency list for poset relation

Figure 2.1   Adjacency list representation of a poset.

for answering queries of the form $x <_c y$ or $x \le y$. Balanced trees are standard data structures and will not be discussed any further. For simplicity, we continue to use linked lists and discuss algorithms when the poset is represented using adjacency lists for (1) the cover relation or (2) the poset relation.

Since the adjacency list corresponds to the cover relation, the query "Does y cover x?" can be answered by simply traversing the linked list for node x. The query "Is $x \le y$?" requires a breadth-first search (BFS) or depth-first search (DFS) starting from node x resulting in time $O(n + |e_{<_c}|)$ as mentioned earlier.

We now give an $O(n + |e_{<_c}|)$ algorithm to compute the join of two elements x and y. The algorithm returns *null* if the join does not exist. To compute the join of x and y, we proceed as follows:

- Step 0: Color all nodes white.
- Step 1: Color all nodes reachable from x as gray. This can be done by a BFS or a DFS starting from node x.
- Step 2: Do a BFS/DFS from node y. Color all gray nodes reached as black.
- Step 3: We now determine for each black node z, the number of black nodes that point to z. Call this number *inBlack*[z] for any node z. This step can be performed in $O(n + |e_{<_c}|)$ by going through the adjacency lists of all black nodes and maintaining cumulative counts for *inBlack* array.
- Step 4: We count the number of black nodes z with *inBlack*[z] equal to 0. If there is exactly one node, we return that node as the answer. Otherwise, we return *null*.

It is easy to see that a node is black iff it can be reached from both x and y. We now show that z equals *join*(x, y) iff it is the only black node with no black nodes pointing to it. Consider the subgraph of nodes that are colored black. If this graph is empty, then there is no node that is reachable from both x and y and therefore *join*(x, y) is null as returned by our method. Otherwise, the subgraph of black nodes is nonempty. Owing to acyclicity and finiteness of the graph, there is at least one node with *inBlack* equal to 0. If there are two or more nodes with *inBlack* equal to 0, then these are incomparable upper bounds and therefore *join*(x, y) does not exist. Finally, if z is the only black node with *inBlack* equal to 0, then all other black nodes are reachable from z because all black nodes are reachable from some black node with *inBlack* equal to 0. Therefore, z is the least upper bound of x and y.

Now assume that the adjacency list of x includes all elements that are greater than or equal to x, i.e., it encodes the poset relation $(e_\leq)$. Generally, the following optimization is made for representation of adjacency lists. We keep the adjacency list in a sorted order. This enables us to search for an element in the list faster. For example, if we are looking for node 4 in the list of node 1 sorted in ascending order and we encounter the node 6, then we know that node 4 cannot be present in the list. We can then stop our search at that point instead of looking through the whole list. This optimization results in a better average case complexity.

Let us now explore complexity of various queries in this representation. To check that y covers x, we need to check that $x \leq y$ and for any z different from x and y such that $x \leq z$, $z \leq y$ is not true. This can be easily done by going through the adjacency lists of all nodes that are in the adjacency list of x and have labels less than y in $O(n + |e_\leq|)$ time.

Checking $x \leq y$ is trivial, so we now focus on computing $join(x, y)$.

- Step 0: We take the intersection of the adjacency lists of nodes x and y. Since lists are sorted, this step can be done in $O(u_x + u_y)$ time where u_x and u_y are the size of the adjacency lists of x and y, respectively. Call this list U.
- Step 1: If U is empty, we return *null*. Otherwise, let w be the first element in the list.
- Step 2: if U is contained in the adjacency list of w, we return w; else, we return *null*.

A further optimization that can lead to reduction in space and time complexity for dense posets is based on keeping intervals of nodes rather than single nodes in adjacency lists. For example, if the adjacency list of node 2 is $\{4, 5, 6, 8, 10, 11, 12\}$, then we keep the adjacency list as three intervals $\{4 - 6, 8 - 8, 10 - 12\}$. We leave the algorithms for computing joins and meets in this representation as an exercise.

2.4 VECTOR CLOCK REPRESENTATION

Of all operations performed on posets, the most fundamental is $leq(x, y)$. We have observed that by storing just the cover relation, we save on space but have to spend more time to check $leq(x, y)$. On the other hand, keeping the entire poset relation can be quite wasteful as the adjacency lists can become large as the number of nodes in the poset increase. We now show a representation that provides a balance between the cover relation and the poset relation. This representation, called vector clock representation, assumes that the poset is partitioned into k chains for some k. Algorithms for partitioning posets into the minimum number of chains is discussed in Chapter 3. For vector clock representation, we do not require the partition to have the least number of chains.

Let there be k chains in some partition of the poset. All elements in any chain are totally ordered and we can rank them from 1 to the total number of elements in the chain. Thus, a node x in chain i with rank r is labeled as a tuple (i, r). Now to store the poset relation, for each element $y \in P$, we assign a vector $y.V$ that can be used for comparing y with other elements. For $y \in P$, we set $y.V$ as follows:

$y.V[i]$ = the rank of the largest element in chain i, which is less than or equal to y.

If no element in chain i is less than or equal to y, then we set $y.V[i]$ to 0. Now, given any element $x = (i, r)$, it is clear that $x \leq y$ iff $r \leq y.V[i]$. Thus, $leq(x, y)$ can be determined in constant time.

Remark: Just as we kept $y.V[i]$ as the rank of the largest element on chain i which is less than or equal to y, we can also keep the dual vector F, defined as follows:
$y.F[i]$ = the rank of the smallest element in chain i which is greater than or equal to y (∞ if no such element).

Given a vector clock representation of a poset, it is an easy exercise to generate adjacency lists for the poset relation.

An example of a poset with its V labels is shown in Figure 2.2. Vector clock representations of posets are especially suited for distributed systems as they can be computed online. In the context of distributed systems, vector clock representations are called the *Fidge and Mattern Vector clocks*.

The algorithm for computing vector clock labels for process P_j is shown in Figure 2.3. The algorithm is described by the initial conditions and the actions taken for each event type. A process increments its own component of the vector clock after each event. Furthermore, it includes a copy of its vector clock in every outgoing message. On receiving a message, it updates its vector clock by taking a component-wise maximum with the vector clock included in the message. In Figure 2.2, when process P_3 receives the message sent by P_1, it takes the maximum of the vectors $(2, 1, 0, 0)$ and $(0, 0, 3, 1)$ to obtain the vector $(2, 1, 3, 1)$.

Thus, the vector clock representation of the poset for a distributed computation on N processes is in fact just N queues of vectors, each queue representing vector clock timestamps of all events in a process.

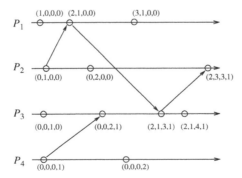

Figure 2.2 Vector clock labeling of a poset for a distributed computation.

```
Pⱼ::
  var
      V: array[1 ... N] of integer
        initially (∀i : i ≠ j : V[i] = 0) ∧ (V[j] = 1);

  send event :
      V[j] := V[j] + 1;

  receive event with vector W
      V[j] := V[j] + 1;
      for i := 1 to N do
          V[i] := max(V[i], W[i]);

  internal event
      V[j] := V[j] + 1
```

Figure 2.3   Vector clock algorithm.

2.5   MATRIX REPRESENTATION

Like a directed graph, a poset can also be represented using a matrix. If there is a poset P with n nodes, then it can be represented by a matrix A of size $n \times n$. As before, we can either represent the cover relation or the poset relation through the matrix. Since in both cases we would be using $O(n^2)$ space, we generally use a matrix representation for the poset relation. Thus, for $x_i, x_j \in P$, $x_i \leq x_j$ iff $A[i,j] = 1$. The main advantage of using the matrix representation is that it can answer the query "Is $x \leq y$?" in $O(1)$ time.

2.6   DIMENSION-BASED REPRESENTATION

The motivation for the dimension-based representation comes from the fact that in the vector clock algorithm, we require $O(k)$ components in the vector where k is bounded by the smallest number of chains required to decompose the poset. As we will see in Chapter 3, Dilworth's Theorem shows that the least number of chains required equals the width of the poset. So, the natural question to ask is if there exists an alternate way of timestamping elements of a poset with vectors that requires less components than the width of the poset and can still be used to answer the query of the form $leq(x, y)$.

Surprisingly, in some cases, we can do with fewer components. For example, consider the poset shown in Figure 2.4(a). Since the poset is just an antichain, the minimum number of chains required to cover the poset is 5. So for using the vector clock representation, we require five components in the vector. But consider the following two linear extensions of the poset : x_1, x_2, x_3, x_4, x_5 and x_5, x_4, x_3, x_2, x_1, shown in

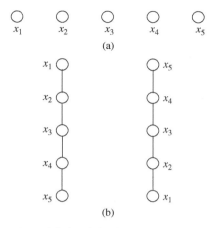

Figure 2.4   (a) An antichain of size 5 and (b) its two linear extensions.

Figure 2.4(b). Using the ranks of the elements in these two linear extensions, we get the following vectors : $(1, 5), (2, 4), (3, 3), (4, 2)$, and $(5, 1)$. These vectors have one-to-one correspondence with the poset order, i.e., they form an antichain. So in this case, we can get away with just 2 components in the vector. This idea of using linear extensions of the poset to assign a vector to each element can be generalized to any poset. The minimum number of linear extensions required is called the **dimension** of the poset. More formally, we first define a realizer of a poset.

Definition 2.2 (Realizer) *A family* $R = \{L_1, L_2, \ldots, L_t\}$ *of linear extensions of a poset P on X is called a* **realizer** *of P if*

$$P = \cap_{L_i \in R} L_i.$$

The dimension of a poset P is the size of the smallest realizer. Determining the dimension of a given poset is NP-hard, whereas determining the width of a poset is computationally easy. For this reason, the dimension based representation is generally not used in distributed systems even though the dimension may be smaller than the width of the poset. The concept of dimension and related results are described in more detail in Chapter 16

2.7   ALGORITHMS TO COMPUTE IRREDUCIBLES

In this section, we briefly consider algorithms for determining irreducibles of a poset. Assume that we have the adjacency list representation of the cover relation. To determine whether x is join-irreducible we first compute $LC(x)$, the set of elements covered by x. Then, we use the following procedure to check if x is join-irreducible.

- Step 1: If $LC(x)$ is singleton, return true;
- Step 2: If $LC(x)$ is empty, then
  if x is the minimum element of the poset, return false, else return true;
- Step 3: If $join(LC(x))$ exists then return false, else return true.

The complexity of this procedure is dominated by the third step that takes $O(n + e_{<_c})$ in the worst case. The proof of correctness of the procedure is left as an exercise.

2.8 INFINITE POSETS

We now consider the representation of (countably) infinite posets for computing applications. Since computers have finite memory, it is clear that we will have to use finite representation for these posets. We assume that the infinite poset is "periodic" (a concept that will be explained later) to enable us finite representation of infinite posets. Our representation is motivated by the need for modeling infinite distributed computations.

To this end, we introduce the notion of *p-diagram* (poset diagram). A p-diagram is a type of a graph with some of the vertices defined to be *recurrent*. Each recurrent vertex, in effect, models an infinite number of elements of the poset. In addition, the graph has two types of edges -forward edges and shift edges that will be defined later. Formally,

Definition 2.3 (p-diagram) *A p-diagram Q is a tuple (V, F, R, B), where V is a set of vertices or nodes, F (forward edges) is a subset of $V \times V$, R (recurrent vertices) is a subset of V, and S (shift edges) is a subset of $R \times R$ with the following constraints:*

- *The graph (V, F) is acyclic, and*
- *If u is a recurrent vertex and $(u, v) \in F$ or $(u, v) \in S$, then v is also recurrent.*

Figure 2.6(a) is an example of a p-diagram. The recurrent vertices and non-recurrent vertices in the p-diagram are represented by hollow circles and filled circles, respectively. The forward edges are represented by solid arrows and the shift edges by dashed arrows.

Each p-diagram represents an infinite poset $(X, \leq)$ defined as follows. X consists of two types of elements. First, for all vertices $u \in V$, we have elements u^1 in X. Further, for all vertices $u \in R$, we add an infinite number of elements $\{u^i | i \geq 2\}$. It is clear that when R is empty we get a finite poset and when R is nonempty we get an infinite poset. The set R captures periodic part of the infinite poset.

We now define $\leq$ relation of the poset based on the given p-diagram. The relation $\leq$ is the smallest reflexive transitive relation that satisfies:

- if $(u, v) \in F$ and $u \in R$, then $\forall i : u^i \leq v^i$,
- if $(u, v) \in F$ and $u \notin R$, then $u^1 \leq v^1$, and

- if $(u, v) \in S$, then $u^i \leq v^{i+1}$.

We now have the following theorem.

Theorem 2.4 $(X, \leq)$ *as defined above is a reflexive poset.*

Proof: We show that $\leq$ is reflexive, transitive, and antisymmetric. It is reflexive and transitive by construction. We now show that $\leq$ as defined earlier does not create any nontrivial cycle (cycle of size greater than one). Any cycle in elements of the poset with the same index would imply cycle in (V, F). Thus, any cycle would have elements with at least two indices. However, the relation $\leq$ never makes a higher indexed element smaller than a lower indexed element.

∎

Let us now consider some examples.

1. The set of natural numbers with the usual order can be modeled using the p-diagram shown in Figure 2.5(a), where
   $V = \{u\}; F = \{\}; S = \{(u, u)\}; R = \{u\}$.
   Note that this poset has infinite height and width equal to 1.
2. The set of natural numbers with no order can be modeled as shown in Figure 2.5(b) with
   $V = \{u\}; F = \{\}; S = \{\}; R = \{u\}$.
3. Figure 2.6 shows an example of a p-diagram along with the corresponding infinite poset. This p-diagram captures infinite behavior of a distributed computation.

We cannot expect finite p-diagrams to be able to model all infinite posets. We now give some examples of posets that cannot be represented using p-diagrams.

(a)   (b)

Figure 2.5   (a,b) Trivial examples of p-diagrams.

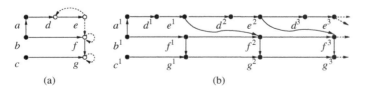

(a)   (b)

Figure 2.6   (a) A p-diagram and (b) its corresponding infinite poset.

1. The set of all integers (including negative integers) under the usual order relation cannot be represented using a p-diagram. The set of integers does not have any minimal element. Any poset defined using a p-diagram is well-founded.

2. Consider the set of all natural numbers with the order that all even numbers are less than all the odd numbers. This poset cannot be represented using a p-diagram. In this poset, the set of elements that cover some element may be infinite. For example, the number 2 is covered by an infinite number of elements. In a p-diagram, an element can only have a bounded number of lower and upper covers.

The following properties of a p-diagram posets are easy to show.

Lemma 2.5 *A poset P defined by a p-diagram has the following properties:*

1. *P is well-founded.*

2. *There exists a constant k such that the size of the set of upper covers and lower covers of every element is bounded by k.*

Runs of a distributed computation generated by a finite number of processes have finite width. The following lemma characterizes those p-diagrams for which the corresponding posets have finite width.

Lemma 2.6 *A poset P defined by a p-diagram has finite width iff for every recurrent vertex there exists a cycle in the graph $(R, F \cup S)$.*

Proof: If every recurrent vertex v is in a cycle, then we get that the set

$$\{v^i | i \geq 1\}$$

is totally ordered. This implies that the poset can be decomposed into a finite number of chains and therefore has a finite width. Conversely, if there exists any recurrent vertex v that is not in a cycle, then v^i is incomparable to v^j for all i, j. Then, the set

$$\{v^i | i \geq 1\}$$

forms an antichain of infinite size. Thus, P has infinite width.

■

Algorithms to check whether $x \leq y$ or x covered by y are left as an exercise.

2.9 PROBLEMS

2.1. Design algorithms for performing the common poset operations for the matrix representation and analyze their time complexity.

2.2. Give efficient algorithms for calculating the join and meet of the elements of a poset using the dimension representation.

2.3. Give parallel and distributed algorithms for topological sort.

2.4. Give parallel and distributed algorithms for computing the poset relation from the cover relation.

2.5. Give parallel and distributed algorithms for computing $x \sqcup y$ in various representations.

2.6. Give an efficient algorithm to convert a vector clock representation of poset into an adjacency list representation of the poset relation.

2.7. (Open) How many different (non-isomorphic) posets can be defined on n elements?

2.8. (Open) Given two posets P and Q, what is the complexity of checking whether they are isomorphic?

2.9. Give an efficient algorithm that takes a poset as input and returns all its irreducibles and dissectors.

2.10. Give efficient algorithms to determine $x \sqcup y$, $leq(x, y)$ and $iscoveredby(x, y)$ for elements x and y in a p-diagram.

2.11. Give an algorithm to compute the width of a p-diagram.

2.10 BIBLIOGRAPHIC REMARKS

The reader is referred to the book by Cormen, Leiserson, Rivest, and Stein [CLRS01] for details on topological sort and adjacency representation of graphs. Vector clock representation in distributed systems is due to Fidge [Fid89] and Mattern [Mat89]. The dimension-based representation of posets is due to Dushnik and Miller [DM41]. The discussion of p-diagrams is taken from the paper by Agarwal, Garg, and Ogale [AGO10].

3

DILWORTH'S THEOREM

3.1 INTRODUCTION

Of all the results in lattice theory, perhaps the most famous is Dilworth's Theorem for decomposition of a poset. Dilworth's Theorem belongs to the special class of results, called *min–max* results, which relate a maximal value in a structure to a minimal value. Dilworth's Theorem states that the minimum number of chains a poset can be partitioned into equals the maximum size of an antichain. In this chapter, we cover this result and associated algorithms.

3.2 DILWORTH'S THEOREM

We first present a proof of Dilworth's Theorem due to Galvin [Gal94].

Theorem 3.1 *([Dil50]) [Dilworth's Theorem] Any finite poset $P = (X, \leq)$ of width w can be decomposed into w chains. Furthermore, w chains are necessary for any such decomposition.*

Proof: We begin by proving that w chains are necessary and that it is not possible to decompose the poset into less than w chains. Consider the longest antichain (of length w). Each element of this antichain must belong to a separate chain in the chain decomposition of the poset and hence we need at least w chains.

Introduction to Lattice Theory with Computer Science Applications, First Edition. Vijay K. Garg.
© 2015 John Wiley & Sons, Inc. Published 2015 by John Wiley & Sons, Inc.

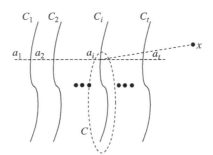

Figure 3.1 Decomposition of P into t chains.

We now show that w chains are indeed sufficient to completely partition the poset. The proof is by induction on n, the size of the poset. The base case $n = 1$ is simple because a poset containing one element can be partitioned into one chain containing that element.

Consider a poset P of size n. Let x denote a maximal element of P. Consider the subposet $P' = (X - \{x\}, \leq)$. Since this is a poset of size less than n, by the induction hypothesis, we can decompose it into t disjoint chains where t is the width of P'. Let $C_1, ..., C_t$ denote the chains obtained after decomposition. We are required to prove that either P has an antichain of size $t + 1$ or P is a union of t chains.

Let a_i be the maximal element of C_i, which is part of some antichain of size t. The set $A = \{a_1, ..., a_t\}$ forms an antichain. To see this, consider an antichain containing a_j. There exists $b_i \in C_i$, which belongs to this antichain because any antichain of size t must have exactly one element from each chain C_i. Since a_i is the maximum element in the chain C_i which is part of some antichain of size t, $b_i \leq a_i$. Therefore, $b_i || a_j$ implies that $a_i \not\leq a_j$.

We now compare x with all the elements of A. If $A \cup \{x\}$ forms an antichain, then the width of P is $t + 1$ and the chain decomposition of P is $C_1, ..., C_t, \{x\}$. Otherwise, there exists $a_i \in C_i$ such that $a_i < x$ for some i. The set $C = \{y \in C_i \mid y \leq a_i\}$ forms a chain in P. Since a_i is the maximal element in C_i that is a part of some t-sized antichain in P, the width of $Q = (X - C, \leq)$ is less than t. Then, by the induction hypothesis, we can partition Q into $t - 1$ chains. Hence along with C, this forms a decomposition of P into t chains (Figure 3.1).   ■

Any partition of a poset into chains is also called a **chain cover** of the poset.

3.3 APPRECIATION OF DILWORTH'S THEOREM

This was one of our first nontrivial proofs in the book. A delightful result such as Dilworth's Theorem must be savored and appreciated. We now look at a few questions that naturally arise out of the above proof which will help the reader understand the proof better.

For any nontrivial proof, the reader should try out special cases. For example, in Dilworth's Theorem, one may consider the special case of posets of height 1 (i.e., a bipartite graph). In this case, one obtains the Konig–Egervary Theorem discussed in Section 3.8.

In any substantial proof, it is generally useful to find lemmas that can be abstracted out of this proof and reused in other proofs. In the proof of Dilworth's Theorem, the key ingredient was to prove that the set A is an antichain. This gives us the following result.

Theorem 3.2 *Let A_w be the set of all antichains of size w in a finite poset P of width w. Let $\{C_1, C_2, ..., C_w\}$ be a decomposition of P into w chains. For Y, any antichain of size w, let $Y[i]$ denote the element in Y from chain C_i. We define an order $\preceq$ on A_w as follows:*

$$Y \preceq Z \overset{\text{def}}{=} \forall i : Y[i] \le Z[i] \quad \text{for all } Y, Z \in A_w,$$

Then, $(A_w, \preceq)$ is a lattice.

Proof: Given $Y, Z \in A_w$, we define a set formed by

$$W[i] := min(Y[i], Z[i]).$$

We first show that $W \in A_w$. It is sufficient to show that $W[i] || W[j]$ for any i and j. By symmetry, it is sufficient to show that $W[i] \not< W[j]$. Without loss of generality, let $W[i] = Y[i]$. If $W[j] = Y[j]$, then $W[i] \not< W[j]$ follows from $Y \in A_w$. If $W[j] = Z[j]$, then $W[i] \not< W[j]$ follows from $Z[j] \le Y[j]$ and $Y[i] \not< Y[j]$. It is easy to see that W is the meet of Y and Z.

A dual argument holds for the join of Y and Z. ∎

To appreciate a nontrivial theorem, one must look for alternative proofs. For example, we used induction on the size of the poset in our proof. Here we give another proof which is based on removing a chain instead of an element as in Galvin's proof. This is closer to Dilworth's original proof [Dil50].

Sketch of an Alternative Proof: Let P be a poset of width k. For induction, we assume that any poset with smaller cardinality of width w or less can be partitioned into w chains. If P is an empty relation (i.e., has no comparable elements), then P has exactly k elements and can be trivially decomposed into k chains. Otherwise, consider a chain $C = \{x, y\}$ where x is a minimal element and y a maximal element of P. If the width of $P - C$ is less than k, we are done because we can use that partition combined with C to get the desired partition. If the width of $P - C$ is k, then there exists an antichain A of size k in the subposet $P - C$. We consider the subposets $U[A]$ and $D[A]$. Since $x \notin U[A]$ and $y \notin D[A]$, we know that both $U[A]$ and $D[A]$ are strictly smaller than P. By induction, each of these sets can be partitioned into k chains and since $U[A] \cap D[A] = A$, we can combine these chains to form the partition of the original set. ∎

3.4   DUAL OF DILWORTH'S THEOREM

In lattice theory, one must also explore the duals of any nontrivial theorem. For Dilworth's Theorem, we get the following result.

Theorem 3.3 *([Mir71]) Any poset $P = (X, \leq)$ of height h can be decomposed into h antichains. Furthermore, h antichains are necessary for any such decomposition.*

Proof: All minimal elements of a poset form an antichain. When we delete this antichain, the height of the poset decreases by exactly one. By continuing this procedure, we get the desired decomposition. The necessity part follows from the fact that no two elements of a chain can be in the same antichain.

∎

3.5   GENERALIZATIONS OF DILWORTH'S THEOREM

We can generalize Dilworth's Theorem in the following manner:

1. Go from finite posets to infinite ones.
2. Generalize the theorem to directed graphs.
3. Decompose the poset into other structures, like k-families. A k-family in a poset P is a subposet containing no chains of size $k + 1$. So, an antichain forms a $1-$family. We can try to generalize the dual of Dilworth's Theorem to this structure.

Different proofs and their generalizations can be found in the literature. We refer the interested reader to West [Wes04].

3.6   ALGORITHMIC PERSPECTIVE OF DILWORTH'S THEOREM

In practical applications, it may not be sufficient to prove existence of a chain partition. One may be required to compute it. Thus, from an algorithmic perspective, one can look at the following questions:

1. How can we convert the proof of the theorem into an algorithm for chain decomposition of a poset?
2. Given any algorithm for chain decomposition, we analyze its time and space complexity. The natural question to ask is if we can improve the algorithm complexity or prove lower bounds on the time and space complexity.
3. Given any sequential algorithm, one can study variations of the algorithm that cater to different needs. A *parallel* algorithm tries to speed up the computation by using multiple processors. A *distributed* algorithm assumes that the information about the poset is distributed across multiple machines. An *online* algorithm assumes that the elements of the poset are presented one at a time,

and we maintain a chain decomposition at all times. The new element is inserted into one of the existing chains or into a new chain. The online algorithm cannot change the existing chain decomposition and as a result may require more chains than an offline algorithm. An *incremental* algorithm also assumes that elements of the poset are presented one at a time. The algorithm must compute the chain decomposition as we are presented with the new element. However, the algorithm is free to rearrange existing elements into chains when a new element arrives. The key issue here is to avoid recomputing the chain decomposition for the entire poset whenever a new element is presented.

We will explore such algorithmic questions in Section 4.2. For now, we look at some applications of Dilworth's Theorem.

3.7   APPLICATION: HALL'S MARRIAGE THEOREM

In this section, we show the relationship between the problem of chain partition of a poset and matching in a bipartite graph. This relationship allows us to use the bipartite matching algorithms for chain-partition and vice versa.

We first describe an application of Dilworth's Theorem to combinatorics. We are given a set of m girls $G = \{y_1, ..., y_m\}$ and n boys $B = \{x_1, ..., x_n\}$ with $m \leq n$. Each girl y_i has a set of boys $S(y_i)$ whom she is willing to marry. The aim is to find a condition on these sets so that it is possible to find a pairing of the girls and boys which enables each girl to get married. Each boy chosen from the set $S(y_i)$ must be distinct. This problem is also known as computing the set of distinct representatives.

A solution to this problem is given by the following theorem. Let $I \subseteq G$. Define $S(I) = \bigcup_{y_i \in I} S(y_i)$.

Theorem 3.4 *[Hall's Theorem] The necessary and sufficient condition for the above-mentioned set of distinct representatives problem is* $\forall I \subseteq G, |S(I)| \geq |I|$.

Proof: The necessary part of the condition is trivial because if I is smaller than $S(I)$ then there will not be enough boys for pairing off with the girls. To prove that the above-mentioned condition is sufficient, we assume that the given condition holds and view the S relation as a poset of height 1 (Figure 3.2). This forms a bipartite poset. If we can split it into n chains then we are done. Thus, we need to prove that there is no antichain in the poset of size greater than $|B| = n$. Let A be an antichain of the poset and $I = A \cap G$ (all the girls included in the antichain A). Since A is an antichain, it does not contain an element belonging to $S(I)$. Hence, $|A| \leq |I| + |B| - |S(I)| \leq |B|$ as $|I| \leq |S(I)|$ from Hall's condition. Thus, the maximum size of an antichain is $|B| = n$. By Dilworth's Theorem, the poset can be partitioned into n chains. Since the antichain B is maximal, each chain in such a partition must contain exactly one point of B. Thus, we can take the chains in the partition of the poset, which contain points of G. These give the desired pairings of boys and girls such that all the girls can get married. This proves the sufficiency of the given condition.

∎

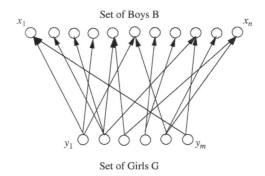

Set of Girls G

Figure 3.2   Hall's Marriage Theorem.

3.8   APPLICATION: BIPARTITE MATCHING

We now show applications of Dilworth's Theorem to bipartite matching. A **matching** in a graph $G = (V, E)$ is a subset of edges $E' \subseteq E$ such that no two edges in E' have any vertex in common. A **vertex cover** in a graph is a subset of vertices $V' \subseteq V$ such that for every edge $(x, y) \in E$, either $x \in V'$ or $y \in V'$.

Theorem 3.5 (Konig–Egervary Theorem[Kon31, Ege31]) *In a bipartite graph, the maximum size of a matching equals the minimum size of a vertex cover.*

Proof: Let $G = (L, R, E)$ be the bipartite graph with a total of $n = |L| + |R|$ vertices. View this bipartite graph as a poset with vertices in L as the minimal vertices and R as the maximal vertices. Any chain decomposition of this poset can have chains of size either 1 or 2. We observe that

1. Any chain cover of size $m \leq n$ is equivalent to existence of a matching of size $n - m$.
2. Any antichain in the poset corresponds to an independent set in the graph. Thus, the complement of an antichain corresponds to a vertex cover of the graph. Hence, existence of any antichain of size m is equivalent to existence of a vertex cover of size $n - m$.

From Dilworth's theorem, the size of the biggest antichain equals the size of the smallest chain cover. Therefore, the size of the smallest vertex cover equals the size of the largest matching.

∎

The above-mentioned construction shows that by using chain decomposition, one can solve the problem of bipartite matching. Now, we consider the converse. Assume that we have an algorithm for bipartite matching. How do we use it for chain decomposition? This relationship between chain decomposition and bipartite matching is based on the idea of a strict split of a poset.

Definition 3.6 (Strict Split of a Poset) *Given a poset P, the* **strict split** *of the poset P, denoted by S(P) is a bipartite graph (L, R, E) where $L = \{x^- | x \in P\}$, $R = \{x^+ | x \in P\}$, and $E = \{(x^-, y^+) | x < y \text{ in } P\}$.*

We state the following theorem due to Fulkerson [Ful56] whose proof is left as an exercise.

Theorem 3.7 *Any matching in S(P) can be reduced to a chain cover of P.*

Thus, one can use any algorithm for bipartite matching to determine a chain cover. There are many techniques available for bipartite matching. One can use *augmenting path* algorithms that start with the trivial matching and increase the size of the matching one edge at a time. In a graph of n vertices and m edges, these algorithms take $O(mn)$ time. Hopcroft and Karp have given an $O(m\sqrt{n})$ algorithm for bipartite matching [HK71].

It is important to note that bipartite matching can also be solved by a more general technique of computing max-flows which itself is a special case of linear programming.

3.9   ONLINE DECOMPOSITION OF POSETS

Dilworth's Theorem states that a finite poset of width k requires at least k chains for decomposition [Dil50]. However, constructive proofs of this result require the entire poset to be available for the partition. The best known *online* algorithm for partitioning the poset is due to Kierstead [Kie81] which partitions a poset of width k into $(5^k - 1)/4$ chains. The lower bound on this problem, due to Szemérdi (1982), states that there is no online algorithm that partitions all posets of width k into fewer than $\binom{k+1}{2}$ chains.

We will focus on a special version of the problem where the elements are presented in a total order consistent with the poset order. Felsner [Fel97] has shown that even for the simpler problem, the lower bound of $\binom{k+1}{2}$ holds. As an insight into the general result, we show how any algorithm can be forced to use 3 chains for a poset of width 2. Consider the poset given in Figure 3.3. Initially, two incomparable elements x and y are presented to the chain decomposition algorithm. It is forced to assign x and y to different chains. Now an element z greater than both x and y is presented. If the algorithm assigns z to a new chain, then it has already used three chains for a poset of width 2. Otherwise, without loss of generality, assume that the algorithm assigns z to x's chain. Then, the algorithm is presented an element u, which is greater than x and incomparable to y and z. The algorithm is forced to assign u to a new chain and hence the algorithm uses three chains for a poset of width 2.

Furthermore, Felsner showed the lower bound to be strict and presented an algorithm that requires at most $\binom{k+1}{2}$ chains to partition a poset. We present a simple algorithm, owing to Agarwal and Garg [AG05], which partitions a poset into at most $\binom{k+1}{2}$ chains and requires at most $O(k^2)$ work per element.

Figure 3.3   A poset of width 2 forcing an algorithm to use three chains for decomposition.

```
var
        B_1, ... , B_k: sets of queues
            ∀i : 1 ≤ i ≤ k, |B_i| = i
            ∀i : q ∈ B_i, q is empty

When presented with an element z:
        for i = 1 to k
            if ∃q ∈ B_i : q is empty or q.head < z
                insert z at the head of q;
                if i > 1
                    swap the set of queues B_{i-1} and B_i \ {q};
```

Figure 3.4   Chain partitioning algorithm.

The algorithm for online partitioning of the poset into at most $\binom{k+1}{2}$ chains is shown in Figure 3.4. The algorithm maintains $\binom{k+1}{2}$ chains as queues partitioned into k sets $B_1, B_2, ..., B_k$ such that B_i has i queues. Let z be the new element to be inserted. We find the smallest i such that z is comparable with heads of one of the queues in B_i or one of the queues in B_i is empty. Let this queue in B_i be q. Then, z is inserted at the head of q. If i is not 1, queues in B_{i-1} and $B_i \setminus \{q\}$ are swapped. Every element of the poset is processed in this manner, and in the end, the nonempty set of queues gives us the decomposition of the poset.

The following theorem gives the proof of correctness of the algorithm.

Theorem 3.8 *The algorithm in Figure 3.4 partitions a poset of width k into $\binom{k+1}{2}$ chains.*

Proof: We claim that the algorithm maintains the followings invariant:

(I) For all i: Heads of all nonempty queues in B_i are incomparable with each other.

Initially, all queues are empty and so the invariant holds. Suppose that the invariant holds for the first m elements. Let z be the next element presented to the algorithm. The algorithm first finds a suitable i such that z can be inserted into one of the queues in B_i.

Suppose the algorithm was able to find such an i. If $i = 1$, then z is inserted into B_1 and the invariant is trivially true. Assume $i \geq 2$. Then, z is inserted into a queue q in B_i which is either empty or has a head comparable with z. The remaining queues in B_i are swapped with queues in B_{i-1}. After swapping, B_i has $i - 1$ queues from B_{i-1} and the queue q, and B_{i-1} has $i - 1$ queues from $B_i \setminus \{q\}$. The heads of queues in B_{i-1} are incomparable as the invariant I was true for B_i before z was inserted. The heads of queues in B_i which originally belonged to B_{i-1} are incomparable to each other because of the invariant I. The head of q, z, is also incomparable to the heads of these queues as i was the smallest value such that the head of one of the queues in B_i was comparable to z. Hence, the insertion of the new element still maintains the invariant.

If the algorithm is not able to insert z into any of the queues, then all queue heads and in particular, queue heads in B_k are incomparable to z. Then, z along with the queue heads in B_k form an antichain of size $k + 1$. This leads to a contradiction as the width of the poset is k. Hence, the algorithm is always able to insert an element into one of the queues and the poset is partitioned into fewer than $\binom{k+1}{2}$ chains. ∎

Note that our algorithm does not need the knowledge of k in advance. It starts with the assumption of $k = 1$, i.e., with B_1. When a new element cannot be inserted into B_1, we have found an antichain of size 2 and B_2 can be created. Thus, the online algorithm uses at most $\binom{k+1}{2}$ chains in decomposing posets without knowing k in advance.

This algorithm can be easily extended for online chain decomposition when the new elements are either maximal elements or minimal elements of the poset seen so far (see Problem 7).

3.10   A LOWER BOUND ON ONLINE CHAIN PARTITION

We now show a lower bound on the number of chains required for online chain partition in the worst case. We will cast our problem in terms of a game between Alice and Bob where Alice corresponds to the algorithm that does the online chain partition and Bob corresponds to the adversary that provides the partial order. The goal for Alice is to use as few chains as possible and for Bob to force Alice to use as many chains as possible. We will require Bob to present elements of the poset only in increasing order. We now claim:

Theorem 3.9 *There exists a strategy for Bob that can force Alice to use $\binom{k+1}{2}$ chains.*

Proof: Let the chains of the poset produced by decomposition be C_i and $top(i)$ be the maximal element of the chain C_i. If x is the maximal element of the poset, then *private(x)* is the set of chains C_i such that $top(i) \leq x$ and $top(i) \not\leq y$ for all maximal elements $y \neq x$.

Induction Hypothesis : For every positive integer k, there is a strategy $S(k)$ for Bob so that the poset P presented so far is of width k and has exactly k maximal elements $x_1, \ldots, x_k$ such that for all i, $|private(x_i)| \geq i$.

Base Case : For $k = 1$, we use one element from process 1. The hypothesis holds for this case.

Induction Step : Suppose we have strategy $S(k)$. We construct $S(k + 1)$ using $S(k)$ as follows:

1. Run strategy $S(k)$. This phase ends with an order Q_1 with maximal elements $x_1, \ldots, x_k$, $|private(x_i)| \geq i$.

2. Run strategy $S(k)$ again. This time every new element is made greater than each of $x_1, \ldots, x_{k-1}$ and their predecessors but incomparable to rest of the elements in Q_1. In particular, the new elements are incomparable to elements in $top(i)$ for $C_i \in private(x_k)$.
   This phase ends with an order Q_2 with $k + 1$ maximal elements $y_1, \ldots, y_k, x_k$. At this point, there are at least i chains in $private(y_i)$ and an additional k chains in $private(x_k)$. At this point, Alice has already used $\binom{k+2}{2} - 1$ chains ($\binom{k+1}{2}$ chains for $private(y_i)$ for all i and k chains for $private(x_k)$).

3. Add a new element z so that z is greater than all elements of Q_2. For the chain C_i to which z is assigned, it holds that $i \notin private(x_k)$ or $i \notin private(y_k)$. Without loss of generality, assume that $i \notin private(x_k)$. Now $private(z)$ has chains from x_k and the chain to which z belongs. So $|private(z)| \geq k + 1$. We refer to z as z_{k+1} from now on.

4. In this final phase, run strategy $S(k)$ again with all new elements greater than $y_1, \ldots, y_k$. This phase ends with maximal elements $z_1 \ldots, z_{k+1}$ so that $|private(z_i)| \geq i$.

This completes the proof of the theorem as Alice has used at least $\binom{k+2}{2}$ chains.

∎

3.11   PROBLEMS

3.1. Prove that in any poset of size $n \geq sr + 1$, there exists a chain of length $s + 1$ or an antichain of length $r + 1$. Use the first part to prove the following result known as Erdos–Szekeres Theorem: In any sequence A of n different real numbers where $n \geq sr + 1$, A has either a monotonically increasing subsequence of $s + 1$ terms or a monotonically decreasing subsequence of $r + 1$ terms.

3.2. Give an algorithm for chain decomposition of a poset based on Galvin's proof of Dilworth's Theorem.

3.3. In Section 3.3, we considered the lattice of all antichains of size equal to the width of the poset. Is that lattice distributive?

3.4. In Section 3.3, we considered the set of all antichains of size equal to the width of the poset. Instead consider, $\mathcal{A}(\mathcal{P})$ the set of all antichains of a poset P. Given two antichains A and B, define $A \leq B$ iff $D[A] \subseteq D[B]$. Show that $(\mathcal{A}(\mathcal{P}), \leq)$ is a distributive lattice.

3.5. Consider the set of all *maximal* antichains of a finite poset. Is it a lattice under the order relation defined in Exercise 4?

3.6. Prove Theorem 3.7.

3.7. In the online chain decomposition algorithm, when a new element y arrives, we know that y is a maximal element of the poset seen so far. Now consider a weaker property where we only know that y is either a maximal element or a minimal element. Give an online chain decomposition algorithm for this case. (Hint: It is sufficient to maintain $2\binom{k+1}{2} - 1$ chains in the online decomposition.)

3.8. Give an algorithm to find the maximum element of A_n defined in Theorem 3.2.

3.12 BIBLIOGRAPHIC REMARKS

Dilworth's Theorem is taken from [Dil50]. It is a prime example of min–max structure theorems that relate a minimum value (the number of chains to cover a poset) to a maximum value (the size of the biggest antichain). Dilworth's Theorem is a special case of min-cut max-flow theorem, which itself is a special case of the duality theorem for linear programming. The paper [BFK+12] provides a survey of online chain partitions of orders.

4

MERGING ALGORITHMS

4.1 INTRODUCTION

In Chapter 3, we proved Dilworth's Theorem for partitioning a poset into the least number of chains. We now give an efficient algorithm to compute this partition that is especially useful in distributed systems. This algorithm is based on reducing the number of chains in a given chain partition whenever possible. To determine optimal chain composition, we begin with the trivial chain partition in which each element of the poset is a one element chain. By repeatedly reducing the number of chains, we arrive at the optimal chain partition. The number of chains in the final partition also gives us the width of the poset.

4.2 ALGORITHM TO MERGE CHAINS IN VECTOR CLOCK REPRESENTATION

Assume that we have a poset corresponding to a distributed computation. This poset is represented using vector clocks for each element. Furthermore, we will assume that the given poset P is partitioned into N chains, $P_1, P_2, \ldots P_N$ corresponding to N processes. The algorithm uses queues to represent the initial chains. Each queue is stored in increasing order so the head of a queue is the smallest element in the queue. The initial chain partition may not be optimal and may even be the trivial partition with each element in a chain by itself. Our goal is to determine if there exists an antichain of size at least K, for any given integer K.

Introduction to Lattice Theory with Computer Science Applications, First Edition. Vijay K. Garg.
© 2015 John Wiley & Sons, Inc. Published 2015 by John Wiley & Sons, Inc.

```
function FindAntiChain (K: integer, P₁, .., P_N: queues)
    while the number of queues is greater than K − 1
        choose K queues which have been merged least number of
        times;
        merge K queues into K − 1 queues;
        if not successful return the antichain;
    end;
    return "no antichain of size K;"
```

Figure 4.1   Function that determines if an antichain of size K exists.

From Dilworth's Theorem, it follows that P can be partitioned into $K - 1$ chains if and only if there does not exist an antichain of size at least K. So, our problem is reduced to taking the N chains P_i, $1 \leq i \leq N$, and trying to merge them into $K - 1$ chains. The approach we take is to choose K chains and try to merge them into $K - 1$ chains. After this step, we have $N - 1$ chains left. We do this step ("choose K chains, merge into $K - 1$ chains") $N - K + 1$ times. If we fail on any iteration, then P could not be partitioned into $K - 1$ chains and there exists an antichain of size K or more.

The algorithm *FindAntiChain* (Figure 4.1) calls the *Merge* function $N - K + 1$ times. The *Merge* function takes K queues as input and returns $K - 1$ queues if successful. If not, then an antichain has been found and is given by the heads of the returned queues.

There are two important decisions in this algorithm. The first is how to choose the K chains for the merge operation. The answer follows from classical merge techniques used for sorting. We choose the chains that have been merged the least number of times. (Alternatively, one can use the K smallest queues. We have used the metric "merged least number of times" for convenience in the complexity analysis.) This strategy reduces the number of comparisons required by the algorithm.

The second and more important decision is how to implement *Merge*. The merge is performed by repeatedly removing an element from one of the K input chains and inserting it in one of the $K - 1$ output chains. An element will be moved from the input to the output if it is smaller than an element on the head of some other input chain. The problem is deciding on which output chain to place the element.

Note that this is trivial for $K = 2$, when two input queues are merged into a single output queue as is done in the merge sort. For $K > 2$, the number of output queues is greater than one, and the algorithm needs to decide which output queue the element needs to be inserted in. The simple strategy of inserting the element in any output queue does not work as shown in Figure 4.2, where there are three input queues (P_1, P_2, and P_3), which need to be merged into two output queues (Q_1 and Q_2). Suppose we use a simple strategy, which results in the operations listed in the following. Initially, Q_1 and Q_2 are empty. Each operation moves an element from the head of P_1, P_2, or P_3 to one of the two output queues. Note that we can only move the head of P_i if it is smaller than the head of some other queue P_j. The operations we perform are as follows:

P1	P2	P3
a:(1,0,0)	d:(0,1,0)	f:(2,0,0)
b:(1,1,0)	e:(2,2,0)	g:(2,3,0)
c:(1,2,0)		

Q1	Q2

(a)

P1	P2	P3
		f:(2,0,0)
	e:(2,2,0)	g:(2,3,0)

Q1	Q2
a:(1,0,0)	d:(0,1,0)
b:(1,1,0)	
c:(1,2,0)	

(b)

Q1	Q2
a:(1,0,0)	d:(0,1,0)
f:(2,0,0)	b:(1,1,0)
e:(2,2,0)	c:(1,2,0)
g:(2,3,0)	

(c)

Figure 4.2 An example of a failed naive strategy. (a) The initial configuration. (b) The point at which the strategy fails: there is nowhere to insert $(2,0,0)$. (c) This example can be merged into two chains.

1. $(1,0,0) < (2,0,0)$. So move $(1,0,0)$ to some output queue, say Q_1.
2. $(0,1,0) < (1,1,0)$. So move $(0,1,0)$ to some output queue, say Q_2.
3. $(1,1,0) < (2,2,0)$. So move $(1,1,0)$ to some output queue, say Q_1.
4. $(1,2,0) < (2,2,0)$. So move $(1,2,0)$ to some output queue, say Q_1.
5. $(2,0,0) < (2,2,0)$. So move $(2,0,0)$ to some output queue, but which one?

Notice that we have worked ourselves into a corner because when we decide to move $(2,0,0)$ there is no output queue in which we can insert it. The output queues must be sorted since they represent chains. This is done by inserting the elements in increasing order, but $(2,0,0)$ is not larger than the tails of any of the output queues. Thus we have nowhere to insert it.

This situation does not imply that the input queues cannot be merged. In fact in this case they can be merged into two queues as shown in Figure 4.2(c). It merely implies that we did not intelligently insert the elements into the output queues. The function *FindQ* chooses the output queue without running into this problem. A discussion of *FindQ* is deferred until after we describe the details of the *Merge* function.

The *Merge* function compares the heads of each input queue with the heads of all other queues. Whenever it finds a queue whose head is less than the head of another queue, it marks the smaller of the two to be deleted from its input queue and inserted in one of the output queues. It repeats this process until no elements can be deleted from an input queue. This occurs when the heads of all the queues are incomparable, that is, they form an antichain. Note that it may be the case that some input queues are empty. If none are empty, then we have found an antichain of size K. The heads of the input queues form the antichain. If one or more are empty, the merge operation (which is not complete yet) will be successful. All that is left to do is to take the nonempty input queues and append them to the appropriate output queues. This is done by the *FinishMerge* function whose implementation is not described because it is straightforward.

The *Merge* algorithm is shown in Figure 4.3. Note that it only compares the heads of queues, which have not been compared earlier. It keeps track of this in the variable ac, which is a set of indices indicating those input queues whose heads are known to form an antichain. Initially, ac is empty. The *Merge* algorithm terminates when either ac has K elements or one of the input queues is empty.

The first *for* loop in *Merge* compares the heads of all queues that are not already known to form an antichain. That is, we compare each queue not in ac to every other queue. This avoids comparing two queues that are already in ac. Suppose $e_i = head(P_i)$ and $e_j = head(P_j)$ and inside the first *for* loop, it is determined that $e_i < e_j$. This implies that e_i is less than all elements in P_j. Thus, e_i cannot be in an antichain with any element in P_j and therefore cannot be in any antichain of size K, which is a subset of the union of the input queues. Thus, we can safely move e_i to an output queue, which eliminates it from further consideration. The set *move* records which elements will be moved from an input queue to an output queue. The array *bigger* records the larger of the two elements that were compared. In this example, $bigger[i]$ equals j, implying that the head of P_j is bigger than the head of P_i. This information is used by *FindQ* to choose the output queue where the head of P_i will be inserted.

The second *for* loop just moves all elements in *move* to an output queue. Consider the state of the program just before the second *for* loop begins. If the head, e, of an input queue is not marked to be moved, then e is not less than the head of any other input queue or else it would have been marked to be moved. This implies that any two elements which are not moved are concurrent, which in turn implies that the set of heads which are not moved form an antichain. This antichain is recorded in ac for the next iteration of the *while* loop.

We now return to describing how *FindQ* works. The formal description of *FindQ* is shown in Figure 4.4. Given the queue that contains the element to be moved, and the queue with which this element was compared (it must be smaller than the head of another queue in order to move it), the procedure *FindQ* determines which output queue to use. The *FindQ* function takes three parameters:

G: an undirected graph called *queue insert graph*

i: the input queue from which the element x is to be deleted

j: the queue in which all elements are bigger than x.

A "queue insert graph" is used to deduce the queue in which the next element is inserted. It has K vertices and exactly $K - 1$ edges. An edge corresponds to an output queue and a vertex corresponds to an input queue. Therefore, each edge (i,j) has a label, $label(i,j) \in \{1, \dots, K - 1\}$, which identifies the output queue it corresponds with. No labels are duplicated in the graph, thus each output queue is represented exactly once. Similarly, each input queue is represented exactly once.

function Merge($P_1, ..., P_K$: queues): $Q_1, ..., Q_{K-1}$: queues;
const all = {1,...K};
var ac,move: subsets of all;
       bigger: array[1..K] of 1..K;
       G: initially any acyclic graph on K vertices;
begin
       ac := ∅;
       while (|ac|≠ K ∧ ¬(∃i : $1 \leq i \leq K$: empty(P_i))) **do**
              move := {};
              for i ∈ all - ac **and** j ∈ all **do**
                     if $head(P_i) < head(P_j)$ **then**
                            move := move ∪ {i};
                            bigger[i] := j;
                     end;
                     if $head(P_j) < head(P_i)$ **then**
                            move := move ∪ {j};
                            bigger[j] := i;
                     end;
              endfor
              for i ∈ move **do**
                     dest := FindQ(G,i,bigger[i]);
                     x := deletehead(P_i);
                     insert(Q_{dest}, x);
              endfor
              ac := all - move;
       endwhile
       if (∃i : empty(P_i)) **then**
              FinishMerge($G, P_1, ... P_K, Q_1, ... Q_{K-1}$);
              return ($Q_1, ... , Q_{K-1}$);
       else
              return ($P_1, ... , P_K$);// merge not possible
       end
end

Figure 4.3 Generalized merge procedure for posets.

An edge (i,j) between vertex i and vertex j means that the heads of P_i and P_j are both bigger than the tail of $Q_{label(i,j)}$. The goal is to ensure that for any input queue (i.e., any vertex) there exists an output queue (i.e., an edge) in which the head of the input queue can be inserted. This constraint is equivalent to the requirement that every vertex has at least one edge adjacent to it. It is also equivalent to the requirement that the graph is a tree (i.e., acyclic) since there are K nodes and $K - 1$ edges.

```
function FindQ(G: graph; i,j:1..K): label;
  add edge (i,j) to G;
  (i,k) := the edge such that (i,j) and (i,k) are part of the same cycle in G;
  remove edge (i,k) from G;
  label(i,j) := label(i,k);
  return label(i,j);
end
```

Figure 4.4   Function *FindQ* that finds the output queue to insert an element.

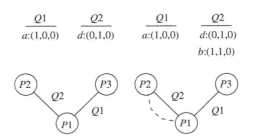

Figure 4.5   Using a queue insert graph to find the output queue.

FindQ uses the queue insert graph as follows. Consider the function call *FindQ(G, i, j)*. The element to be deleted is $e_i = head(P_i)$, and it is smaller than $e_j = head(P_j)$ (i.e., $bigger[i] = j$). *FindQ* adds the edge (i, j) to G. Since G was a tree before adding edge (i, j), it now contains exactly one cycle that includes (i, j). Let (i, k) be the other edge incident on vertex i, which is part of this cycle (it is possible that $k = j$). *FindQ* deletes (i, k) and adds (i, j) and then sets the label of (i, j) equal to the label of (i, k). *FindQ* then returns the label associated with the new edge. This label indicates which queue e_i will be inserted in.

Consider our previous example with the naive algorithm. It made a bad decision when it placed element $(1, 1, 0)$ on Q_1. Figure 4.5 shows the state of the queues and of the graph before and after the correct decision made by *FindQ*. Element $(1, 1, 0)$ is in P_1 and is less than the head of P_2. Thus, the edge $(1, 2)$ is added to the graph (dashed line in Figure 4.5). It forms a cycle with the other edge $(1, 2)$, which is labeled with Q_2. We copy this label to the new edge, delete the old edge and return Q_2, indicating that $(1, 1, 0)$ should be inserted in Q_2.

An important invariant of the queue insert graph is that given any edge (i, j) and the output queue associated with it, the queue is empty or the tail of the queue is less than all elements in input queues P_i and P_j. This is stated and proven in Lemma 4.1 and is used later to show that the output queues are always sorted.

Lemma 4.1   *If* $(i, j) \in G$, *then*

$$empty(Q_{label(i,j)}) \lor (\forall e : e \in P_i \cup P_j : tail(Q_{label(i,j)}) \leq e).$$

Proof: Initially, the lemma holds since all output queues are empty. Now assume that the lemma holds and we need to insert $e_i = head(P_i)$ into output queue Q_l where $l = FindQ(G, i, j)$ and $j = bigger[i]$. Since $j = bigger[i]$, we know $e_i \leq head(P_j)$. Since P_i and P_j are sorted, we know $e_i \leq e$ for any element $e \in P_i \cup P_j$. After moving e_i to Q_l, the tail of Q_l will be e_i and the lemma will still hold.   ∎

The merge operation must produce sorted output queues. Lemma 4.2 proves that our algorithm meets this requirement.

Lemma 4.2 *If the elements are inserted in the output queues using FindQ, then all output queues are always sorted.*

Proof: Initially, all output queues are empty. Now assume that each output queue is sorted and we need to move $e_i = head(P_i)$ to an output queue. The *FindQ* procedure will return $Q_{label(i,j)}$, where (i, j) is some edge in G. By Lemma 4.1, the tail of this queue is less than or equal to e_i. Thus, after inserting e_i in Q_l, Q_l is still sorted. No other output queues are modified, thus the lemma still holds.   ∎

4.3   AN UPPER BOUND FOR DETECTING AN ANTICHAIN OF SIZE K

In this section, we analyze the time complexity based on the number of comparisons required by the algorithm, that is, the number of times the heads of two queues are compared in the *Merge* function.

Theorem 4.3 *The maximum number of comparisons required by the above-mentioned algorithm is $KMN(K + \log_\rho N)$ where $\rho = K/(K - 1)$.*

Proof: We first calculate the complexity of merging K queues into $K - 1$ queues. From the *Merge* algorithm, it is clear that each element must be in ac before it passes to an output queue and it requires K comparisons to be admitted to ac. Thus, if the total number of elements to be merged is l, then l elements must pass through ac on their way to the output queue for a total of Kl comparisons.

Initially, $l \leq KM$ but the queues grow for each successive call to *Merge*. At this point, our technique of rotating the list of queues to be merged is useful. Let $level.i$ denote the maximum number of merge operations that any element in P_i has participated in. The algorithm rotates $Qlist$ to ensure that in each iteration the K queues with the smallest level numbers will be merged. Initially, there are N queues at level 0. Each of the first N/K merge operations reduces K queues with level 0 to $K - 1$ queues with level 1. This pattern continues until there are $2K$ queues left, at which time the maximum level will be $log_\rho N$ where ρ is the reducing factor and equals $K/(K - 1)$. Merging the remaining $2K$ queues into $K - 1$ queues adds K more levels. Thus, the maximum level of any final output queue is $K + log_\rho N$. So, there are at most MN elements, each of which participates in at most $K + log_\rho N$ merge operations at a cost of K comparisons per element per merge. Therefore, the maximum number of comparisons required by the above-mentioned algorithm is $KMN(K + log_\rho N)$.   ∎

Note that for the special case when $K = 2$, the complexity is $O(MN \log N)$. Further, if $M = 1$ and $K = 2$, this reduces to the well-known merge sort algorithm with the complexity of $O(N \log N)$ comparisons.

4.4   A LOWER BOUND FOR DETECTING AN ANTICHAIN OF SIZE K

In this section, we provide a lower bound on the number of comparisons required by any algorithm to solve the above-mentioned problem. The lower bound is proved by defining an adversary which produces a set of input queues that forces the merge algorithm to use at least KMN comparisons, where M is the number of elements in the largest input queue.

Theorem 4.4 *Let* $(P, \leq)$ *be any partially ordered finite set of size MN. We are given a decomposition of P into N sets* $P_1, ...P_N$ *such that each* P_i *is a chain of size M. Any algorithm that determines if there exists an antichain of size K must make at least* $\Omega(KMN)$ *comparisons.*

Proof: We use an adversary argument. Let $P_i[s]$ denote the sth element in the queue P_i. The adversary will give the algorithm P_i's with the following characteristic:

$$(\forall i,j,s \; : \; P_i[s] < P_j[s + 1]).$$

Formally, on being asked to compare $P_i[s]$ and $P_j[t]$, $(s \neq t)$ the adversary uses:

> **if** $(s < t)$ **then** return $P_i[s] < P_j[t]$
> **if** $(t < s)$ **then** return $P_j[t] < P_i[s]$.

Thus, the above-mentioned problem reduces to M independent instances of the problem that checks if a poset of N elements has a subset of size K containing pairwise incomparable elements. If the algorithm does not completely solve one instance, then the adversary chooses that instance to show a poset consistent with all its answers but different in the final outcome.

We now show that the number of comparisons to determine whether any poset of size N has an antichain of size K is at least $N(K - 1)/2$. The adversary will give that poset to the algorithm that has either $K - 1$ or K chains such that any pair of elements in different chains are incomparable. In other words, the poset is a simple union of either $K - 1$ or K chains. The adversary keeps a table *numq* such that *numq[x]* denotes the number of questions asked about the element x. The algorithm for the adversary is shown in Figure 4.6.

Given any two elements x and y, when the algorithm asks the relationship between x and y, the adversary returns that the elements are incomparable if the algorithm has not asked $K - 1$ questions related to x or y. When the algorithm asks $(K - 1)^{th}$ question about any element, we know that there is at least one chain in which no element has been compared with x so far. This is because there are $K - 1$ chains and x has been compared with at most $K - 2$ elements. In this case, x is inserted in that chain. This insertion is consistent with all the answers provided so far because x is

```
var
        numq: array[1, ..., N] of integers, initially, ∀i : 1, ... , N, numq[i] = 0;
/* number of questions asked about element x */

function  compare (x, y:elements)
        numq[x]++; numq[y]++;
        if (numq[x] = K − 1) then
                chain[x] := chain in which no element has been compared
                with x so far;
        if (numq[y] = K − 1) then
                chain[y] := chain in which no element has been compared
                with y so far;
        if (numq[x] < K − 1) or (numq[y] < K − 1) then
                return x||y;
        if (chain[x] ≠ chain[y]) then
                return x||y;
        else
                if x inserted earlier than y then return (x < y);
                else return (y < x);
end
```

Figure 4.6   Algorithm for the adversary.

indeed incomparable with all the elements that it has been compared. When both x and y have already been inserted in chains, then the adversary returns that x and y are incomparable if they are in different chains and comparable if they are in the same chain. In the latter case, it uses the simple order of when the elements were inserted in the chain to return the order between x and y.

We show that if the algorithm does not ask $K − 1$ questions about any element x, the adversary can produce a poset inconsistent with the answer of the algorithm. If the algorithm answered that no antichain of size K exists, then the adversary can produce an antichain that includes one element from each of the $K − 1$ chains and the element x. On the other hand, if the algorithm answered that an antichain exists, then the adversary could put x and all other elements for which $K − 1$ questions have not been asked in $K − 1$ chains.

Since each comparison involves two elements, we get that the algorithm must ask at least $N(K − 1)/2$ questions for each level. Thus, overall, any algorithm must make at least $MN(K − 1)/2$ comparisons.

∎

It is easy to see that the lower bound is not tight. If we choose $M = 1$ and $K = 2$, we get the lower bound of $N/2$. However, the lower bound of $N \log N$ is well known for this case.

4.5   AN INCREMENTAL ALGORITHM FOR OPTIMAL CHAIN DECOMPOSITION

In this section, we briefly outline a strategy for optimal chain decomposition when elements of the poset arrive one at a time. Assume that we have seen poset P so far and that we have an optimal chain decomposition $\{C_1, C_2, ..., C_t\}$ of P. Let the new element that arrives be x and our goal is to determine optimal chain decomposition of $P' := P \cup \{x\}$. We determine for each chain C_i, the largest and the smallest element that is concurrent with x (by using binary search). If no such element exists then, x can be inserted into C_i. Otherwise, we consider the subposet Q formed by elements in P that are concurrent with x. The elements in $P - Q$ consists of chains $\{U_1, U_2, ..., U_t\}$ and $\{L_1, L_2, ..., L_t\}$ such that all elements in U_i are bigger than x and all elements in L_i are smaller than x.

If there is any antichain of size t in Q, then that antichain together with x forms an antichain of size $t + 1$. In this case, we have an optimal chain partition by keeping x in a separate chain. Otherwise, t chains in Q can be merged into $t - 1$ chains. Moreover, it can be shown that the resulting $t - 1$ chains are such that they can be combined with $t - 1$ smaller chains and $t - 1$ larger chains (see Problem 4). By inserting x into the remaining smaller and the remaining larger chain, we get an optimal chain partition of P'.

4.6   PROBLEMS

4.1. Consider the following greedy algorithm for chain decomposition. Choose any longest chain in the poset. Remove the chain from the poset and repeat the process till the poset becomes empty. Show that the greedy algorithm may not return a decomposition of the poset into the least number of chains.

4.2. Give an efficient algorithm to return the minimum antichain of size K of a poset with width K where the ordering between antichains is based on the relation $\preceq$ defined in Theorem 3.2.

4.3. Give an efficient incremental algorithm for chain partition under *linear extension hypothesis*. Assume that elements of a poset arrive one at a time such that the new element x that arrives is a maximal element of the poset seen so far. Your algorithm should maintain the optimal chain partition after each arrival.
(Hint: Maintain the minimum antichain A of size w, where w is the width of the current poset. Show that the chains below A do not change when x is merged.)

4.4. For the incremental algorithm in Section 4.5, show how will you merge t chains of Q into $t - 1$ chains such that the resulting $t - 1$ chains can be combined with $t - 1$ of the smaller chains and $t - 1$ of the larger chains. (Hint: Use the spanning tree and FindQ algorithm appropriately.)

4.7 BIBLIOGRAPHIC REMARKS

The algorithm to merge k chains into $k - 1$ chains is taken from [TG97]. Bogart and Magagnosc solve the chain reduction problem by using the concept of a reducing sequence. We have not discussed that algorithm in this book and refer the interested readers to [FJN96]. Incremental algorithms for optimal chain partitions are discussed in [IG06].

5

LATTICES

5.1 INTRODUCTION

Given a poset, the two most fundamental derived operations on the elements of the poset are the join and the meet operations. As we have seen earlier, join and meet operations may not exist for all subsets of the poset. This observation motivates the notion of lattices that occur in many different contexts. Let us recall the definition of a lattice from Chapter 1.

Definition 5.1 (Lattice) *A poset* $(X, \leq)$ *is a* **lattice** *iff* $\forall x, y \in X : x \sqcup y$ *and* $x \sqcap y$ *exist.*

If $\forall x, y \in X : x \sqcup y$ exists, then we call it a *sup semilattice*. If $\forall x, y \in X : x \sqcap y$ exists, then we call it an *inf semilattice*.

In our definition of a lattice, we have required the existence of *lub*'s and *glb*'s for sets of size two. This is equivalent to the requirement of the existence of *lub*'s and *glb*'s for sets of finite size by using induction (see Problem 5.6).

We now give many examples of lattices that occur naturally.

- The set of natural numbers under the relation *divides* forms a lattice. Given any two natural numbers, the greatest common divisor (gcd) and the least common multiple (lcm) of those two numbers correspond to the sup and inf, respectively.
- The family of all subsets of a set X, under the relation $\subseteq$ (i.e., the poset $(2^X, \subseteq)$) forms a lattice. Given any two subsets Y, Z of X, the sets $Y \cup Z$ and $Y \cap Z$ (corresponding to sup and inf) are always defined.

Introduction to Lattice Theory with Computer Science Applications, First Edition. Vijay K. Garg.
© 2015 John Wiley & Sons, Inc. Published 2015 by John Wiley & Sons, Inc.

- The set of rationals or reals forms a lattice with the $\leq$ relation. This is a totally ordered set and sup and inf correspond to the *max* and *min* for a finite subset.
- The set of n-dimensional vectors over $\mathbb{N}$ with component-wise $\leq$ relation forms a lattice. Componentwise $\leq$ of two vectors $(x_1, x_2, \ldots x_n)$, $(y_1, y_2, \ldots y_n)$ is defined as

$$(x_1, x_2, \ldots x_n) \leq (y_1, y_2, \ldots y_n) \equiv \forall i : x_i \leq y_i.$$

The sup and inf operations correspond to component-wise maximum and minimum.

It is important to note that a poset may be a lattice, but it may have sets of infinite size for which sup and inf may not exist. A simple example is that of the set of natural numbers under the natural $\leq$ relation. There is no sup of the set of even numbers, even though sup and inf exist for any finite set. Another example is the set of rational numbers, Q. Consider the set $\{x \in Q \mid x \leq \sqrt{2}\}$. The least upper bound of this set is $\sqrt{2}$, which is not a rational number. A lattice for which any subset has lub and glb defined is called a **complete lattice**. An example of a complete lattice is the set of real numbers extended with $+\infty$ and $-\infty$. We will discuss complete lattices in greater detail in Chapter 6.

5.2 SUBLATTICES

A set $S \subseteq L$ is a sublattice of a given lattice $L = (X, \leq)$ iff:

$$\forall a, b \in S : \sup(a, b) \in S \wedge \inf(a, b) \in S.$$

In the above-mentioned definition, the sup and the inf operations are with respect to the original lattice L. For S to be a sublattice, S being a subset and a lattice is not sufficient. In addition to S being a lattice, sup and inf operations must be inherited from the lattice L.

Examples

1. In Figure 5.1, the shaded elements in lattices (i) and (ii) form sublattices, while those in (iii) and (iv) do not.
2. Any one-element subset of a lattice is a sublattice. More generally, any chain in a lattice is a sublattice.
3. A subset M of a lattice L may be a lattice in its own right without being a sublattice of L; see Figure 5.1 (iii) for an example. The shaded elements in (iii) is not a sublattice because $a, b \in S$, however $a \sqcup b \notin S$.

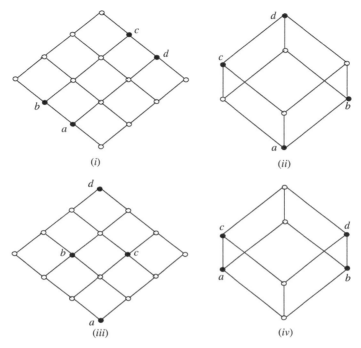

Figure 5.1   Examples: lattices and sublattices.

5.3   LATTICES AS ALGEBRAIC STRUCTURES

So far, we have looked at a lattice as a special type of poset, $P = (X, \leq)$ with $\sqcup$ and $\sqcap$ defined based on the $\leq$ relation.

An alternative method of studying lattices is to start with a set equipped with the $\sqcup$ and $\sqcap$ operators and define $\leq$ relation based on these operations. Consider any set X with two algebraic operators $\sqcup$ and $\sqcap$. Assume that the operators satisfy the following properties:

$(L1)$ $a \sqcup (b \sqcup c) = (a \sqcup b) \sqcup c$ (associativity)

$(L1)^{\delta}$ $a \sqcap (b \sqcap c) = (a \sqcap b) \sqcap c$

$(L2)$ $a \sqcup b = b \sqcup a$ (commutativity)

$(L2)^{\delta}$ $a \sqcap b = b \sqcap a$

$(L3)$ $a \sqcup (a \sqcap b) = a$ (absorption)

$(L3)^{\delta}$ $a \sqcap (a \sqcup b) = a.$

	a	b	c	d	e	f	g
a	a	$a \sqcap b$	$a \sqcap c$	$a \sqcap d$	$a \sqcap e$	$a \sqcap f$	$a \sqcap g$
b	$b \sqcup a$	b	$b \sqcap c$	$b \sqcap d$	$b \sqcap e$	$b \sqcap f$	$b \sqcap g$
c	$c \sqcup a$	$c \sqcup b$	c	$c \sqcap d$	$c \sqcap e$	$c \sqcap f$	$c \sqcap g$
d	$d \sqcup a$	$d \sqcup b$	$d \sqcup c$	d	$d \sqcap e$	$d \sqcap f$	$d \sqcap g$
e	$e \sqcup a$	$e \sqcup b$	$e \sqcup c$	$e \sqcup d$	e	$e \sqcap f$	$e \sqcap g$
f	$f \sqcup a$	$f \sqcup b$	$f \sqcup c$	$f \sqcup d$	$f \sqcup e$	f	$f \sqcap g$
g	$g \sqcup a$	$g \sqcup b$	$g \sqcup c$	$g \sqcup d$	$g \sqcup e$	$g \sqcup f$	g

Figure 5.2   Table notation for the algebra $(X, \sqcup, \sqcap)$.

Theorem 5.2 *Let $(X, \sqcup, \sqcap)$ be a nonempty set with the operators $\sqcup$ and $\sqcap$ that satisfy $(L1) - (L3)$ earlier. We define the operator $\leq$ on X by*

$$a \leq b \equiv (a \sqcup b = b).$$

Then,

- $\leq$ *is reflexive, antisymmetric, and transitive*
- $\sup(a, b) = a \sqcup b$
- $\inf(a, b) = a \sqcap b$.

Proof: Left as an exercise.

∎

The algebra $(X, \sqcup, \sqcap)$ can be represented by an $n \times n$ table, where $|X| = n$. It may seem as though two $n \times n$ tables are needed, one for $\sqcup$ and one for $\sqcap$. However, a single $n \times n$ table suffices, with one half used for $\sqcup$ and the other for $\sqcap$, as shown in Figure 5.2. By commutativity, $a \sqcup b = b \sqcup a$, and $a \sqcap b = b \sqcap a$, so populating both halves of the table for the same operation is redundant. In addition, by absorption, $a \sqcup a = a \sqcap a = a$, so the diagonal elements of the table agree for $\sqcup$ and $\sqcap$.

5.4   BOUNDING THE SIZE OF THE COVER RELATION OF A LATTICE

In this section, we give a bound on the number of edges in the cover relation of a lattice. Consider a poset with n elements. Let e_c be the number of edges in the cover relation and $e_\leq$ be the number of edges in the poset relation.

Then, it is clear that $e_c \leq e_\leq \leq n^2$. We prove that $e_c \leq n^{3/2}$.

Theorem 5.3 *For a lattice L,*

$$n - 1 \leq e_c \leq n^{3/2}.$$

Proof: The lower bound is clear because every element in the lattice has at least one lower cover (except the smallest element). We show the upper bound.

Consider two distinct elements $x, y \in L$. Let $B(x)$ denote the set of elements covered by x. $B(x) \cap B(y)$ cannot have more than one element because that would violate the lattice property. Let $B'(x) = B(x) \cup \{x\}$. Hence,

$$|B'(x) \cap B'(y)| \le 1.$$

Let

$$L = \{x_0, \dots, x_{n-1}\},$$
$$b_i = |B(x_i)|.$$

Because there is no pair of elements in common between $B'(x)$ and $B'(y)$ for distinct x and y, we get

$$\sum_{i=0}^{n-1} \binom{b_i + 1}{2} \le \binom{n}{2}.$$

Simplifying, we get

$$\sum_{i=0}^{n-1} (b_i^2 + b_i) \le n^2 - n.$$

Dropping b_i from the left-hand side and $-n$ from the right-hand side, we get

$$\sum_{i=0}^{n-1} b_i^2 < n^2.$$

Since $e_c = \sum b_i$, we get

$$\left(\frac{e_c}{n}\right)^2 = \left(\frac{\sum b_i}{n}\right)^2 \le \frac{\sum b_i^2}{n} \le \frac{n^2}{n} = n.$$

The first inequality follows from Cauchy–Schwarz inequality.
   Therefore,

$$e_c^2 \le n^3.$$

■

5.5   JOIN-IRREDUCIBLE ELEMENTS REVISITED

We have defined join-irreducible elements of a poset in Chapter 1. Since lattices are posets with some additional properties, the same definition carries over. In fact, the concept of join-irreducible elements is more natural in the setting of lattices where the join operator between elements is always defined. In this section, we revisit join-irreducibles in lattices to show some of their useful properties. We use $J(L)$ to denote the set of join-irreducible elements of lattice L.

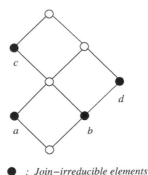

Figure 5.3   Join-irreducible elements: $J(L) = \{a, b, c, d\}$.

For finite lattices, the elements with only one lower cover are join-irreducible elements (see Problem 3).

In the lattice shown in Figure 5.3, a, b, c, and d are join-irreducible. In a chain, all elements except the least element are join-irreducible.

In a finite Boolean lattice, the lattice of all subsets of a given finite set, only the atoms (elements that cover the bottom element) are join-irreducible.

We now show how join-irreducible elements help us reduce complexity of various operations. It is easily shown that for all posets:

$$a \leq b \equiv \forall z : z \leq a \Rightarrow z \leq b.$$

The advantage of the next lemma is that it only requires comparisons between join-irreducible elements and not all elements $\leq a$.

Lemma 5.4 *For a finite lattice L, $a \leq b$ is equivalent to $\forall x : x \in J(L) : x \leq a \Rightarrow x \leq b$.*

Proof: For the forward direction, $a \leq b$ and $x \leq a$ implies, for any x, $x \leq b$ by transitivity. For the reverse direction, denote by $h(z)$ the *height* of z, i.e., the length (number of edges) of the *longest* path from z to inf L in the cover graph (well-defined, since L is a finite lattice). We will prove the property

$$P(a) := \forall b : ((\forall x : x \in J(L) : x \leq a \Rightarrow x \leq b) \Rightarrow a \leq b)$$

for all $a \in L$ by *strong* induction on $h(a)$. Given a, consider an arbitrary b and assume

(LHS) $\forall x : x \in J(L) : x \leq a \Rightarrow x \leq b$ and (IH) $P(c)$ holds for all c with $h(c) < h(a)$.

(1) If $h(a) = 0$, then $a = \inf L \leq b$, and $P(a)$ is vacuously true.
(2) If a is join-irreducible, then, using $x := a$ in (LHS), $a \leq b$ follows, and $P(a)$ is again vacuously true.

(3) Now assume $h(a) > 0$ and a not join-irreducible. Then, there exist $c \neq a, d \neq a$ such that $a = c \sqcup d$. Since $c \neq a$, we can conclude that $h(a) \geq h(c) + 1$ (h measures *longest* paths!). By (IH), $P(c)$ holds, i.e., $\forall b : ((\forall x : x \in J(L) : x \leq c \Rightarrow x \leq b) \Rightarrow c \leq b)$. We will use $P(c)$ to show $c \leq b$: assume $x \in J(L)$ with $x \leq c$, then $x \leq c \sqcup d = a$, hence $x \leq a$, thus, by (LHS), $x \leq b$. Property $P(c)$ delivers that $c \leq b$. Similarly, one can derive $d \leq b$, hence $c \sqcup d \leq b$, and with $a = c \sqcup d$, we obtain $a \leq b$.

∎

The following result strengthens the statement that $a = \sqcup_{x \leq a} x$.

Lemma 5.5 *For a finite lattice L and any $a \in L$,*

$$a = \bigsqcup \{x \in J(L) : x \leq a\}.$$

Proof: Let $T = \{x \in J(L) : x \leq a\}$. We have to show that $a = \text{lub}(T)$.

Since any $x \in T$ satisfies $x \leq a$, a is an upper bound on T. Consider *any* upper bound u:

$\quad u$ is an upper bound on T
$\equiv\quad$ { Definition of upper bound }
$\quad x \in T \Rightarrow x \leq u$
$\equiv\quad$ { Definition of T }
$\quad (x \in J(L) \wedge x \leq a) \Rightarrow x \leq u$
$\equiv\quad$ { Elementary propositional logic: $(a \wedge b) \Rightarrow c \equiv a \Rightarrow (b \Rightarrow c)$ }
$\quad x \in J(L) \Rightarrow (x \leq a \Rightarrow x \leq u)$
$\equiv\quad$ { Lemma 5.4 }
$\quad a \leq u,$

So, a is in fact the least upper bound on T.

∎

Notice one special case: since $a := \inf L$ is not considered join-irreducible, the lemma confirms that $\inf L = \bigsqcup \emptyset$.

5.6 PROBLEMS

5.1. Show that a poset $P = (X, \leq)$ is a lattice iff for all finite subsets $Y \subseteq X$, $\sup Y$ and $\inf Y$ exist.

5.2. Show that the bound for e_c can be improved when L is distributive, i.e., show that if L is distributive then

$$e_c \leq \frac{n \log_2 n}{2}.$$

5.3. Show that in finite lattices an element is join-irreducible iff it has only one lower cover.

5.7   BIBLIOGRAPHIC REMARKS

Most of the material in this chapter is quite standard and can be found in Birkhoff [Bir67], and Davey and Priestley [DP90]. The description of the bound on the size of the cover relation follows the reference Freese, Jaroslav, and Nation [FJN96].

6

LATTICE COMPLETION

6.1 INTRODUCTION

We have seen that lattices are nicer structures than general posets because they allow us to take the meet and the join for any pair of elements in the set. What if we wanted to take the join and the meet of arbitrary subsets? Complete lattices allow us to do exactly that. All finite lattices are complete, so the concept of complete lattices is important only for infinite lattices. In this chapter, we first discuss complete lattices and show many ways in which complete lattices arise in mathematics and computer science. In particular, *topped* ∩–*structures* and *closure operators* give us complete lattices.

Next we consider the question: What if the given poset is not a complete lattice or even a lattice? Can we embed it into a complete lattice? This brings us to the notion of lattice completion which is useful for both finite and infinite posets.

6.2 COMPLETE LATTICES

Recall the definition of a complete lattice.

Definition 6.1 (Complete Lattice) *A poset $P = (X, \leq)$ is a* **complete lattice** *iff for all subsets $Y \subseteq X$, sup Y and inf Y exist.*

Finite lattices are always complete. When X is infinite, then $(X, \leq)$ may be a lattice but not a complete lattice. Note that we require sup Y and inf Y to exist for all subsets

Introduction to Lattice Theory with Computer Science Applications, First Edition. Vijay K. Garg.
© 2015 John Wiley & Sons, Inc. Published 2015 by John Wiley & Sons, Inc.

(not just finite subsets). For example, consider the set of natural numbers under the usual order. This poset is a lattice but not a complete lattice because sup is not defined for subsets Y such as the set of all odd numbers. Note that in some cases, a lattice can be easily made complete by adding a few "artificial" elements. For example, we can add a special element "∞" to the set of natural numbers. The set $\mathbb{N} \cup \{\infty\}$ is a complete lattice. It may not be enough to add finite number of elements to complete a lattice. For example, the set of rationals with the elements ∞ and $-\infty$ is not a complete lattice. Consider the subset $Y = \{x \in X | x^2 \leq 2\}$. This set has no supremum in the set of rationals.

In the definition of complete lattices, note that when Y is the empty set, the requirement that inf Y exist corresponds to existence of the ⊤ element. Similarly, when Y is the empty set, sup Y equals the ⊥ element.

The following lemma provides us a way of showing that a lattice is complete by only proving that the inf exists for any subset, saving us half the work.

Lemma 6.2 (Half-work Lemma) *A poset P is a complete lattice iff inf S exists for every $S \subseteq P$.*

Proof: The forward direction ($\Rightarrow$) is easy.

To show $\Leftarrow$, we need to prove that sup S exists for every S. To do so, we will formulate sup S in terms of the inf of some other set.

Consider the set T of upper bounds of S, i.e.,

$$T = \{x \in X \mid \forall s \in S : s \leq x\}.$$

Now let $a = \inf T$. We claim that $a = \sup S$. From the definition of T, we get that $\forall s \in S : \forall t \in T : s \leq t$. Since $a = \inf T$, it follows that $\forall s \in S : s \leq a$. Thus, a is an upper bound of S.

Further, for any upper bound t of S, we know that $t \in T$. Therefore, $a \leq t$ because $a = \inf T$. Thus, $a = \sup S$.

∎

Note that the set T in the proof may be empty. In that case, a would be the top element of P.

6.3   CLOSURE OPERATORS

We find from experience that good structures tend to have multiple, equivalent ways of defining them. This is good for us in at least two ways. First, it provides multiple ways of characterizing the structure, hence offering us more flexibility in doing proofs. In addition, it may provide us efficient algorithms for dealing with the structures. Here, we study two alternative definitions for complete lattices and then show their equivalence. The first definition is based on closure operators.

Given a set X, we denote the set of all subsets of X (the power set of X) by 2^X. We now define closure operators on the set 2^X.

Definition 6.3 (Closure Operator) *A map* $C : 2^X \mapsto 2^X$ *is a closure operator iff it satisfies*

1. $\forall A \subseteq X, A \subseteq C(A)$ *(increasing)*
2. $\forall A, B \subseteq X, A \subseteq B \Rightarrow C(A) \subseteq C(B)$ *(monotone)*
3. $\forall A \subseteq X, C(C(A)) = C(A)$ *(idempotent)*.

We now give some examples of the closure operator.

1. Given a poset $P = (X, \leq)$ and any subset $Y \subseteq X$, let

$$C(Y) = \{x \in X \mid \exists y \in Y : x \leq y\}.$$

   $C(Y)$ adds to Y all elements that are smaller than some element in Y. It is easy to verify that C is a closure operator.
2. Our next example is from the theory of formal languages. Let Σ be any alphabet and $L \subseteq \Sigma^*$ be a language (set of finite strings) defined over Σ. Then, **Kleene closure** of L consists of all finite strings that can be obtained by concatenation of strings in L. Thus, Kleene closure for a language L is defined as

$$C(L) = \{x.y \mid x \in L \wedge y \in L\},$$

   where the operator . means concatenation. It is easy to verify that Kleene closure satisfies all requirements of the closure operator.

Before we show the relationship between complete lattices and closure operators, we present yet another alternate definition, called *topped ∩–structures*.

6.4   TOPPED ∩–STRUCTURES

The second definition of a complete lattice is based on topped ∩–structures.

Definition 6.4 (Topped ∩–Structure) *For a set* X, *let* $\mathcal{L} \subseteq 2^X$. $\mathcal{L}$ *is a topped ∩–structure iff the following hold:*

1. $X \in \mathcal{L}$
2. $[\forall i \in I : A_i \in \mathcal{L}] \Rightarrow (\bigcap_{i \in I} A_i \in \mathcal{L})$, *where* I *is any indexing set.*

Thus, a topped ∩–structure is a set of sets that contains the original set and is closed under arbitrary intersection. From the Half-work Lemma, it is clear that topped ∩–structures form a complete lattice under the relation $\subseteq$.

We now show that closure operators are equivalent to topped ∩–structures.

Theorem 6.5 *Let* C *be a closure operator defined on* 2^X. *Let* $\mathcal{L}(C) = \{A \subseteq X : C(A) = A\}$ *be a family of subsets in* 2^X. *Then* $\mathcal{L}(C)$ *is a topped* $\cap$–*structure. Conversely, let* $\mathcal{L}$ *be a topped* $\cap$–*structure. Then,*

$$C_{\mathcal{L}}(A) = \cap\{B \in \mathcal{L} | A \subseteq B\}$$

is a closure operator.

Proof: Left as an exercise.

∎

6.5   DEDEKIND–MACNEILLE COMPLETION

For any poset P, sup or inf may not be defined for all subsets of elements of P. We would like to find a complete lattice that has P embedded in it (see Fig. 6.1). We now turn to one such completion, the *Dedekind–MacNeille completion* (also called *normal completion* or *completion by cuts* (figure 6.1)).

To define the notion of cuts, we first recall the definitions of down sets, up sets, upper bounds, and lower bounds.

$$y \in D[x] \;\equiv\; y \leq x \qquad \text{(down set)} \qquad (6.1)$$

$$y \in U[x] \;\equiv\; x \leq y \qquad \text{(up set)} \qquad (6.2)$$

$$y \in A^u \;\equiv\; \forall x \in A : x \leq y \qquad \text{(upper bounds)} \qquad (6.3)$$

$$y \in A^l \;\equiv\; \forall x \in A : y \leq x \qquad \text{(lower bounds)} \qquad (6.4)$$

Also recall that $D[x]$ is an order ideal. It is called the *principal ideal* of x. Similarly, $U[x]$ is an order filter. It is called the *principal filter* of x.

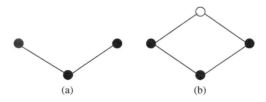

(a)   (b)

Figure 6.1   (a) A poset. (b) Its completion (the unshaded vertex is the added element).

Figure 6.2   A poset that is not a complete lattice.

The Dedekind–MacNeille completion will henceforth be referred to as the *DM* completion; the *DM* completion of a specific poset *P* will be denoted as *DM(P)*. The *DM* completion is based on a closure operator. Since we know that closure operators are equivalent to complete lattices, we know that applying the *DM* completion to *P* will give us our desired result. Before continuing, we use A^{ul} for $(A^u)^l$. We now define a *cut*.

Definition 6.6 (Cut of a Poset) *For a poset $P = (X, \leq)$, a subset $A \subseteq X$ is a* **cut** *if $A^{ul} = A$.*

Consider the poset in Figure 6.2. For $A = \{a, b, c\}$, we have $A^u = \{c\}$ and $A^{ul} = \{a, b, c\}$, so A is a cut. On the other hand, for $A = \{b, c\}$, we have $A^u = \{c\}$ and $A^{ul} = \{a, b, c\} \neq A$, so A is not a cut.

Remark 6.7 *A cut of a poset $P = (X, \leq)$ can also be defined as a pair (A, B) with $A, B \subseteq X$ such that $A^u = B$ and $B^l = A$. The reader can verify that both definitions are equivalent.*

We are now ready to define *DM(P)*.

Definition 6.8 (Dedekind–MacNeille Completion of a Poset) *For a given poset $P = (X, \leq)$, the Dedekind–MacNeille completion of P is the poset formed with the set of all the cuts of P under the set inclusion. Formally,*

$$DM(P) = (\{A \subseteq X : A^{ul} = A\}, \subseteq).$$

For the poset in Figure 6.2, the set of all cuts is

$$\{\{\}, \{a\}, \{b\}, \{a, b\}, \{a, b, c\}, \{a, b, d\}, \{a, b, c, d\}\}.$$

The poset formed by these sets under the $\subseteq$ relation is shown in Figure 6.3. This new poset is a complete lattice. Our original poset *P* is embedded in this new structure. We also note that the set of cuts forms a topped ∩–structure.

Lemma 6.9 *If A and B are cuts of a poset P, then so is $A \cap B$.*

Proof: Left as an exercise.

■

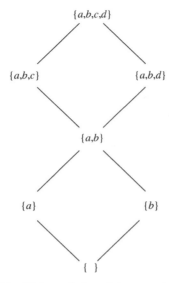

Figure 6.3   The *DM* completion of the poset from Figure 6.2.

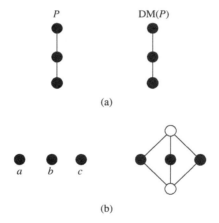

Figure 6.4   Two posets and their *DM* completions.

Figure 6.4 illustrates some more *DM* completions.

There are other ways to embed a poset *P* in a complete lattice. One way is via ideals; Figure 6.5 shows the complete lattice that embeds the poset from Figure 6.4(b). Notice that the embedding by ideals yields a larger lattice than that by *DM* completion. This is an important property of the *DM* completion: *DM(P)* results in the *smallest* complete lattice that embeds *P*.

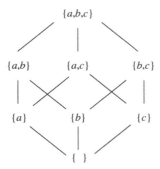

Figure 6.5 The complete lattice via order ideals that embeds the poset from Figure 6.4(b).

6.6 STRUCTURE OF DEDEKIND—MACNEILLE COMPLETION OF A POSET

In this section, we explore the structure of $DM(P)$ for a poset P and exhibit a mapping that show embedding of P into $DM(P)$. We show calculational style of proofs in this section. To facilitate such proofs, we give lemmas to eliminate or introduce inf and sup symbols as follows.

Lemma 6.10 *Assuming* inf A *exists:* $x \leq \inf A \equiv \forall a \in A : x \leq a$.

Lemma 6.11 *Assuming* sup A *exists:* $x \geq \sup A \equiv \forall a \in A : x \geq a$.

To manipulate formulae, it is also desirable to remove the "$\forall$" symbols:

Lemma 6.12 $(x \leq y) \equiv (\forall z : z \leq x \Rightarrow z \leq y)$.

The forward direction holds due to transitivity $\leq$. The backward direction can be shown by substituting x for z and reflexivity of $\leq$.

We are now ready to prove results about the structure of $DM(P)$. We first show that for any $x \in P$, $D[x]$ is a cut and therefore belongs to $DM(P)$.

Lemma 6.13 $\forall x \in P : D[x]^{ul} = D[x]$.

Proof:
We show that
$$D[x]^u = U[x]. \tag{6.5}$$

By duality:
$$U[x]^l = D[x]. \tag{6.6}$$

Therefore, the result follows from (6.5) and (6.6). To prove (6.5): $\quad y \in D[x]^u$
$\equiv \quad$ {definition of upper bound as in (6.3)}
$\quad \forall z : z \in D[x] : z \leq y$

$\equiv$ {definition of D as in (6.1)}
    $\forall z : z \leq x : z \leq y$
$\equiv$ {rules of predicate calculus}
    $\forall z : z \leq x \Rightarrow z \leq y$
$\equiv$ {property of $\leq$}
    $x \leq y$
$\equiv$ {definition of U as in (6.2)}
    $y \in U[x]$.

∎

Therefore, $D[x]$ is a map from P to $DM(P)$. We now show that $D[.]$ preserves all least upper bounds and greatest lower bounds in P.

Lemma 6.14 *Assume* inf A *exists. Then:*

$$\bigcap_{\forall a \in A} D[a] = D[\inf A].$$

Proof: $x \in \bigcap_{a \in A} D[a]$
$\equiv$ {$\cap = \forall$ }
    $\forall a \in A : x \in D[a]$
$\equiv$ {definition of D as in (6.1)}
    $\forall a \in A : x \leq a$
$\equiv$ {Lemma 6.10}
    $x \leq \inf A$
$\equiv$ {definition of D as in (6.1)}
    $x \in D[\inf A]$.

∎

From lemmas 6.13 and 6.14, we know that there is a mapping from P to $DM(P)$, which maps any element $x \in P$ to $D[x]$ that preserves the least upper bounds and the greatest lower bounds. We next want to show that $DM(P)$ contains only the elements necessary to complete P. To this end, we first define the notion of *join-dense* subsets.

Definition 6.15 (Join-Dense) *Let P, Q be posets such that $P \subseteq Q$. P is **join-dense** in Q, if every element $x \in Q$ is expressible as join of a subset $A \subseteq P$.*

The notion of **meet-dense** can be defined dually.

We now have the following theorem that characterizes Dedekind–MacNeille completion.

Theorem 6.16 *Let P be any poset. Let $f : P \rightarrow DM(P)$ be the order-embedding of P into $DM(P)$ given by $f(x) = D[x]$. Then, $f(P)$ is join-dense and meet-dense in $DM(P)$. Moreover, if L is a complete lattice such that P is meet-dense and join-dense in L, then L is isomorphic to $DM(P)$.*

Proof: The proof is left as an exercise.

∎

6.7　AN INCREMENTAL ALGORITHM FOR LATTICE COMPLETION

We now discuss algorithms for constructing DM completion of a poset.

Let P be a poset and L be its Dedekind–MacNeille lattice completion. In this section, we present an incremental algorithm for lattice completion in implicit representation in which both P and L are represented using vectors. Suppose that a new element x is added to P with the constraint that x is not less than or equal to any of the existing elements. Our goal is to compute the lattice completion, L' of $P' = P \cup \{x\}$ given P and L. When P is a singleton, then its completion is itself. By adding one element at a time in any linear order that is consistent with the partial order, we can use the incremental algorithm for lattice completion of any poset.

Our incremental strategy for the lattice completion is as follows. We show that all the elements of L other than the top element of L are also contained in L'. The top element of L would be either retained or modified for L'. Therefore, except for the top, our algorithm will simply add elements to L to obtain L'.

Lemma 6.17 *Let S be a normal cut of $P = (X, \leq)$ such that $S \neq X$. Then S is also a normal cut of $P' := P \cup \{x\}$ where x is a maximal element of P'.*

Proof: Let $T = S^u$ in P. This implies that $T^l = S$ in P because S is a normal cut of P. Since $S \neq X$, T is nonempty (because if T is empty, $T^l = X$ which is not equal to S).

If $S \subseteq D[x]$, then S^u in P' equals $T \cup \{x\}$. We need to show that $S^{ul} = S$ in P', i.e., $(T \cup \{x\})^l = S$ in P'. The set $(T \cup \{x\})^l = T^l \cap D[x]$. Since x is a maximal element, we know that $x \notin T^l$. Since $T^l = S$ and $S \subseteq D[x]$, $T^l \cap D[x] = S$. Hence, S is a normal cut of P'.

If $S \nsubseteq D[x]$, then S^u in P' equals T. Since T is nonempty, and $T^l = S$ in P, we get that $T^l = S$ in P' as well. Hence, S is a normal cut of P'. ∎

Our algorithm for DM construction is shown in Figure 6.6. Whenever a new element x arrives, we carry out three steps. In step 1, we process Y, the top element of L; in step 2, we add a normal cut corresponding to the principal ideal of x; and, in step 3, we process the remaining elements of L. The goal of step 1 is to ensure that L' has a top element. The goal of step 2 is to ensure that all principal ideals of P' are in L'. The goal of step 3 is to ensure that L' is closed under intersection. In step 3, we first check if x covers more than one element. If it does not, then we do not have to go over all normal cuts in L because of the following claim.

Lemma 6.18 *If x covers at most one element in P, then for any normal cut $W \in L$, $min(W, D[x]) \in L$ assuming $\{\} \in L$.*

Proof: If x does not cover any element of P, then $D[x] = \{x\}$ and $W \cap D[x] = \{\}$, which is assumed to be in L. Now suppose that x covers just one element y, then $D[x] = \{x\} \cup D[y]$. Therefore, $W \cap D[x] = W \cap D[y]$. Since both W and $D[y]$ are normal cuts of L, so is $W \cap D[y]$. ∎

Input: a nonempty finite poset P, its DM-completion L, element x
Output: $L' :=$ DM-completion of $P \cup \{x\}$

$D[x] :=$ the vector clock for x;
$Y := top(L)$;
$newTop := max(D[x], Y)$;
// **Step 1**: Ensure that L' has a top element
      if $Y \in P$ then $L' := L \cup \{newTop\}$;
      else $L' := (L - Y) \cup \{newTop\}$;

// **Step 2**: Ensure that $D[x]$ is in L'
      if $(D[x] \neq newTop)$ then $L' := L' \cup \{D[x]\}$;

// **Step 3**: Ensure that all meets are defined
      if x does not cover any element in P then
          $L' := L' \cup \{\mathbf{0}\}$; // add zero vector
      else if x covers more than one element in P then
          for all normal cuts $W \in L$ do
              if $min(W, D[x]) \notin L'$ then $L' := L' \cup min(W, D[x])$;

Figure 6.6 Incremental algorithm IDML for DM construction.

We call the incremental algorithm for DM lattice construction We now show the correctness of the algorithm, i.e., L' is precisely the DM lattice for P'.

Theorem 6.19 *The algorithm IDML (Incremental DM Lattice Construction) computes DM completion of P' assuming that L is a DM completion of P.*

Proof: We first show that all cuts included in L' are normal cuts of P'. In step 1, we add to L' all cuts of L except possibly $top(L)$, and $max(D[x], Y)$. All elements of L except possibly $top(L)$ are normal cuts of P' from Lemma 6.17. The cut $max(D[x], Y)$ is a cut of P' because it includes all elements of P'. In step 2, we add cut $D[x]$ to L', which is a normal cut of P' because it is a principal ideal of P'. In step 3, we only add cuts of the form $min(W, D[x])$. Since both W and $D[x]$ are normal cuts of P', and the set of normal cuts are closed under intersection, we get that $min(W, D[x])$ is also a normal cut of P'.

We now show that all normal cuts of P' are included in L'. Let S be a normal cut of P'. Let Q be the set of all principal ideals of P'. By our construction, L' includes all principal ideals of P' (because of step 2). It is sufficient to show that L' is closed under joins and meets. Since we have the top element in L', it is sufficient to show closure under meets. Let S and T be two normal cuts in L'. If both S and T are in L, then $S \cap T$ is in L and therefore also L'. Now, assume that $S \in L' - L$. Therefore, $S = W \cap D[x]$ for some $W \in L$. If $T \in L$, then $S \cap T = W \cap D[x] \cap T = (W \cap T) \cap D[x]$. Since $(W \cap T) \in L$, we get that $S \cap T \in L'$ because of step 3. If $T \in L' - L$, then it can be written as $W' \cap D[x]$ for some $W' \in L$. Therefore, $S \cap T = W \cap D[x] \cap W' \cap D[x] = (W \cap W') \cap D[x]$. Since $(W \cap W') \in L$, we again get that $S \cap T \in L'$. Since L' contains all principal ideals of P' and is closed under meet and join, we get that all normal cuts of P' are included in L'.

∎

Note that our algorithm also gives an easy proof for the following claim.

Lemma 6.20 *The number of normal cuts of $P \cup \{x\}$ is at most twice the number of normal cuts of P plus two.*

Proof: For every cut in L, we add at most one more cut in step 3 of the algorithm. Further, we add at most one cut in step 1 and one additional cut in step 2.

∎

We now discuss the time complexity of the IDML algorithm. Let m be the size of the lattice L. The time complexity of the IDML algorithm is dominated by step 3. Assuming that L is kept in a sorted order (for example, in the lexicographically sorted order) in a binary balanced tree, the operation of checking whether $min(W, S) \in L$ can be performed in $O(w \log m)$, where w is the width of the poset P'. For any element for which we traverse the lattice L, we take $O(wm \log m)$ time. If the element x covers only one element (or no elements), then we take $O(w \log m)$ time. Suppose that there are r events in the poset that cover at least two events. In a distributed computation, only *receive* events would have this property. Then, to compute DM lattice of a poset P, we can repeatedly invoke IDML algorithm in any total order consistent with P. Therefore, we can construct DM lattice of a poset P of width w with r elements of lower cover of size at least two in $O(rwm \log m)$.

We also note here that given a poset P, to construct its DM-lattice, we can restrict our attention to its subposet of irreducible elements because DM-completion of P is identical to DM-completion of the subposet containing all its join and meet irreducibles.

We have presented the algorithm based on computing closure under intersections. It is clear that by considering the complements of the sets, we can also construct the lattice via union closure. Formally, for poset $P = (X, \leq)$, let the basis $\mathbb{B}$ be defined as

$$\mathbb{B} = \{X - D[x] | x \in X\}.$$

Let $\mathcal{F}$ be defined as the family of sets obtained by taking union of some number of sets in $\mathbb{B}$. We leave it as an exercise to show that $(\mathcal{F}, \supseteq)$ is isomorphic to $DM(P)$.

6.8 BREADTH FIRST SEARCH ENUMERATION OF NORMAL CUTS

In some distributed computing applications, we may be interested not in storing the DM lattice but simply enumerating all the elements of the lattice or storing only those elements of the lattice that satisfy a given property. Recall that the size of the DM-Lattice may be exponential in the size of the poset in the worst case. Algorithm

---

Input: a finite poset P
Output: Breadth First Enumeration of elements of DM-completion of P
G := bottom element ;
S := TreeSet of VectorClocks initially $\{G\}$ with *levelCompare* order;
(1)   **while** (S is notEmpty)
(2) H := remove the smallest element from S;
(3)   output(H);
(4)   **foreach** event e enabled in H do;
(5) K := the smallest normal cut containing $Q := H \cup \{e\}$;
(6)   if K is not in S, then add K to S;

         int **function** *levelCompare*(VectorClock a, VectorClock b)
(1)   if ($a.sum() > b.sum()$) return 1;
(2)   else if ($a.sum() < b.sum()$) return -1;
(3)   **for** (int $i = 0$; $i < a.size()$; i++)
(4)   if ($a[i] > b[i]$) return 1;
(5)   if ($a[i] < b[i]$) return -1;
(6)   **return** 0;

Figure 6.7   Algorithm BFS-DML for BFS enumeration of DM-Lattice.

IDML has space complexity of $O(mw \log n)$ to store the lattice L (there are m elements in the lattice, and each element is represented using a w-dimensional vector of entries of size $O(\log n)$). We now give an algorithm BFS-DML that does not require storing the entire lattice.

The algorithm BFS-DML views the lattice as a directed graph and generates its elements in the breadth first order. It is different from the traditional BFS algorithm on a graph because we do not store the graph or keep data that is proportional to the size of the graph (such as the nodes already visited). Let $Layer(k)$ be the set of nodes in the graph that are at distance k from the bottom element of the lattice. Let w_L be the size of the largest set $Layer(k)$. Then, the space required by BFS-DML is $O(w_L w \log n)$.

The algorithm BFS-DML is shown in Figure 6.7. The set S is used to store the set of nodes that have been generated but have not been explored yet. The set is kept in a balanced binary tree so that it is easy to check if some element is already contained in the set. We maintain the invariant that the set S contains only the normal cuts of the poset P. The elements in the binary search tree are compared using the function *levelCompare* shown in Figure 6.7. For any vector a corresponding to a consistent cut, the function $a.sum()$ returns the number of events in the consistent cut. At lines (1) and (2) of the function *levelCompare*, we define a consistent cut to be smaller than the other if it has fewer elements. Lines (3)–(5) impose a lexicographic order on all consistent cuts with equal number of elements. As a result, the function *levelCompare* imposes a total order on the set of all consistent and normal cuts.

The main BFS traversal of normal cuts, shown in lines (1)–(6), exploits the fact that there is a unique least normal cut that contains any consistent cut. The algorithm removes normal cuts from S in the *levelCompare* order. Let H be the smallest vector in this order (line 2). It finds that all consistent cuts reachable from H by executing a single event e (line 4). It adds all normal cuts that corresponds to "closure" of consistent cuts $H \cup \{e\}$ at line (5). We need to ensure that no normal cut is enumerated twice. At line (6), we check if a normal cut is already part of S. It can be shown that this check is sufficient to ensure that no normal cut is enumerated twice (due to the definition of *levelCompare* and the BFS order of traversal).

We now discuss the complexity of the BFS algorithm. At line (4), since there are w processes, there can be at most w events enabled on any normal cut H. Checking whether an event is enabled in H requires that the events that happened-before e in poset P are included in H. This check requires $O(w)$ comparisons in the worst case.

To find the smallest normal cut containing $Q := H \cup \{e\}$, we simply compute Q^u. Recall,

$$Q^u = \cap_{f \in Q} U[f]$$

Since $f \leq g$ is equivalent to $U[g] \subseteq U[f]$, we can restrict our attention to maximal elements of Q, i.e.,

$$Q^u = \cap_{f \in \text{maximal}(Q)} U[e].$$

Since P is represented using w chains, there are at most w maximal elements and therefore we can compute Q^u in $O(w^2)$ operations. We now take $R := Q^u$ and compute R^l, again using $O(w^2)$ operations. Thus, step (5) can be implemented in $O(w^2)$.

To check if the resulting normal cut K is not in S, we exploit the tree structure of S to perform it in $O(w \log |S|)$, which is $O(w \log w_L)$ in the worst case. Hence, the total time complexity of BFS algorithm is $O(mw(w^2 + w \log w_L)) = O(mw^2(w + \log w_L))$. The main space complexity of the BFS algorithm is the data structure S, which is $(w_L w \log n)$. Note that the size of S is proportional to the size of the layer of the lattice in BFS enumeration (w_L) and is much smaller than the size of the lattice m used in the IDML algorithm.

6.9 DEPTH FIRST SEARCH ENUMERATION OF NORMAL CUTS

Another useful technique to enumerate elements of the lattice is based on the DFS order. In BFS enumeration, the storage required is proportional to the width of the lattice, whereas in DFS enumeration, the storage required is proportional to the height of the lattice. Given any poset with n elements, the width of its lattice of normal cuts may be exponential in the size of the poset, but the height is always less than or equal to n. Hence, the DFS enumeration may result in exponential savings in space.

The algorithm for DFS enumeration is shown in Figure 6.8. From any normal cut, we explore all enabled events to find the normal cuts. There are at most w enabled events and for each event it takes $O(w^2)$ time to compute the normal cut K at line

```
        Input: a finite poset P, starting state G
        Output: DFS Enumeration of elements of DM-completion of P
(1)            output(G);
(2)            foreach event e enabled in G do
(3)                K := smallest normal cut containing Q := G ∪ {e};
(4)                M := get-Max-predecessor(K) ;
(5)                if M = G then
(6)                    DFS-NormalCuts(K);


        function VectorClock get-Max-predecessor(K) {
        //takes K as input vector and returns its maximum predecessor normal cut
(1)        H = MinimalUpperBounds(K); // H := Kᵘ
(2)        // find the maximal predecessor using normal cuts in the dual poset
(3)        foreach event f enabled in the cut H in Pᵈ do
(4)            temp_f := advance on event f in Pᵈ from cut H;
(5)            // get the set of lower bounds on temp_f
(6)            pred := MaximalLowerBounds(temp_f) using Hˡ;
(7)            if (levelCompare(pred, maxPred) = 1) then maxPred = pred;
(8)        return maxPred;
```

Figure 6.8   Algorithm DFS-DML for DFS enumeration of DM-lattice.

(3). Since we are not storing the enumerated elements explicitly, we need a method to ensure that the same normal cut is not visited twice.

Let $pred(K)$ be the set of all normal cuts that are covered by K in the lattice. We use the total order $levelCompare$ defined in Section 6.8 on the set $pred(K)$. We make a recursive call on K from the normal cut G iff G is the maximum normal cut in $pred(K)$ in the $levelCompare$ order. Line (4) finds the maximum predecessor M using the traversal on the dual poset P^d. The dual of a poset $P = (X, \leq)$ is defined as follows. In the poset P^d, $x \leq y$ iff $y \leq x$ in P. It is easy to verify that S is a normal cut in P iff S^u is a normal cut in P^d. The function $get\text{-}Max\text{-}Predecessor$, shown in Figure 6.8, uses expansion of a normal cut in the poset P^d to find the maximum predecessor. The function $get\text{-}Max\text{-}predecessor$ works as follows. At line (1), we compute $H = K^u$, which is the normal cut in P^d corresponding to K. Our goal is to compute all predecessors of K in P that corresponds to all successors of H in P^d. To find successors of H, we consider each event f enabled in H in P^d. At line (4), we compute the consistent cut $temp_f$. The closure of $temp_f$ in P^d equals $temp_f^{ul}$ in P^d. Equivalently, we can compute $temp_f^{lu}$ in P. The closed set $temp_f^{lu}$ in P^d corresponds to the closed set $temp_f^{lul}$ in P. However, from Problem 4, we know that $temp_f^{lul}$ is equal to $temp_f^{l}$. Therefore, by computing $temp_f^{l}$ for each f enabled in H, we get all the predecessors of K in P^d. Since there can be w events enabled in H in P^d, and it takes $O(w^2)$ time to compute each predecessor, it would take $O(w^3)$ to determine the maximum predecessor. However, since $temp_f$ and H differ on a single event, we can compute $temp_f^{l}$ using $H^l = K$ in $O(w)$ time. By this observation, the complexity of computing max-predecessor reduces to $O(w^2)$, and the total time complexity to determine whether K can be inserted is $O(w^2)$.

In line (5) of DFS-DML, we traverse K using recursive DFS call only if M equals G. Since the complexity of steps (3) and step (4) is $O(w^2)$, the overall complexity of processing a normal cut G is $O(w^3)$ due to the *foreach* at line (2). Since there are m normal cuts, we get the total time complexity of DFS-DML algorithm as $O(mw^3)$.

The main space requirement of the DFS algorithm is the stack used for recursion. Every time the recursion level is increases, the size of the normal cut increases by at least 1. Hence, the maximum depth of the recursion is n. Therefore, the space requirement is $O(nw \log n)$ bits because we only need to store vectors of dimension w at each recursion level. Hence, the DFS algorithm takes significantly less space than the BFS algorithm.

6.10   APPLICATION: FINDING THE MEET AND JOIN OF EVENTS

Suppose that there are two events x and y on different processes that correspond to faulty behavior. It is natural to determine the largest event, z, in the computation that could have affected both x and y. The event z is simply the meet of events x and y if it exists in the underlying computation. For example, in Figure 6.9(a), suppose that the faulty events are $\{d, e\}$. In this case, the "root" cause of faults of these events could be event a. In the vector clock representation, the root cause is $(1, 0, 0)$ in the DM lattice. Now consider the case when the set of faulty events is $\{e, f\}$. In this case, the underlying computation does not have a unique maximum event that affects both e and f. It can be seen in Figure 6.9(a) that both the events b and c could be the "root" cause of the events e and f. This is exactly what we would get from the lattice of normal cuts. The largest normal cut that is smaller than both events e with vector clock $(1, 2, 1)$ and event f with vector clock $(0, 1, 2)$ equals the vector $(0, 1, 1)$, which correctly identifies the set of events that affect both e and f.

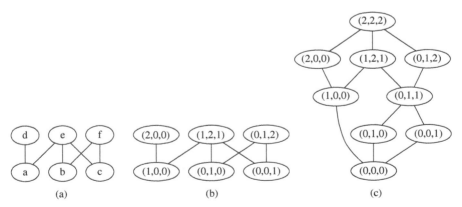

Figure 6.9 (a) The original poset. (b) Equivalent representation using vector clocks. (c) Its Lattice of normal cuts.

Dual to the previous application, we may be interested in the smallest event z that happened-after a subset of events. In a distributed system, an event z can have the knowledge of event x only if x happened-before event z. If two events x and y happened on different processes, we may be interested in the minimum event z that knows about both x and y. In this case, z corresponds to the join of events x and y if it exists in the underlying computation.

6.11 APPLICATION: DETECTING GLOBAL PREDICATES IN DISTRIBUTED SYSTEMS

The key problem in detecting global predicates of a distributed computation is that the lattice of ideals (or consistent cuts) L_I may be exponential in the size of the poset. The lattice of normal cuts, L_{DM}, of a poset P is a suborder of the L_I (every normal cut is consistent, but every consistent cut may not be normal). Its size always lies between the size of the poset P and the size of the lattice of consistent cuts of P. In particular, it may be exponentially smaller than L_I. We now show that a class of predicates can be efficiently detected by traversing the lattice of normal cuts rather than L_I.

The class of predicates we discuss are based on the idea of knowledge in a distributed system [HM84]. We define knowledge predicates based on the happened-before relation. We use the notation $G[i]$ to refer to events of G on process i.

Definition 6.21 *Given a distributed computation, or equivalently a poset $(P, \leq)$, we say that everyone knows the predicate B in the consistent cut G, if there exists a consistent cut H such that H satisfies B and for every process i there exists an event e in $G[i]$ such that all events in H happened before e. Formally, $E(B, G) \equiv \exists H : B(H) \wedge \forall i \exists e \in G[i] : \forall f \in H : f \leq e$. We also define $E(B) \equiv \exists G : E(B, G)$.*

Intuitively, the above-mentioned definition says that a predicate is known to everyone in the system if every process has a consistent cut in its past in which B was true. The definition captures the fact that in a distributed system, a process can know about remote events only through a chain of messages.

We now show that instead of traversing L_I we can traverse L_{DM} to detect $E(B)$ for any global predicate B.

Theorem 6.22 *Let B be any global predicate and G be a consistent cut such that $E(B, G)$. Then, there exists a normal cut N such that $E(B, N^u)$.*

Proof: Since everyone knows B in G, by the definition of "everyone knows," we get that there exists a consistent cut $H \subseteq G$ such that B is true in H and every process in G knows H. Let $\mathcal{K}$ be the set of all consistent cuts that know H. The set is nonempty because $G \in \mathcal{K}$. Furthermore, it is easy to show that the set $\mathcal{K}$ is closed under intersection. The least element K of the set $\mathcal{K}$ corresponds to the minimal elements of the filter H^u. Hence, we conclude that $E(B, K)$.

Define N to be the consistent cut corresponding to H^{ul}. It is clear that N is a normal cut because it corresponds to the closure of H. Moreover, $N^u = H^{ulu} = H^u = K$.

The first equality holds by the definition of N and the second equality holds due to properties of u and l operators. Since K equals N^u, from $E(B, K)$, we get that $E(B, N^u)$.

∎

6.12 APPLICATION: DATA MINING

Lattice theory has been used quite extensively for analysis of **concepts** in data mining applications. Suppose that we have a set of **objects** G each of which has one or more **attributes** from the set M. Can we automatically infer a **concept** from the knowledge of which objects have which attributes? These concepts are studied in the branch of mathematics called **formal concept analysis** which has many applications in data mining.

Definition 6.23 (Context) *A **context** R is a triple (G, M, I), where G is the set of objects, M is the set of attributes, and I is the relation between G and M, i.e., $I \subseteq G \times M$.*

Given any set of objects $A \subseteq G$, we can define the set of attributes common to all objects in A as

$$A^u = \{m \in M | \forall g \in A : (g, m) \in I\}$$

Similarly, given a set of attributes, $B \subseteq M$, we define the set of objects that all have those attributes

$$B^l = \{g \in G | \forall m \in B : (g, m) \in I\}$$

.

As an example, consider any poset $P = (X, \leq)$. We can treat this poset as a context $(X, X, \leq)$, where the set of objects and attributes are X and the binary relation is the poset relation on P. Note that in this example, our notation for A^u and B^l is consistent with the definition of upper bounds (A^u) and lower bounds (B^l) defined earlier.

Conversely, given a context (G, M, I), we can create a bipartite poset $P = (X, \leq)$ of height two with X as union of G and M and $x \leq y$ iff object x has attribute y.

We can now define a concept.

Definition 6.24 (Concept) *A **concept** of a context $R = (G, M, I)$ is a pair (A, B) such that $A^u = B$ and $B^l = A$.*

For the context $(X, X, \leq)$ for any poset $P = (X, \leq)$, a concept is identical to the *normal cut* of a poset.

We can put a partial order on the set of concepts as follows:

$$(A_1, B_1) \leq (A_2, B_2) \overset{\text{def}}{=} A_1 \subseteq A_2$$

It can be easily shown that $A_1 \subseteq A_2$ is equivalent to $B_1 \supseteq B_2$.

We have seen earlier that the set of normal cuts of P is a complete lattice $DM(P)$ (the smallest complete lattice containing P). Similarly, the set of concepts form a complete lattice (called the **concept lattice**) under the relation $\leq$ defined on concepts.

Given a context, by constructing DM completion of the poset corresponding to the context, we can generate the concept lattice.

6.13   PROBLEMS

6.1. Assume $\sup A$ exists in P. Show that

$$A^{ul} = D[\sup A].$$

6.2. Consider a poset $(X, \leq)$. Assume that for $S \subseteq X$, $\inf S$ exists. Let $y = \inf S$. Show that $\forall x \in X : x \leq y \Leftrightarrow \forall s \in S : x \leq s$.

6.3. Consider $S, T \subseteq X$, where X is a poset. Show that $\sup S \leq \inf T \Rightarrow \forall s \in S, \forall t \in T : s \leq t$.

6.4. Show that for any subset A of a poset, $A^l = A^{lul}$ and dually $A^u = A^{ulu}$.

6.5. Show that the completion of the set of rational numbers using cuts results in the set of real numbers.

6.6. Prove or disprove that every cut of a poset is also its order ideal.

6.7. Show that $(\mathcal{F}, \supseteq)$ defined in Section 6.7 is isomorphic to $DM(P)$.

6.8. Show that if A_1 and A_2 are cuts of a poset P, then so is $A_1 \cap A_2$.

6.9. Prove Theorem 6.16.

6.14   BIBLIOGRAPHIC REMARKS

Most of the material in this chapter is quite standard and can be found in Davey and Priestley [DP90]. The main difference from the standard treatment is that we have used calculational proofs for many of the results. Our discussion of algorithms for DM completion follows [Gar12].

7

MORPHISMS

7.1 INTRODUCTION

In this chapter, we study homomorphisms between lattices. Many of the concepts and results are analogous to those typically studied in group and ring theory. For example, the concept of lattice homomorphism is analogous to that of group homomorphism. These concepts have natural applications in the theory of distributed systems. In particular, we show applications in predicate detection.

7.2 LATTICE HOMOMORPHISM

We begin by defining functions that preserve the order structure.

Definition 7.1 (Monotone function) *Given two posets $P = (X, \leq_P)$ and $Q = (Y, \leq_Q)$, a function $f : X \to Y$ is called* monotone *iff*

$$\forall x, y \in X : x \leq_P y \Rightarrow f(x) \leq_Q f(y)$$

The concept of preserving order can be extended to preserving meet and join operations.

Introduction to Lattice Theory with Computer Science Applications, First Edition. Vijay K. Garg.
© 2015 John Wiley & Sons, Inc. Published 2015 by John Wiley & Sons, Inc.

Definition 7.2 (Lattice homomorphism) *Given two lattices L_1 and L_2, a function $f : L_1 \to L_2$ is a* **lattice homomorphism** *if f is* **join-preserving** *and* **meet-preserving***, that is, $\forall x, y \in L_1$:*

$$f(x \sqcup y) = f(x) \sqcup f(y) \quad and \quad f(x \sqcap y) = f(x) \sqcap f(y).$$

The property of preserving joins (or meets) is stronger than that of preserving the partial order. This fact is shown in the following lemma.

Lemma 7.3 *If f is join-preserving, then f is monotone.*

Proof: Let $x, y \in L_1$. We show that $x \leq y$ implies $f(x) \leq f(y)$ assuming that f is join-preserving.

$$
\begin{aligned}
& x \leq y \\
\equiv\ & \{ \text{ Connecting Lemma } \} \\
& (x \sqcup y) = y \\
\Rightarrow\ & \{ \text{ applying } f \text{ on both sides } \} \\
& f(x \sqcup y) = f(y) \\
\Rightarrow\ & \{ f \text{ is join-preserving } \} \\
& (f(x) \sqcup f(y)) = f(y) \\
\equiv\ & \{ \text{ Connecting Lemma } \} \\
& f(x) \leq f(y).
\end{aligned}
$$

■

It is left as an exercise for the reader to prove that if f is meet-preserving, then it is monotone.

7.3   LATTICE ISOMORPHISM

Definition 7.4 (Lattice isomorphism) *Two lattices L_1 and L_2 are* **isomorphic** *(denoted by $L_1 \approx L_2$) iff there exists a bijection f from L_1 to L_2, which is a lattice homomorphism.*

Theorem 7.5 *L_1 and L_2 are isomorphic iff there exists a bijective $f : L_1 \to L_2$ such that both f and f^{-1} are monotone.*

Proof: We leave the forward direction as an exercise. We prove the backward direction. Let f be a bijection from L_1 to L_2 such that f and f^{-1} are monotone. We show that f preserves joins and meets.

1. We first show that $\forall a, b \in L_1 : f(a) \sqcup f(b) \leq f(a \sqcup b)$

$\quad$ *true*
$\Rightarrow \quad$ { definition of join }
$\quad (a \leq (a \sqcup b)) \wedge (b \leq ((a \sqcup b))$
$\Rightarrow \quad$ { monotone f }
$\quad f(a) \leq f(a \sqcup b) \wedge f(b) \leq f(a \sqcup b)$
$\Rightarrow \quad$ { definition of join }
$\quad f(a) \sqcup f(b) \leq f(a \sqcup b)$.

2. We now show that $\forall a, b \in L_1 : f(a) \sqcup f(b) \geq f(a \sqcup b)$.
It is sufficient to show that for any $u \in L_2$,
$(f(a) \sqcup f(b)) \leq u \Rightarrow f(a \sqcup b) \leq u$

$\quad (f(a) \sqcup f(b)) \leq u$
$\Rightarrow \quad$ { definition of join }
$\quad (f(a) \leq u) \wedge (f(b) \leq u)$
$\Rightarrow \quad$ { f^{-1} is monotone }
$\quad (a \leq f^{-1}(u)) \wedge (b \leq f^{-1}(u))$
$\Rightarrow \quad$ { definition of join }
$\quad (a \sqcup b) \leq f^{-1}(u)$
$\Rightarrow \quad$ { monotone f }
$\quad f(a \sqcup b) \leq u$.

The proof for $\sqcap$ is dual.

$\blacksquare$

In Figure 7.1, f is monotone, but L_1 and L_2 are not isomorphic. Observe that, although f preserves the order, it does not preserve the meet and join operations. For example, $f(b \sqcup c) \neq f(b) \sqcup f(c)$.

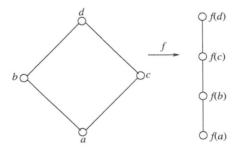

Figure 7.1   Monotone f.

7.4 LATTICE CONGRUENCES

Lattice homomorphisms can also be understood using the notion of lattice congruences. Informally, a congruence on a lattice (or any algebra) is an equivalence relation that preserves lattice operations (operations of the algebra, respectively). Recall that a binary relation θ on a set X is an equivalence relation iff θ is reflexive, symmetric, and transitive.

The general structure of an equivalence relation is easy to understand because of the well-known correspondence between an equivalence relation and partitions of a set. An equivalence relation partitions a set into disjoint subsets called **equivalence classes** or **blocks**. A block $[x]_\theta$ consists of all elements in X that are related to x by the relation θ. For example, consider the following relation on the set of natural numbers:

$$\theta_n = \{(x,y)|x = y \bmod n\} \text{ for } n \geq 1.$$

This relation partitions the set of natural numbers into n blocks. Conversely, given a partition of a set into a union of nonempty disjoint subsets, one can easily define an equivalence relation whose equivalence classes are the blocks in the partition.

An equivalence relation on a lattice L, which is compatible with both join and meet operations is called a congruence on L. Formally,

Definition 7.6 (Lattice Congruence) *An equivalence relation θ on a lattice L is a congruence iff for all $x, y \in L$, $x \equiv_\theta y$ implies that*

1. $\forall z : (z \sqcup x) \equiv_\theta (z \sqcup y)$
2. $\forall z : (z \sqcap x) \equiv_\theta (z \sqcap y)$.

The following lemma is left as an exercise.

Lemma 7.7 *Let θ be a congruence of lattice L; then*

1. $(a \equiv_\theta b) \wedge (a \leq c \leq b)) \Rightarrow a \equiv_\theta c$
2. $a \equiv_\theta b$ *iff* $(a \sqcap b) \equiv_\theta (a \sqcup b)$.

Example 7.8 *Consider the lattice L with four elements $\{a, b, c, d\}$ shown in Figure 7.1. Suppose we define an equivalence relation θ with two blocks $\{a, b\}$ and $\{c, d\}$. It can be verified that θ is a lattice congruence. For example, $c \equiv_\theta d$ implies that $a \sqcup c$ and $a \sqcup d$ are also equivalent under θ.*

Now consider another equivalence relation β with three blocks $\{a, b\}$, $\{c\}$, and $\{d\}$. The relation β is not a congruence because even though a and b are equivalent under β, $a \sqcup c$, and $b \sqcup c$ are not.

7.5   QUOTIENT LATTICE

Given a congruence θ on a lattice L, we can define *quotient* of L with respect to θ as

$$L/\theta = \{[a]_\theta | a \in L\}.$$

The join and meet operations between the blocks of θ are defined naturally as

$$[a]_\theta \sqcup [b]_\theta = [a \sqcup b]_\theta.$$

Similarly,

$$[a]_\theta \sqcap [b]_\theta = [a \sqcap b]_\theta.$$

The set L/θ together with the meet and join operations defined earlier is called the *quotient lattice* or the *reduced lattice*.

7.6   LATTICE HOMOMORPHISM AND CONGRUENCE

We now show that given a lattice homomorphism, one can define a lattice congruence and vice versa.

Lemma 7.9 *Let L and K be lattices and $f : L \to K$ be a lattice homomorphism. Define the equivalence relation θ on L as follows: $u \equiv_\theta v \iff f(u) = f(v)$. Then θ, called the **kernel** of f and denoted as $\ker f$, is a congruence.*

Proof: We need to show that if $a \equiv_\theta b$ and $c \equiv_\theta d$ then $a \sqcup c \equiv_\theta b \sqcup d$.

$\quad\quad f(a \sqcup c)$
$=\quad \{\, f \text{ is a lattice homomorphism } \}$
$\quad\quad f(a) \sqcup f(c)$
$=\quad \{\, a \equiv_\theta b, c \equiv_\theta d \,\}$
$\quad\quad f(b) \sqcup f(d)$
$=\quad \{\, f \text{ is a lattice homomorphism } \}$
$\quad\quad f(b \sqcup d).$

Therefore, $a \sqcup c \equiv_\theta b \sqcup d$. The proof for $\sqcap$ is dual.

■

The following is a standard algebraic result.

Theorem 7.10 *[Fundamental Homomorphism Theorem] Let L and K be lattices and $f : L \to K$ be a lattice homomorphism. Define $\theta = \ker f$. The mapping $g : L/\theta \to K$ given by $g([a]_\theta) = f(a)$ is well defined and g is an isomorphism between L/θ and K. (Figure 7.2).*

Proof: Left as an exercise.

■

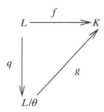

Figure 7.2   Fundamental Homomorphism Theorem.

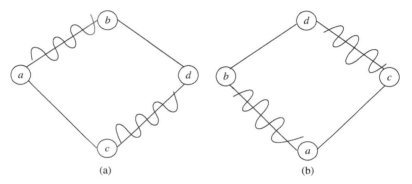

(a)   (b)

Figure 7.3   (a,b) Quadrilateral-closed structures.

7.7   PROPERTIES OF LATTICE CONGRUENCE BLOCKS

In this section, we explore the structure of a congruence block. We show that every congruence block is a *quadrilateral-closed* convex sublattice. To this end, we first define a quadrilateral in a lattice.

The elements a, b, c, and d in a lattice L form a **quadrilateral** $< a, b; c, d >$ iff

1. $a < b$ and $c < d$
2. $(a \sqcup d = b) \wedge (a \sqcap d = c)$ or,
   $(b \sqcup c = d) \wedge (b \sqcap c = a)$.

We say that a partition corresponding to θ is *quadrilateral-closed* if for every quadrilateral $< a, b; c, d >$, we have that $a \equiv_\theta b$ implies $c \equiv_\theta d$.

Theorem 7.11 *An equivalence relation θ is a congruence iff*

1. *Each block of θ is a sublattice*
2. *Each block is convex*
3. *The blocks are quadrilateral-closed.*

Proof: First assume that θ is a congruence relation. We show the following.

1. Each block A of θ is a sublattice.
   We need to show that $\forall a, b \in A : (a \sqcup b \in A) \wedge (a \sqcap b \in A)$

   $\qquad a \equiv_\theta b$

   $\Rightarrow \quad \{ \text{take join with } a \}$

   $\qquad a \sqcup a \equiv_\theta b \sqcup a$

   $\equiv \quad \{ \text{join is idempotent} \}$

   $\qquad a \equiv_\theta b \sqcup a.$

   The proof for closure under the meet operation is similar.

2. Each block is convex.
   We show that $\forall a,\ b \in A : (a \leq c \wedge c \leq b) \Rightarrow c \in A$

   $\qquad a \equiv_\theta b$

   $\Rightarrow \quad \{ \text{taking join with } c \}$

   $\qquad a \sqcup c \equiv_\theta b \sqcup c$

   $\Rightarrow \quad \{ a \leq c, c \leq b \}$

   $\qquad c \equiv_\theta b.$

3. The blocks are quadrilateral-closed.
   It is sufficient to show that $a \equiv_\theta b \Rightarrow c \equiv_\theta d$, where $< a, b; c, d >$ is a quadrilateral.
   Assume that $(a \sqcup d = b) \wedge (a \sqcap d = c)$. The proof when $(b \sqcup c = d) \wedge (b \sqcap c = a)$ hold is similar. We are given that $a \sqcap d = c$. Moreover, since $(a \sqcup d = b)$, we get that $d \leq b$. Hence, $b \sqcap d = d$. Since $a \sqcap d = c$ and $b \sqcap d = d$, we get that $a \equiv_\theta b \Rightarrow c \equiv_\theta d$ (because θ is a congruence).
   The converse, i.e, conditions (1–3) imply that θ is a congruence class, is left as an exercise.
   ∎

7.8   APPLICATION: MODEL CHECKING ON REDUCED LATTICES

We now show an application of congruences to checking temporal logic formulas on Kripke structures (state transition graphs) that form a lattice. System properties and specifications are assumed to be expressed in temporal logic such as CTL_{-X} (a restricted version of the *computation tree logic (CTL)*, which does not have the *next-time* operator X). The temporal logic formulas allow one to express properties on the computation sequences (or paths) of the program. We do not deal with the structure and semantics of the logic except to observe that formulas may make assertions on the paths in the state transition graphs.

One of the difficulties in mechanically checking a formula over a graph is that the number of states (or global states in a distributed system) may be prohibitively large. One possible approach to alleviate this problem is to group together global states that have the same state with respect to the property that we wish to verify. For example, if we are interested in detecting the property of reaching a global state such that $(x^2 + y > 10)$, then it would simplify the problem of detection if we can group

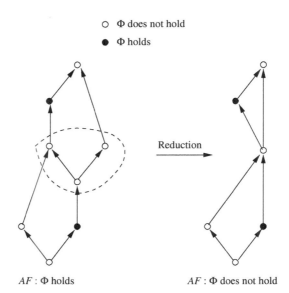

○ Φ does not hold
● Φ holds

Reduction

AF : Φ holds   AF : Φ does not hold

Figure 7.4   Simple reduction of state graph does not preserve path based formulas.

together states that have the same x and y values. Doing this will induce an equivalence relation on the lattice and partition it into equivalence classes. However, the
structure formed by collapsing together the equivalence class elements may not preserve the temporal logic formula. We are interested in exact reductions in the sense
that a property holds in the original state lattice iff it holds in the reduced state lattice.
Collapsing a "contiguous" set of states may not give exact reduction. We demonstrate
this by a simple example of a global state graph in Figure 7.4. The black nodes represent states at which Φ holds. The property we are trying to verify is that every path
from the initial state to the final state goes through a state in which Φ holds. It is clear
from the Figure that the property holds in the original graph on the left but not on the
reduced graph on the right.

We will show that if the equivalence class forms a congruence, then one can indeed
use the reduced lattice. Consider a global state lattice L, the congruence θ, and the
reduced lattice L/θ. Then corresponding to every path P from bottom to top in L/θ,
there is a corresponding path in the original lattice L from its bottom to top and vice
versa. In the following discussion, we use $\prec_L$ to denote the cover relation in a lattice
L. To prove the equivalence of paths between L and L/θ, we need Lemma 7.13 which
states that two states in the reduced graph have a cover relation between them if and
only if they contain states that have a cover relation between them. Using this, we
prove the equivalence of paths in Lemma 7.14. We first need the following lemma.

Lemma 7.12 *Given two congruence classes A and B in L/θ, let $(a_\perp, a_\top)$ and $(b_\perp, b_\top)$
be the bottom and top element pairs of A and B, respectively. If B covers A in L/θ,
then there exists a path from $a_\top$ to $b_\top$ in L consisting only of nodes in A and B.*

Proof: Since B covers A in L/θ, there exist elements $c \in A$ and $d \in B$ such that $c \leq d$ in L. Since $c \leq a_\top$, we get that $c \leq d \sqcap a_\top \leq a_\top$. From convexity of A, we get that $d \sqcap a_\top \in A$. Consider the quadrilateral $< d \sqcap a_\top, a_\top; d, d \sqcup a_\top >$. From the quadrilateral-closed property of congruences, we get that $d \sqcup a_\top \in B$. This implies that $d \sqcup a_\top \leq b_\top$. Therefore $a_\top \leq b_\top$. Hence, there exists a path from $a_\top$ to $b_\top$ in L.

It remains to be shown that the path consists only of nodes belonging to A or B. Pick any $e \in L$ such that it is on the path from $a_\top$ to $b_\top$. Thus, $a_\top \leq e \leq b_\top$ and since $A \prec_{L/\theta} B$, hence by property of the covering relation either $e \in A$ or $e \in B$, which yields the desired result.

■

Lemma 7.13 *Let $A, B \in L/\theta$, then*

$$A \prec_{L/\theta} B$$

iff there exist $m, n \in L$ such that

$$n \in A, \ m \in B \text{ and } n \prec_L m.$$

Proof: The forward direction of the proof follows from Lemma 7.12 as follows: We assume that $A \prec_{L/\theta} B$. Thus, by Lemma 7.12, there exists a path from $a_\top$ to $b_\top$ in L consisting only of nodes in A and B. The first element in the path is $a_\top$ and let the second element on the path be b. Clearly $b \in B$ and $a_\top \prec_L b$. Thus, there exist $m, n \in L$ such that $n \in A$, $m \in B$ and $n \prec_L m$.

To prove the converse, we assume that $A, B \in L/\theta$ and there exist $m, n \in L$ such that $n \in A$, $m \in B$ and $n \prec_L m$. Let us assume that there exists $C \in L/\theta$ such that $A <_{L/\theta} C <_{L/\theta} B$ (Figure 7.5).

Because $n \prec_L m$, we cannot have $n \leq c_\top \leq m$ (from the definition of cover relation). Thus $\neg(c_\top \leq m)$. (Figure 7.5(b)). Since $C \prec_{L/\theta} B$, $c_\top < b_\top$ from Lemma 7.12. Therefore, $\neg(m \leq c_\top)$ (otherwise, $m \leq c_\top \leq b_\top$ implies $c_\top \in B$ due to convexity). Hence, $m \parallel c_\top$.

Since $n \prec_L m$, $m \parallel c_\top$, and $n \leq c_\top$, it follows that $m \sqcap c_\top = n$. It can be now verified that $< m, m \sqcup c_\top; n, c_\top >$ forms a quadrilateral in L.

Now we show that $m \sqcup c_\top \in B$. This follows from convexity of B because $m \leq m \sqcup c_\top \leq b_\top$.

Since $m \sqcup c_\top \equiv_\theta m$, hence from the quadrilateral-closed property of congruences we have, $n \equiv_\theta c_\top$. Therefore, $c_\top \in A$. This contradicts our assumption that there exists $C \in L/\theta$ such that $A <_{L/\theta} C <_{L/\theta} B$.

■

Now we can prove that there is a one-to-one correspondence between paths of L and L/θ. The first part of the lemma says that for any path in L/θ, if we look at the preimages of the nodes on the path (corresponding to inverse of the lattice homomorphism function f), then there exists a subset of these preimage nodes, which

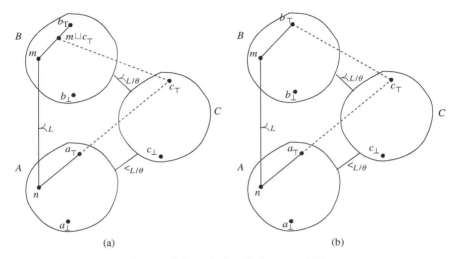

Figure 7.5   (a,b) Proof of Lemma 7.13

also forms a path in L. Since f is defined to preserve values of variables relevant to the property being detected, this enables us to prove that detecting temporal formula in L is equivalent to detecting temporal formulae in L/θ. Similarly, the second part of the lemma proves that for every path in L, if we look at the image of the nodes on the path, then they form a corresponding path in L/θ.

Lemma 7.14 *[Equivalence of Paths] Let f be the lattice homomorphism corresponding to θ.*

1. *If $P = (P_1, ..., P_k)$ is a path from bottom to top in L/θ, then there exists a path Q in L such that $Q \subseteq \{q \in L : \exists i \in [1, k] : q \in f^{-1}(P_i)\}$.*
2. *If $Q = (q_1, ..., q_k)$ is a path from bottom to top in L, then the set $P = \{f(q_1), ..., f(q_k)\}$ forms a path from bottom to top in L/θ (Figure 7.6 illustrates the lemma).*

Proof:

1. Consider the set $f^{-1}(P_i)$. For any $i \in [1, k]$, let x_i and y_i be the bottom and top elements of $f^{-1}(P_i)$, respectively $(f^{-1}(P_i)$, is a sublattice). Note that x_1 and y_k are the bottom and top elements of L. From Lemma 7.12, we get that there is a path from $y_1 \to y_2 \to ... \to y_k$. In addition, since $f^{-1}(P_1)$ is a sublattice, hence there is a path $x_1 \to y_1$. Therefore, there is a path from x_1 (bottom) to y_k (top) in L.
2. Let $f(q_{i,1}), ..., f(q_{i,l})$ be the sequence obtained from P after removing duplicate nodes. From the definition of $f(q_{i,k})$ and $f(q_{i,k+1})$, there exists $m, n \in L$ such that $m \in f(q_{i,k})$, $n \in f(q_{i,k+1})$ and $m \prec_L n$. Then Lemma 7.13 gives us

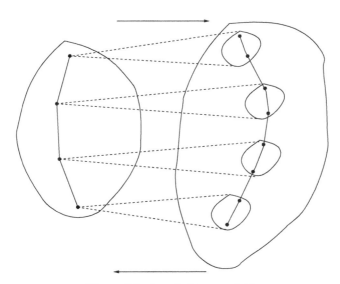

Figure 7.6   Proof of Lemma 7.14.

that $f(q_{i,k}) \prec_{L/\theta} f(q_{i,k+1})$ and in general $f(q_{i,1}) \prec_{L/\theta} \cdots \prec_{L/\theta} f(q_{i,l})$ and thus this forms the desired path.

■

7.9   PROBLEMS

7.1. Let L_1 and L_2 be lattices and $f : L_1 \to L_2$ be a map. Show that the following are equivalent:

(a) f is order-preserving;

(b) $\forall a, b \in L : f(a \sqcup b) \geq f(a) \sqcup f(b)$;

(c) $\forall a, b \in L : f(a \sqcap b) \geq f(a) \sqcap f(b)$.

In particular, if f is a homomorphism, then f is order preserving.

7.2. Prove that if f is meet-preserving, then f is monotone.

7.3. Prove the forward direction of Theorem 7.5.

7.4. Let $Eq(X)$ be the set of all equivalence relations defined on a set X. For any two elements θ_1, θ_2 of $Eq(X)$, we define θ_1 to be less than or equal to θ_2 iff $\theta_1 \subseteq \theta_2$. Show that $Eq(X)$ forms a complete lattice under this order. (Hint: Show that it is a topped $\cap$-closed structure.)

7.5. Prove Lemma 7.7.

7.6. Prove the Fundamental Homomorphism Theorem (Theorem 7.10).

7.7. Complete the proof of Theorem 7.11.

7.8. ([CG06]) Show that a formula ϕ in temporal logic CTL_{-X} holds in L iff it holds in L/θ, where θ is the congruence class corresponding to all nontemporal subformulas in ϕ.

7.10   BIBLIOGRAPHIC REMARKS

The discussion on lattice homomorphisms and congruence lattices is quite standard. The reader is referred to Grätzer [Grä03] for various proofs. The application of lattice congruences to model checking is taken from Chakraborty and Garg [CG06].

8

MODULAR LATTICES

8.1 INTRODUCTION

We describe a special class of lattices called modular lattices. Modular lattices are numerous in mathematics; for example, the lattice of normal subgroups of a group is modular, the lattice of ideals of a ring is modular, and so is the finite-dimensional vector space lattice. Distributive lattices are a special class of modular lattices. The set of all consistent global states in a distributed computation forms a distributive lattice and is therefore a modular lattice.

In this chapter, we first introduce both modular and distributive lattices to show the relationship between them. Later, we focus on modular lattices. Distributive lattices are considered in detail in Chapter 9.

8.2 MODULAR LATTICE

Definition 8.1 (Modular Lattice) L *is* **modular** *if* $\forall a, b, c \in L : a \geq c \Rightarrow a \sqcap (b \sqcup c) = (a \sqcap b) \sqcup c$.

The definition says that if $c \leq a$, then one can bracket the expression $a \sqcap b \sqcup c$ either way.

We will show that all distributive lattices are modular. Recall that a lattice L is distributive if $\forall a, b, c : a \sqcap (b \sqcup c) = (a \sqcap b) \sqcup (a \sqcap c)$.

Introduction to Lattice Theory with Computer Science Applications, First Edition. Vijay K. Garg.
© 2015 John Wiley & Sons, Inc. Published 2015 by John Wiley & Sons, Inc.

In this definition, the equality can be replaced by $\leq$ because of the following observation.

Lemma 8.2 *For all lattices,* $a \sqcap (b \sqcup c) \geq (a \sqcap b) \sqcup (a \sqcap c).$

Proof: We know that

1. $a \sqcap (b \sqcup c) \geq (a \sqcap b)$
2. $a \sqcap (b \sqcup c) \geq (a \sqcap c)$

Combining (1) and (2), we get

$a \sqcap (b \sqcup c) \geq (a \sqcap b) \sqcup (a \sqcap c).$

∎

A similar observation applies to the definition of modular lattices as shown by the following lemma.

Lemma 8.3 *For all lattices,* $a \geq c \Rightarrow a \sqcap (b \sqcup c) \geq (a \sqcap b) \sqcup c.$

Proof: $a \geq c \Rightarrow (a \sqcap c) = c$

Using Lemma 8.2 it follows that $a \sqcap (b \sqcup c) \geq (a \sqcap b) \sqcup c.$

∎

We can now show the relationship between the modularity condition and the distributivity condition for lattices.

Theorem 8.4 *L is distributive implies that L is modular.*

Proof: L is distributive
   $\equiv$ { definition of a distributive lattice }
         $\forall a, b, c : a \sqcap (b \sqcup c) = (a \sqcap b) \sqcup (a \sqcap c)$
   $\Rightarrow$ { $a \geq c$ is equivalent to $a \sqcap c = c$ }
         $\forall a, b, c : a \geq c \Rightarrow a \sqcap (b \sqcup c) = (a \sqcap b) \sqcup c$
   $\equiv$ { definition of a modular lattice }
         L is modular.

∎

8.3   CHARACTERIZATION OF MODULAR LATTICES

We now give examples of lattices that are not modular or modular but not distributive. All lattices of four elements or less are modular. The smallest lattice which is not modular is the **pentagon** (N_5) shown in Figure 1.4(a). In this lattice, $a \geq c$ holds; however, $a \sqcap (b \sqcup c) = a \sqcap 1 = a$, whereas $(a \sqcap b) \sqcup c = 0 \sqcup c = c$.

The **diamond lattice** (M_3) shown in Figure 1.4(b) is modular but not distributive. To see this, note that in the diagram of M_3 we have

$$a \sqcap (b \sqcup c) = a \sqcap 1 = a$$

and $(a \sqcap b) \sqcup (a \sqcap c) = 0 \sqcup 0 = 0.$

Since $a \neq 0$, M_3 is not distributive.

We now focus on modular lattices and list some theorems that characterize modular lattices.

In the definition of modular lattices, if c satisfies $(a \sqcap b) \leq c \leq a$, then we get that $a \sqcap (b \sqcup c) = (a \sqcap b) \sqcup c = c$. The following theorem shows that to check modularity it is sufficient to consider c's that are in the interval $[a \sqcap b, a]$.

Theorem 8.5 *A lattice L is modular iff* $\forall a, b \in L$

$$d \in [a \sqcap b, a] \Rightarrow a \sqcap (b \sqcup d) = d. \tag{8.1}$$

Proof:

First, we show that (8.1) implies that L is modular, i.e.,

$$\forall a, b, c \in L : a \geq c \Rightarrow a \sqcap (b \sqcup c) = (a \sqcap b) \sqcup c.$$

When $c \leq a$ and $a \sqcap b \leq c$, we get that $a \sqcap (b \sqcup c) = (a \sqcap b) \sqcup c$ because the left-hand side equals c from (8.1) and the right-hand side equals c because $(a \sqcap b) \leq c$.

Now suppose $c \leq a$ but $a \sqcap b \leq c$ is false (see Figure 8.1). We define $d = (a \sqcap b) \sqcup c$. Clearly $d \in [a \sqcap b, a]$.

Consider $a \sqcap (b \sqcup d)$. Replacing the value of d in (8.1) we get

$$a \sqcap (b \sqcup ((a \sqcap b) \sqcup c)) = (a \sqcap b) \sqcup c. \tag{8.2}$$

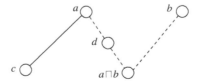

Figure 8.1   Proof of Theorem 8.5.

Now consider $a \sqcap (b \sqcup c)$. Using the fact that $c \leq (a \sqcap b) \sqcup c$ we get

$$a \sqcap (b \sqcup c) \leq a \sqcap (b \sqcup ((a \sqcap b) \sqcup c)). \qquad (8.3)$$

Combining (8.2) and (8.3), we get $a \sqcap (b \sqcup c) \leq (a \sqcap b) \sqcup c$.

Since $a \sqcap (b \sqcup c) \geq (a \sqcap b) \sqcup c$ holds for all lattices (Lemma 8.3), we get

$$a \sqcap (b \sqcup c) = (a \sqcap b) \sqcup c.$$

Hence, L is modular.

Showing the other side, that modularity implies condition (8.1) is trivial and is left as an exercise.

∎

The following lemma is useful in proving the Pentagon theorem, which gives a characterization of modular lattices using the absence of a sublattice isomorphic to a pentagon (or N_5).

Lemma 8.6 *For all lattices L, consider any $a, b, c \in L$. Let $v = a \sqcap (b \sqcup c))$ and $u = (a \sqcap b) \sqcup c$. Thus, v and u are expressions obtained by different bracketing of the expression $a \sqcap b \sqcup c$. Then,*

1. $v > u \Rightarrow (v \sqcap b) = (u \sqcap b)$.
2. $v > u \Rightarrow (v \sqcup b) = (u \sqcup b)$.

Proof: We show the first assertion. The proof for the second one is similar.

$$a \sqcap b$$
$$=$$
$$(a \sqcap b) \sqcap b$$
$$\leq$$
$$[(a \sqcap b) \sqcup c)] \sqcap b$$
$$= \quad \{ \text{ definition of } u \}$$
$$u \sqcap b$$
$$\leq \quad \{ v > u \}$$
$$v \sqcap b$$
$$= \quad \{ \text{ definition of } v \}$$
$$(a \sqcap (b \sqcup c)) \sqcap b$$
$$= \quad \{ b \leq b \sqcup c \}$$
$$a \sqcap b.$$

The above-mentioned sequence of inequalities implies that all the intermediate expressions must be equal; therefore, $u \sqcap b = v \sqcap b$.

∎

We are now ready for another characterization of modular lattices due to R. Dedekind.

Theorem 8.7 *[Pentagon Theorem] A lattice L is modular iff it does not contain a sublattice isomorphic to N_5.*

Proof: If L contains N_5, then it clearly violates modularity as shown earlier. Now assume that L is not modular. Then, there exist a, b, c such that $a > c$ and $a \sqcap (b \sqcup c) > (a \sqcap b) \sqcup c$. It can be verified that $b||a$ and $b||c$. For example, $b \leq a$ implies $(a \sqcap b) \sqcup c = b \sqcup c \leq a \sqcap (b \sqcup c)$. The other cases are similar.

We let $v = a \sqcap (b \sqcup c)$ and $u = (a \sqcap b) \sqcup c$. We know that $v > u$. It is easy to verify that $b||u$ and $b||v$. For example, $b < v \equiv b < a \sqcap (b \sqcup c) \Rightarrow (b < a)$.

From Lemma 8.6, $u \sqcup b = v \sqcup b$ and $u \sqcap b = v \sqcap b$.

Thus, $u, v, b, u \sqcup b$, and $u \sqcap b$ form N_5.

■

Modular lattices can also be characterized using an identity on lattices. An advantage of a characterization based on identities is that it allows easy manipulation of expressions: the left-hand side of any identity can be replaced by the right-hand side.

Theorem 8.8 *A lattice L is modular iff $\forall a, b, c \in L$*
$$a \sqcap (b \sqcup (a \sqcap c)) = (a \sqcap b) \sqcup (a \sqcap c).$$

Proof: Substitute $(a \sqcap c)$ for c in the definition 8.1.

■

Consider two incomparable elements a and b as shown in Figure 8.2. Define two intervals $[a, a \sqcup b]$, and $[a \sqcap b, b]$. We can define maps f and g from one interval to the other as follows.

$$f : x \mapsto x \sqcap b$$

$$g : y \mapsto y \sqcup a.$$

Theorem 8.9 *[Diamond Isomorphism Theorem] A lattice L is modular iff $\forall a, b$: f and g as defined earlier are isomorphic.*

Proof: First we show that modularity implies f and g are isomorphic. In order to show that f and g are isomorphic, we need to show that

1. f and g are homomorphic.
2. they are bijective.

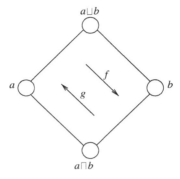

Figure 8.2   Theorem 8.9.

In order to show f is a lattice homomorphism, we show that it is join preserving and meet preserving.

We first show that f is join preserving, that is, $f(x_1 \sqcup x_2) = f(x_1) \sqcup f(x_2)$. Consider the right-hand side

$$f(x_1) \sqcup f(x_2)$$
$$= (x_1 \sqcap b) \sqcup (x_2 \sqcap b)$$
$$= x_2 \sqcap b \; \{x_1 \le x_2\}$$

Now taking the left-hand side, we get

$$f(x_1 \sqcup x_2)$$
$$= (x_1 \sqcup x_2) \sqcap b$$
$$= x_2 \sqcap b. \; \{x_1 \le x_2\}.$$

Hence, f is join preserving. It can be shown similarly that f is also meet preserving. Similarly, g preserves both join and meet. Hence, f and g are lattice homomorphisms.

We now show that f and g are inverses of each other. Consider

$$f \circ g(x)$$
$$= g(f(x))$$
$$= (x \sqcap b) \sqcup a$$
$$= x \sqcap (b \sqcup a) \text{ from modularity}$$
$$= x.$$

Therefore $f = g^{-1}$. Hence, f and g are bijective. This concludes our proof that f and g are lattice isomorphisms. We leave it as an exercise to show the converse.

■

We now give yet another characterization of modular lattices using upper and lower covering conditions.

Definition 8.10 (Upper Covering Condition) *A lattice L satisfies the* **Upper Covering Condition** *iff*

$\forall x, y, z \in L : x <_c y \Rightarrow (x \sqcup z) <_c (y \sqcup z)$. *The Lower Covering Condition is dual.*

Theorem 8.11 *A lattice L is modular iff it satisfies the Upper Covering Condition and the Lower Covering Condition.*

Proof: We leave this proof as an exercise in using the Diamond Isomorphism Theorem.

■

We now define a ranked poset and a graded poset. Some examples are shown in Figure 8.3.

Definition 8.12 (Ranked poset) *A poset is ranked if there exists a ranking function* $r : P \mapsto N$ *such that* $r(x) = r(y) + 1$ *whenever x covers y.*

Definition 8.13 (Graded poset) *A ranked poset is graded if all maximal chains have the same length.*

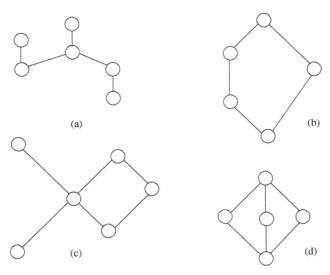

Figure 8.3 (a) A ranked poset, (b) A poset that is not ranked, (c) A ranked and graded poset, and (d) A ranked and graded lattice.

Theorem 8.14 *A lattice L is modular iff L is graded and the ranking function satisfies*

$$r(x) + r(y) = r(x \sqcap y) + r(x \sqcup y).$$

Proof: The proof of the theorem is left as an exercise.

∎

8.4   PROBLEMS

8.1. Show that if L is a graded lattice, then
   (a) $r(x) + r(y) \geq r(x \sqcap y) + r(x \sqcup y)$ is equivalent to the Upper Covering Condition.
   (b) $r(x) + r(y) \leq r(x \sqcap y) + r(x \sqcup y)$ is equivalent to the Lower Covering Condition.

8.2. Complete the proof of Theorem 8.5.

8.3. Show the shearing identity for modular lattices.
   [Shearing Identity] A lattice L is modular iff $\forall x, y, z : x \sqcap (y \sqcup z) = x \sqcap ((y \sqcap (x \sqcup z)) \sqcup z)$.

8.4. Complete the proof of Theorem 8.9.

8.5. Prove Theorem 8.11.

8.6. Prove Theorem 8.14.

8.5   BIBLIOGRAPHIC REMARKS

The book by Gratzer [Grä71, Grä03] contains most of the results in this chapter except for our emphasis on calculational proofs.

9

DISTRIBUTIVE LATTICES

9.1 INTRODUCTION

Recall that a lattice L is distributive if

$$\forall a, b, c \in L : a \sqcap (b \sqcup c) = (a \sqcap b) \sqcup (a \sqcap c). \qquad (9.1)$$

Distributive lattices form one of the most interesting class of lattices. Many lattices that arise in distributed computing and combinatorics are distributive. The set of all consistent global states in a distributed computation forms a distributive lattice. The set of all subsets of any set forms a distributive lattice under the subset relation.

In this chapter, we discuss some of the crucial properties of distributive lattices. Section 9.2 gives a characterization of distributive lattices using forbidden sublattices. In Section 9.4, we discuss a duality between finite distributive lattices and finite posets. Every finite distributive lattice can be recovered from the poset of its join-irreducible elements. This result due to Birkhoff, is known as the fundamental theorem of finite distributive lattices.

9.2 FORBIDDEN SUBLATTICES

Given a modular lattice, the following theorem is useful in determining if the lattice is distributive.

Introduction to Lattice Theory with Computer Science Applications, First Edition. Vijay K. Garg.
© 2015 John Wiley & Sons, Inc. Published 2015 by John Wiley & Sons, Inc.

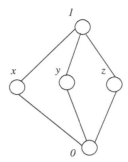

Figure 9.1   Diamond M_3—a nondistributive lattice.

Theorem 9.1 *[Diamond] A modular lattice is distributive iff it does not contain a diamond, M_3, as a sublattice.*

Proof: ($\Rightarrow$): If the lattice contains a diamond, it cannot be distributive because elements of a diamond do not satisfy the distributive law. In Figure 9.1, $x \sqcap (y \sqcup z) = x \sqcap 1 = x$; however, $(x \sqcap y) \sqcup (x \sqcap z) = 0 \sqcup 0 = 0$.

($\Leftarrow$) It is sufficient to prove that every modular nondistributive lattice contains M_3 as a sublattice. Let x, y, z be such that $x \sqcap (y \sqcup z) > (x \sqcap y) \sqcup (x \sqcap z)$.

Define elements a, b, c, d, e as follows:

$$a := (x \sqcap y) \sqcup (y \sqcap z) \sqcup (z \sqcap x)$$
$$b := (x \sqcup y) \sqcap (y \sqcup z) \sqcap (z \sqcup x)$$
$$c := (x \sqcap b) \sqcup a$$
$$d := (y \sqcap b) \sqcup a$$
$$e := (z \sqcap b) \sqcup a.$$

We leave it for the reader to verify that these elements form a diamond.

■

The above-mentioned theorem along with the Pentagon Theorem, Theorem 8.7, prove that a lattice is modular and distributive iff it contains neither a pentagon nor a diamond. This fact gives us a brute force algorithm to determine if a lattice is distributive or modular by enumerating all its sublattices of size 5.

9.3   JOIN-PRIME ELEMENTS

The notion of join-prime elements is useful in the characterization of finite distributive lattices by Birkhoff's Theorem (Theorem 9.4). For any lattice L, a nonzero element x is **join-prime** iff

$$\forall a, b \in L : x \leq a \sqcup b \Rightarrow (x \leq a \lor x \leq b). \tag{9.2}$$

Every join-prime element is also join-irreducible. To see that, assume that x is a join-prime element (9.2), and let $x = a \sqcup b$. Then $x \le a \sqcup b$; hence $x \le a \lor x \le b$. On the other hand, $x = a \sqcup b$ implies $x \ge a \land x \ge b$. From these, it follows that $(x = a) \lor (x = b)$. Hence x is join-irreducible.

For distributive lattices, even the converse holds: every join-irreducible element is also join-prime.

Lemma 9.2 *In a finite distributive lattice L, every join-irreducible element is join-prime.*

Proof: Let x be any join-irreducible element.

$$x \le a \sqcup b$$
$\equiv$ { Connecting Lemma }
$$x = x \sqcap (a \sqcup b)$$
$\equiv$ { L distributive }
$$x = (x \sqcap a) \sqcup (x \sqcap b)$$
$\Rightarrow$ { x join-irreducible}
$$(x = x \sqcap a) \lor (x = x \sqcap b)$$
$\equiv$ { Connecting Lemma }
$$(x \le a) \lor (x \le b).$$

∎

Corollary 9.3 *In a finite distributive lattice L, an element x is join-irreducible iff for all nonempty $V \subseteq L$:*

$$x \le \bigsqcup V \Rightarrow \exists v : v \in V : x \le v. \tag{9.3}$$

Proof: If x is join-irreducible, then for any nonempty $V \subseteq L$, property (9.3) is proved by induction on $|V|$. The case when V is singleton is trivial and the case ($|V| = 2$) makes use of Lemma 9.2. The converse holds trivially.

∎

9.4   BIRKHOFF'S REPRESENTATION THEOREM

Let $J(L)$ denote the set of join-irreducible elements of any lattice L, and $L_I(P)$ denote the set of order ideals of any poset P. Birkhoff's Theorem establishes an isomorphism relationship between a given finite distributive lattice, L, and $L_I(P)$, the set of order ideals of a particular poset, P, namely the poset of join-irreducible elements of L. In general, the poset P is obtained from L as the set of L's join-irreducibles, and L is recovered from P *up to isomorphism* by taking the set of ideals of elements from P. The significance of this theorem lies in the fact that the poset of join-irreducibles of L can be exponentially more succinct than the lattice itself.

Birkhoff's theorem relates finite distributive lattices to posets as follows:

Theorem 9.4 *[Birkhoff's Theorem] Let L be a finite distributive lattice. Then the following mapping from L to the set of ideals of J(L) is an isomorphism:*

$$f : L \to L_I(J(L)), \qquad a \in L \mapsto f(a) = \{x \in J(L) : x \le a\}.$$

Proof: First note that $f(a) \in L_I(J(L))$ because $\le$ is transitive.

Secondly, f is injective (one-one). If $f(a) = f(b)$, then $\bigsqcup f(a) = \bigsqcup f(b)$, hence $a = b$ by Lemma 5.5.

Thirdly, f is surjective (onto). Let $V \in L_I(J(L))$. Consider $a := \bigsqcup V$; we will show that $f(a) = V$. We first show that $f(a) \subseteq V$.

$$x \in f(a)$$
$\equiv$ { definition of $f(a)$ }
$\qquad x$ is join-irreducible and $x \le a$
$\equiv$ { definition of a }
$\qquad x$ is join-irreducible and $x \le \bigsqcup V$
$\Rightarrow$ { Corollary 9.3 }
$\qquad x$ is join-irreducible and $\exists y \in V : x \le y$
$\Rightarrow$ { V is an order ideal }
$\qquad x \in V$

We now show that $V \subseteq f(a)$.

$$v \in V$$
$\Rightarrow$ { definition of V, and $\bigsqcup$ }
$\qquad v$ is join-irreducible and $v \le \bigsqcup V$
$\Rightarrow$ { definition of a }
$\qquad v$ is join-irreducible and $v \le a$
$\Rightarrow$ { definition of $f(a)$ }
$\qquad v \in f(a)$.

Lastly, we show that f preserves the order: if $a \le b$, then $x \le a$ implies $x \le b$, hence $f(a) \subseteq f(b)$. Conversely, $f(a) \subseteq f(b)$ implies $\bigsqcup f(a) \le \bigsqcup f(b)$, which by Lemma 5.5 reduces to $a \le b$. The proof follows from Theorem 7.5.

∎

Figure 9.2 shows a five-element lattice with three join-irreducibles: a, b and c. The set of ideals of the join-irreducibles on the right is isomorphic to the original lattice. Another example is given in Figure 9.3.

Birkhoff's Theorem also makes it possible to translate the numerous properties of a finite distributive lattice L into those of its corresponding poset P and vice versa. For example, the dimension of L is equal to the width of the poset P, and the height of L equals the cardinality of P. It can also be shown easily that L is a Boolean lattice

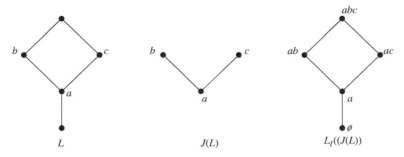

Figure 9.2 A lattice L, its set of join-irreducibles $J(L)$, and their ideals $L_I(J(L))$.

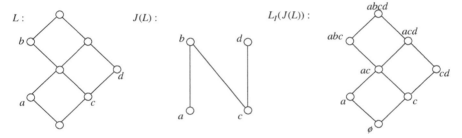

Figure 9.3 A lattice with the "N-poset" as the set of join-irreducibles.

iff P is an antichain, and L is a chain iff P is a chain. We have left such claims as exercises for the reader.

Although we have used join-irreducibles $J(L)$ in Birkhoff's Theorem, the argument can also be carried out with meet-irreducibles of the lattice L, denoted by $M(L)$. We leave the following lemma as an exercise.

Lemma 9.5 *For a finite distributive lattice L, the subposets containing $J(L)$ and $M(L)$ are isomorphic.*

Figure 9.4(b) shows that the statement is not true for a nondistributive lattice: not even the cardinalities of $J(L)$ and $M(L)$ are equal. The lattice in Figure 9.4(a), on the other hand, is distributive, and indeed $J(L)$ and $M(L)$ are isomorphic.

At this point, we should also mention the dual of Birkhoff's Theorem.

Theorem 9.6 *let P be a finite poset. Then the map $g : P \rightarrow J(L_I(P))$ defined by*

$$g(a) = \{x \in P \mid x \leq a\}$$

is an isomorphism of P onto $J(L_I(P))$.

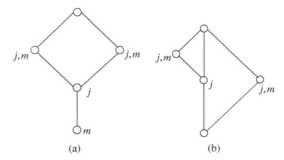

Figure 9.4   (a) Poset of Join- ("*j*") and meet- ("*m*") irreducible elements are isomorphic; (b) Irreducibles in a nondistributive lattice.

9.5   FINITARY DISTRIBUTIVE LATTICES

Birkhoff's Theorem requires the distributive lattice to be finite. In an infinite distributive lattice, there may not be any join-irreducible elements. For example, the lattice of open subsets on the real-line does not have any join-irreducible elements. In the infinite case, prime ideals serve as the "basis" elements. We refer the reader to Davey and Priestley [DP90] for details on that approach.

In computer science applications (such as distributed computing), it is more common to get finitary distributive lattices. A finitary distributive lattice is a locally finite distributive lattice with the bottom element. By following the proof of Birkhoff's Theorem, it can be extended to finitary lattices in the following sense.

Theorem 9.7 *Let P be a poset such that every principal order ideal is finite. Then, the poset of finite order ideals of P is a finitary distributive lattice. Conversely, if L is a finitary distributive lattice and P is its subposet of join-irreducibles, then every principal order ideal of P is finite and L is isomorphic to the lattice of all finite order ideals of P.*

9.6   PROBLEMS

9.1. We saw in Chapter 1 that join-irreducible elements may not always be dissectors. Show that for distributive lattices all join-irreducible elements are also dissectors.

9.2. Show that the poset of join-irreducible elements of a finite distributive lattice L is isomorphic to the poset of meet-irreducible elements of L.

9.3. Show that the height of a finite distributive lattice L equals the size of the subposet $J(L)$.

9.4. Let L be the finite distributive lattice generated by the set of all order ideals of a poset P. Show that

(a) The dimension of L is equal to the width of a poset P.

(b) L is a Boolean lattice iff P is an antichain.

(c) L is a chain iff P is a chain.

9.5. Show that for a finite lattice L, the following are equivalent:

(1) L is distributive.

(2) L is isomorphic to the set of ideals of its join-irreducibles: $L \approx L_I(J(L))$.

(3) L is isomorphic to a lattice of sets.

(4) L is isomorphic to a sublattice of a Boolean lattice.

9.6. Consider a finite lattice. We say that b is a complement of a if $a \sqcap b = 0$ and $a \sqcup b = 1$.

(a) Give an example of a finite distributive lattice that has an element without any complement.

(b) Show that in a finite distributive lattice, if an element a has a complement, then it is unique (i.e. no element in a finite distributive lattice can have two distinct complements).

(c) Give an example of a finite lattice in which an element has two complements.

(d) Show that if a and b have complements a' and b', respectively, in a finite distributive lattice, then $(a \sqcup b)$ also has a complement given by $a' \sqcap b'$.

9.7. Let X be any finite set and T be a total order defined on X. Consider the set of all posets P defined on the set X such that T is a valid linear extension (topological sort) of P. Show that this set is a lattice under $\subseteq$ relation on posets. Is this lattice distributive?

9.7 BIBLIOGRAPHIC REMARKS

The characterization of distributive lattices based on forbidden sublattices and the duality with the set of join-irreducibles is due to Birkhoff [Bir67].

10

SLICING

10.1 INTRODUCTION

In many applications, we are required to enumerate a subset of a given set that satisfies a given property. For example, in a distributed computation, we may be interested in all global states such that they satisfy a given formula (such as violation of mutual exclusion). While studying integer partitions, we may be interested in only those partitions in which the first two parts are equal. In this chapter, we present a method based on finite distributive lattices that allows us to analyze such subsets. This method, called slicing, enables us to produce structures that generate subsets of the finite distributive lattice.

10.2 REPRESENTING FINITE DISTRIBUTIVE LATTICES

From Birkhoff's representation theorem, every finite distributive lattice L can be equivalently represented by the poset of the join-irreducible elements of L (and constructing all the down-sets of that poset). Given any subset S of L, our goal is to compute the poset that represents the smallest sublattice containing S. For this purpose, we use directed graphs instead of posets to represent finite distributive lattices. We show that we can get sublattices by simply adding edges to the original directed graph.

The notion of order ideals of a poset can be extended to graphs in a straightforward manner. A subset of vertices, H, of a directed graph, P, is an *ideal* if it satisfies the

Introduction to Lattice Theory with Computer Science Applications, First Edition. Vijay K. Garg.
© 2015 John Wiley & Sons, Inc. Published 2015 by John Wiley & Sons, Inc.

following condition: if H contains a vertex v and (u, v) is an edge in the graph, then H also contains u. Observe that an ideal of P either contains all vertices in a strongly connected component or none of them. Let $L_I(P)$ denote the set of ideals of a directed graph P. Observe that the empty set and the set of all vertices trivially belong to $L_I(P)$. We call them **trivial** ideals. The following theorem is a slight generalization of the result that the set of ideals of a partially ordered set forms a distributive lattice.

Theorem 10.1 *Given a directed graph P, $(L_I(P); \subseteq)$ forms a distributive lattice.*

Proof: Left as an exercise.

■

Observe that when the directed graph has no edges (i.e., the poset is an antichain), the set of ideals corresponds to the Boolean lattice on the set of vertices. At the other extreme, when the graph is strongly connected, there are only trivial ideals. Since trivial ideals are always part of $L_I(P)$, it is more convenient to deal only with nontrivial ideals of a graph. It is easy to convert a graph P to P' such that there is one-to-one correspondence between all ideals of P and all nontrivial ideals of P'. We construct P' from P by adding two additional vertices $\perp$ and $\top$ such that $\perp$ is the smallest vertex and $\top$ is the largest vertex (i.e., there is a path from $\perp$ to every vertex and a path from every vertex to $\top$). It is easy to see that any nontrivial ideal will contain $\perp$ and not contain $\top$. As a result, every ideal of P is a nontrivial ideal of the graph P' and vice versa. We will deal with only nontrivial ideals from now on and an ideal would mean a nontrivial ideal unless specified otherwise. The directed graph representation of Figure 10.1(a) is shown in Figure 10.1(c).

Figure 10.2 shows another directed graph and its nontrivial ideals. The directed graph in Figure 10.2(a) is derived from Figure 10.1(a) by adding an edge from c to b

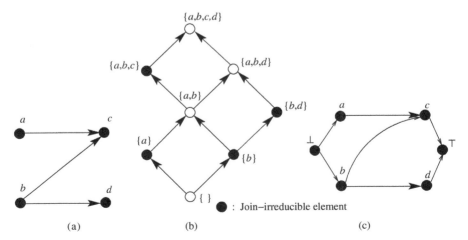

Figure 10.1   (a) P: A partial order. (b) The lattice of ideals. (c) The directed graph P'.

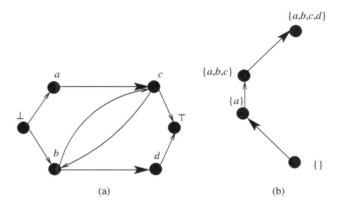

Figure 10.2 (a) A directed graph and (b) the lattice of its nontrivial ideals.

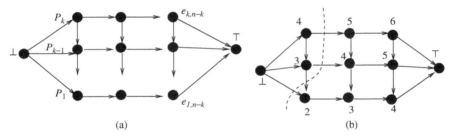

Figure 10.3 (a) The poset or directed graph $\mathcal{K}$ for generating subsets of X of size k. (b) The ideal denoting the subset $\{1, 3, 4\}$.

and adding two additional vertices $\bot$ and $\top$. The resulting set of nontrivial ideals is a sublattice of Figure 10.1(b). In the figure, we have not shown $\bot$ in the ideals because it is implicitly included in every nontrivial ideal.

We use the graph in Figure 10.3 as a running example in this chapter and denote it by $\mathcal{K}$. Let $[n] = \{1..n\}$ and k be an integer between 1 and n (inclusive). Ignoring the vertices $\top$ and $\bot$, $\mathcal{K}$ has k chains and each chain has $n - k$ elements. We call these chains $P_1, \dots, P_k$. In the graph, there are two types of edges. For every chain, there is an edge from the jth element to the $(j + 1)$th element, and an edge from the jth element in P_{i+1} to the jth element in P_i. Therefore, if an ideal of P contains j elements of P_i, then it also contains at least j elements of P_{i+1}.

We show that the ideals of $\mathcal{K}$ are in one-to-one correspondence with all the subsets Y of X of size k. The correspondence between subsets of X and ideals is as follows. If chain P_i has t elements in the ideal, then the element $t + i$ is in the set Y. Thus, chain P_1 chooses a number from $1 \dots n - k + 1$ (because there are $n - k$ elements); chain P_2 chooses the next larger number and so on. Figure 10.3(b) gives an example of the graph for subsets of size 3 of the set $[6]$. The ideal shown corresponds to the subset $\{1, 3, 4\}$. It can also be easily verified that there are $\binom{n}{k}$ nontrivial ideals of this poset.

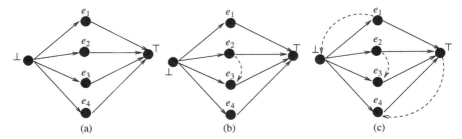

Figure 10.4   Graphs and slices for generating subsets of X when $|X| = 4$.

As yet another example, consider a poset on n elements such that all pairs of elements are mutually incomparable. The graph when n equals 4 is shown in Figure 10.4. We call this graph $\mathcal{B}_n$ and all of its (nontrivial) ideals are in one-to-one correspondence with all subsets of $[n]$.

10.3   PREDICATES ON IDEALS

The slicing technique is crucially based on the notion of predicates on the set of ideals. A predicate is simply a Boolean function from the set of all ideals to $\{0, 1\}$. Equivalently, a predicate specifies a subset of the ideals in which the Boolean function evaluates to 1. In the poset $\mathcal{K}$, "does not contain consecutive numbers" is a predicate, which is either true or false for any ideal. For example, it is true for $\{1, 3, 5\}$ but false for $\{1, 3, 4\}$. In the Boolean lattice of all subsets of $[n]$, $\mathcal{B}_n$, "has size k" is a predicate which is true if the subset has size k and false otherwise.

We now define various classes of predicates. The class of meet-closed predicates is useful because they allow us to compute the least ideal that satisfies a given predicate.

Definition 10.2 (meet-closed Predicates) *A predicate B is meet-closed for a poset or a graph P if*

$$\forall G, H \in L_I(P) : B(G) \wedge B(H) \Rightarrow B(G \sqcap H).$$

The predicate "does not contain consecutive numbers" in the poset $\mathcal{K}$ is meet-closed. For example, let $G = \{1, 3, 7\}$ and $H = \{2, 4, 6\}$. Both G and H satisfy the predicate B, "does not contain consecutive numbers." If we compute the meet of G and H, we get $\{1, 3, 6\}$ which also satisfies B. We will show that this is true for all possible G and H later.

Now consider the predicate "has size k" in the poset $\mathcal{B}_n$. Let $G = \{1, 3\}$ and $H = \{2, 3\}$. Then, $G \sqcap H$ equals $\{3\}$ which has different cardinality. Hence, "has size k" is not a meet-closed predicate in $\mathcal{B}_n$.

It follows from the definition that if there exists any ideal that satisfies a meet-closed predicate B, then there exists the least one obtained by taking the meet of all ideals satisfying B. Note that the predicate *false* that corresponds to the empty subset and the predicate *true* that corresponds to the entire set of ideals are meet-closed predicates.

As another example, define a n-size subset of $[2n]$ to satisfy the predicate Catalan if by putting left parentheses on the specified subset and right parentheses in remaining positions, one gets a well-balanced string of parentheses. For example, the subset $\{1, 3, 4\}$ corresponds to the string "()(())" where left parentheses are at positions 1, 3, and 4. This subset satisfies Catalan predicate, whereas the subset $\{1, 4, 5\}$ does not. We will use $G[i]$ to denote the ith largest element in the set. To formalize a well-balanced expression, note that if $G[i]$ equals k for any $i \in [n]$, then there are $i - 1$ left parentheses and $k - i$ right parentheses to the left of position k. Therefore, G satisfies the Catalan predicate iff for all i

$$G[i] - i \leq i - 1.$$

Or, equivalently

$$G[i] \leq 2i - 1.$$

It is now clear that Catalan is a meet-closed (and join-closed) predicate. If $G[i] \leq 2i - 1$ and $H[i] \leq 2i - 1$, then $min(G[i], H[i]) \leq 2i - 1$.

We now give another characterization of such predicates that will be useful for computing the least ideal that satisfies the predicate. To that end, we first define the notion of a crucial element for an ideal.

Definition 10.3 (Crucial Element) *Let $P = (E, \leq)$ be a poset. For an ideal $G \subsetneq E$ and a predicate B, we define $e \in E - G$ to be crucial for G as:*

$$crucial(G, e, B) \overset{def}{=} \forall \text{ ideals } H \supseteq G : (e \in H) \vee \neg B(H).$$

Intuitively, this means that any ideal H, that is at least G, cannot satisfy the predicate unless it contains e.

Definition 10.4 (Linear Predicates) *A predicate B is linear iff for all ideals $G \subsetneq E$,*

$$\neg B(G) \Rightarrow \exists e \in E - G : crucial(G, e, B).$$

Now, we have

Theorem 10.5 *A predicate B is linear iff it is meet-closed.*

Proof: First assume that B is not closed under meet. We show that B is not linear. Since B is not closed under meets, there exist two ideals H and K such that $B(H)$ and $B(K)$ but not $B(H \sqcap K)$. Define G to be $H \sqcap K$. G is a strict subset of $H \subseteq E$ because $B(H)$ but not $B(G)$. Therefore, G cannot be equal to E. We show that B is not linear by showing that there does not exist any crucial element for G. A crucial element e, if it exists, cannot be in $H - G$ because K does not contain e and still $B(K)$ holds. Similarly, it cannot be in $K - G$ because H does not contain e and still $B(H)$ holds.

It also cannot be in $E - (H \cup K)$ because H does not contain e and still $B(H)$ holds. We conclude that there does not exist any crucial element for G.

Now assume that B is not linear. This implies that there exists $G \subsetneq E$ such that $\neg B(G)$ and none of the elements in $E - G$ is crucial. We first claim that $E - G$ cannot be a singleton. Assume if possible $E - G$ contains only one element e. Then, any ideal H that contains G and does not contain e must be equal to G itself. This implies that $\neg B(H)$ because we assumed $\neg B(G)$. Therefore, e is crucial contradicting our assumption that none of the elements in $E - G$ is crucial. Let $W = E - G$. For each $e \in W$, we define H_e as the ideal that contains G, does not contain e, and still satisfies B. Since W has at least two events, it is easy to see that G is the meet of all H_e. Therefore, B is not meet-closed because all H_e satisfy B but not their meets.

■

Example 10.6 Consider $\mathcal{B}_n$ shown in Figure 10.4(a). The ideals of this graph correspond to subsets of $[n]$ and thus generate the Boolean lattice. Now consider the predicate B defined to be true on G as "If G contains any odd $i < n$, then it also contains $i + 1$." It is easy to verify that B is meet-closed. Given any G for which B does not hold, the crucial elements consist of

$$\{i \mid i \text{ even}, 2 \leq i \leq n, i - 1 \in G, i \notin G\}.$$

Example 10.7 Consider the poset $\mathcal{K}$. Let the predicate B be "G does not contain any consecutive numbers." Consider any G for which B does not hold. This means that it has some consecutive numbers. Let i be the smallest number in G such that $i - 1$ is also in G. If i is on chain P_j, then the next element in P_j is crucial. For example, the ideal $\{1, 3, 4\}$ does not satisfy B. The smallest element whose predecessor is also in G is 4 which is on the chain P_3. Therefore, the second element in P_3 is crucial. In other words, any ideal that satisfies B and is bigger than $\{1, 3, 4\}$ is at least $\{1, 3, 5\}$. If i is the last element in P_j, then any element in $E - G$ can serve as a crucial element because in this case for any H that contains G, $B(H)$ is false.

Our interest is in detecting whether there exists an ideal that satisfies a given predicate B. We assume that given an ideal, G, it is efficient to determine whether B is true for G. On account of linearity of B, if B is evaluated to be false in some ideal G, then we know that there exists a crucial element in $E - G$. We now make an additional assumption called the efficient advancement property.

(Efficient Advancement Property) A predicate B satisfies the efficient advancement property if there exists an efficient (polynomial time) function to determine a crucial element whenever B evaluates to false on any cut.

We now have

```
(1)  boolean function detect(B:boolean_predicate, P:graph)
(2)  var
(3)       G: ideal initially G = {⊥};
(4)
(5)  while (¬B(G) ∧ (G ≠ P)) do
(6)       Let e be such that crucial(e, G, B) in P;
(7)       G := G ∪ {e}.
(8)  endwhile;
(9)  if B(G) return true;
(10) else return false;
```

Figure 10.5   An efficient algorithm to detect a linear predicate.

Theorem 10.8 *If B is a linear predicate with the efficient advancement property, then there exists an efficient algorithm to determine the least ideal that satisfies B (if any).*

Proof: An efficient algorithm to find the *least* cut in which B is true is given in Figure 10.5. We search for the least ideal starting from the ideal $\{\bot\}$. If the predicate is false in the ideal, then we find a crucial element using the efficient advancement property and then repeat the procedure.

■

Assuming that $crucial(e, G, B)$ can be evaluated efficiently for a given graph, we can determine the least ideal that satisfies B efficiently even though the number of ideals may be exponentially larger than the size of the graph. As an example, to find the least ideal in $\mathcal{K}$ that satisfies "does not contain consecutive numbers," we start with the ideal $\{1, 2, 3\}$. Since 1 and 2 are consecutive, we advance along P_2 to the ideal $\{1, 3, 4\}$, which still does not satisfy the predicate. We now advance along P_3 to the ideal $\{1, 3, 5\}$ which is the smallest ideal that satisfies the given predicate.

So far, we have focused on meet-closed predicates. All the definitions and ideas carry over to join-closed predicates. If the predicate B is join-closed, then one can search for the largest ideal that satisfies B in a fashion analogous to finding the least ideal when it is meet-closed.

Predicates that are both meet-closed and join-closed are called regular predicates.

Definition 10.9 (Regular Predicates) *A predicate is regular if the set of ideals that satisfy the predicate forms a sublattice of the lattice of ideals.*

Equivalently, a predicate B is *regular* with respect to P if it is closed under $\sqcup$ and $\sqcap$, i.e.,

$$\forall G, H \in L_I(P) : B(G) \wedge B(H) \Rightarrow B(G \sqcup H) \wedge B(G \sqcap H)$$

The set of ideals that satisfy a regular predicate forms a sublattice of the lattice of all ideals. Since a sublattice of a distributive lattice is also distributive, the set of ideals that satisfy a regular predicate forms a distributive lattice. From Birkhoff's theorem, we know that a distributive lattice can be equivalently represented using the poset of its join-irreducible elements. The poset of join-irreducible elements provides a compact way of enumerating all ideals that satisfy the predicate and will be useful in efficient solving of combinatorial problems.

There are two important problems with this approach of finding the set of ideals that satisfy a given predicate. First, what if the predicate is not regular? Is it still possible to represent the set of ideals satisfying B compactly? Second, we need to calculate the structure that captures the set of ideals satisfying B efficiently. These problems are addressed in the following section.

The notion of a slice will be used to represent the subset of ideals that satisfy B in a concise manner. The slice of a directed graph P with respect to a predicate B (denoted by $slice(P, B)$) is a graph derived from P such that all the ideals in $L_I(P)$ that satisfy B are included in $L_I(slice(P, B))$. Note that the slice may include some additional ideals that do not satisfy the predicate. Formally,

Definition 10.10 (Slice) *A slice of a graph P with respect to a predicate B is the directed graph obtained from P by adding edges such that:*

(1) it contains all the ideals of P that satisfy B and
(2) of all the graphs that satisfy (1), it has the least number of ideals.

We first show that given a distributive lattice L generated by the graph (poset) P, every sublattice of L can be generated by a graph obtained by adding edges to P.

Theorem 10.11 *Let L be a finite distributive lattice generated by the graph P. Let L' be any sublattice of L. Then, there exists a graph P' that can be obtained by adding edges to P that generates L'.*

Proof: Our proof is constructive. We show an algorithm to compute P'. For every vertex $e \in P$, let $I(e)$ be the set of ideals of P containing e. Since L is the set of all ideals of P, we can view $I(e)$ as a subset of L. In rest of the proof, we will not distinguish between an ideal of the graph P and the corresponding element in lattice L. Let $I(e, L')$ be the subset of $I(e)$ that is contained in L', i.e., $I(e, L') = I(e) \cap L'$. On the basis of the set $I(e, L')$, we define $J(e, L')$ as follows. If $I(e, L')$ is empty, then $J(e, L')$ is defined to be the trivial ideal of P that includes the $\top$ element. Otherwise, $J(e, L')$ is defined as the least element of $I(e, L')$. Since L' is a sublattice, it is clear that if the set of ideals that include e are in L', then their intersection (meet) also includes e and is in L'. Thus, $J(e, L')$ is well defined.

Note that $J(\bot, L')$ corresponds to the least element of L' and $J(\top, L')$ corresponds to the trivial ideal that includes $\top$.

Now, we add the following edges to the graph P. For every pair of vertices e, f such that $J(e, L') \le J(f, L')$, we add an edge from e to f. We now claim that the resulting graph P' generates L'.

Pick any nontrivial ideal G of P', i.e., an ideal that includes $\bot$ and does not include $\top$. We show that $G = \cup_{e \in G} J(e, L')$. This will be sufficient to show that $G \in L'$ because G is a union of ideals in L' and L' is a lattice. Since $e \in J(e, L')$, it is clear that $G \subseteq$

$\cup_{e \in G} J(e, L')$. We show that $G \supseteq \cup_{e \in G} J(e, L')$. Let $f \in J(e, L')$ for some e. This implies that $J(f, L') \subseteq J(e, L')$ because $J(f, L')$ is the least ideal containing f in L'. By our algorithm, there is an edge from f to e in P', and since G is an ideal of P' that includes e, it also includes f. Thus $G \supseteq \cup_{e \in G} J(e, L')$.

Conversely, pick any element G of L'. We show that G is a nontrivial ideal of P'. Since $L' \subseteq L$ and L correspond to nontrivial ideals of P, it is clear that G is a nontrivial ideal of P. Our obligation is to show that it is a nontrivial ideal of P' as well. Assume, if possible, G is not a nontrivial ideal of P'. This implies that there exists vertices e, f in P' such that $f \in G$, $e \notin G$ and (e, f) is an edge in P'. The presence of this edge in P', but not in P implies that $J(e, L') \subseteq J(f, L')$. Since $f \in G$ and $G \in L'$, from definition of $J(f, L')$, we get that $J(f, L') \subseteq G$. However, this implies $J(e, L') \subseteq G$, i.e., $e \in G$, a contradiction.

∎

Now, the following result is easy.

Theorem 10.12 *For any P and B, slice(P, B) exists and is unique.*

Proof: First note that intersection of sublattices is also a sublattice. Now given any predicate B consider all the sublattices that contain all the ideals that satisfy B. The intersection of all these sublattices gives us the smallest sublattice that contains all the ideals. From Theorem 10.11, we get that there exists a graph that generates this sublattice.

∎

The procedure outlined in the above-mentioned proof is not efficient because it requires us to take intersection of all bigger sublattices. We now show how to efficiently compute slices for the predicates for which there exists an efficient detection algorithm. The slicing algorithm is shown in Figure 10.6. It takes as input a graph P and a Boolean predicate B. The algorithm constructs the slice by adding edges to the graph P. For this purpose, it initializes in line (3) a graph R as P. In rest of the function, edges are added to R, which is finally returned.

The addition of edges is done as follows. For every pair of vertices, e and f, in the graph P, the algorithm constructs Q from P by adding edges from f to $\bot$ and $\top$ to e. Owing to these edges in Q, all nontrivial ideals of Q contain f and do not contain e. We now invoke the detection algorithm on Q. If the detection algorithm returns false, then we know that there is no nontrivial ideal of P that contains f but does not contain e. Therefore, all ideals that satisfy B have the property that if they include f, they also include e. Hence, we add an edge from e to f in the graph R. We continue this procedure for all pairs of vertices. Theorem 10.13 shows the correctness of this procedure.

Theorem 10.13 *Let P be a directed graph. Let R be the directed graph output by the algorithm in Figure 10.6 for a predicate B. Then R is the slice of P with respect to B.*

```
(1)  graph function computeSlice(B:boolean_predicate, P: graph)
(2)  var
(3)      R: graph initialized to P;
(4)  begin
(5)      for every pair of nodes e, f in P do
(6)          Q := P with the additional edges (f, ⊥) and (⊤, e);
(7)          if detect(B, Q) is false
(8)              add edge (e,f) to R;
(9)      endfor
(10)     return R;
(11) end;
```

Figure 10.6   An efficient algorithm to compute the slice for a predicate B.

Proof: Let $L_I(P, B)$ denote the set of ideals of P that satisfy B. We first show that $L_I(R) \supseteq L_I(P, B)$. Adding an edge (e, f) in R eliminates only those ideals of P that contain f but do not contain e. However, all those ideals do not satisfy B because the edge (e, f) is added only when $detect(B, Q)$ is false. Thus, all the ideals of P that satisfy B are also the ideals of R.

Next, we show that the $L_I(R)$ is the smallest sublattice of $L_I(P)$ that includes $L_I(P, B)$. Let M be a graph such that $L_I(M) \supseteq L_I(P, B)$. Assume that if possible $L_I(M)$ is strictly smaller than $L_I(R)$. This implies that there exists two vertices e and f such that there is an edge from e to f in M but not in R. Since R is output by the algorithm, $detect(B, Q)$ is true in line (7); otherwise, an edge would have been added from e to f. But, this means that there exists an ideal in P, which includes f, does not include e, and satisfies B. This ideal cannot be in $L_I(M)$ due to the edge from e to f contradicting our assumption that $L_I(P, B) \subseteq L_I(M)$.   ∎

Theorem 10.13 allows us to compute the slice for any predicate that can be detected efficiently. For example, relational predicates can be detected efficiently using max-flow techniques [CG95].

When the predicate is known to be linear, we can use a more efficient and direct algorithm to compute the slice as shown in Figure 10.7. The algorithm determines for every element $e \in P$, the least order ideal of P that includes e and satisfies B. Since B is a linear predicate and the condition "includes e" is also linear, it follows that least is well-defined whenever there are satisfying cuts. The correctness of this algorithm is left as an exercise.

10.4   APPLICATION: SLICING DISTRIBUTED COMPUTATIONS

Since the set of all consistent global states form a distributive lattice, we can use the slicing method to represent a subset of interesting global states. For regular predicates,

```
(1)    graph function computeSlice(B:linear_predicate, P: graph)
(2)    var
(3)        R: graph initialized to P;
(4)    begin
(5)        for every element e in P do
(6)            let J(e, B) be the least order ideal of P that satisfies B
               and includes e;
(7)            for every f ∈ J(e, B) do
(8)                add edge (f, e) to R;
(9)            endfor
(10)       endfor
(11)       return R;
(12) end;
```

Figure 10.7   An efficient algorithm to compute the slice for a linear predicate B.

the slice would correspond to the exact set of satisfying consistent global states. For nonregular predicates, the slice would correspond to the smallest sublattice containing the set of satisfying global states. Examples of regular predicates in a distributed computation are as follows.

- There are no "token" messages in transit.
- Every "request" message has been "acknowledged" in the system.
- All processes are green and all channels are empty.

Slicing can be used to facilitate predicate detection as illustrated by the following scenario. Consider a predicate B that is a conjunction of two clauses B_1 and B_2. Now, assume that B_1 is such that it can be detected efficiently but B_2 has no structural property that can be exploited for efficient detection. An efficient algorithm for locating *some* consistent cut satisfying B_1 cannot guarantee that the cut also satisfies B_2. Therefore, to detect B, without computation slicing, we are forced to explore the set of all consistent global states of the computation. With computation slicing, however, we can first compute the slice for B_1. If only a small fraction of consistent cuts satisfy B_1, then instead of detecting B in the computation, it is much more efficient to detect B in the slice. Therefore, by spending only polynomial amount of time in computing the slice, we can throw away an exponential number of consistent cuts.

10.5 PROBLEMS

10.1. Prove Theorem 10.1.

10.2. Give a directed graph such that all its nontrivial ideals are in one-to-one correspondence with all the subsets of $[n]$, which contain 1 whenever they contain 2.

10.3. Compute the slice of the graph in the previous question for subsets, which always contain $n - 1$.

10.4. Show that whenever B is linear, the order ideal $J_B(e)$ defined as the least order ideal that satisfies B and includes e is a join-irreducible element of the slice of order ideals that satisfy B. Conversely, every join-irreducible elements of the slice is of the form $J_B(e)$ for some e.

10.5. Show the correctness of the algorithm in Figure 10.7.

10.6. Given slices for predicates B_1 and B_2 with respect to a computation P, give algorithms to compute slices for $B_1 \wedge B_2$, $B_1 \vee B_2$, and $\neg B_1$.

10.7. Often, we are interested in temporal properties relating to the sequence of states during an execution rather than just the initial and final states. For example, the liveness property in the dining philosophers problem, "a philosopher, whenever gets hungry, eventually gets to eat," is a temporal property. We say that a consistent cut C satisfies $EF(B)$ if B holds for some consistent cut on some path from C to the final consistent cut. We say that a consistent cut C satisfies $EG(B)$ (respectively $AG(B)$) if B holds for all cuts on some (respectively all) path from C to the final consistent cut. Given a distributed computation, and a slice for a regular predicate B, give algorithms to compute slice for $EF(B)$ and $AG(B)$.

10.6 BIBLIOGRAPHIC REMARKS

The definition of slicing is from Garg and Mittal [GM01], Mittal and Garg [MG01b]. The algorithm in Figure 10.6 is from Mittal, Sen, and Garg [MSG07].

11

APPLICATIONS OF SLICING TO COMBINATORICS

11.1 INTRODUCTION

A combinatorial problem usually requires enumerating, counting, or ascertaining existence of structures that satisfy a given property B in a set of structures L. We now show that slicing can be used for solving such problems mechanically and efficiently. Specifically, we give an efficient (polynomial time) algorithm to enumerate, count, or detect structures that satisfy B when the total set of structures is large but the set of structures satisfying B is small. We illustrate the slicing method by analyzing problems in integer partitions, set families, and the set of permutations.

Consider the following combinatorial problems:

(Q1) Count the number of subsets of the set $[n]$ (the set $\{1 \ldots n\}$), which have size m and do not contain any consecutive numbers.

(Q2) Enumerate all integer partitions less than or equal to the partition $(\lambda_1, \lambda_2, \ldots, \lambda_n)$ in which λ_1 equals λ_2.

(Q3) Give the number of permutations of $[n]$ in which i less than or equal to j implies that the number of inversions of i is less than or equal to the number of inversions of j.

Our goal in this chapter is to show how such problems can be solved *mechanically* and *efficiently* for any fixed values of the parameters n and m.

Introduction to Lattice Theory with Computer Science Applications, First Edition. Vijay K. Garg.
© 2015 John Wiley & Sons, Inc. Published 2015 by John Wiley & Sons, Inc.

It is important to note that someone trained in combinatorics may be able to solve all of these problems efficiently (and the reader is encouraged to solve these problems before reading further). Our emphasis is on techniques that can be applied mechanically. On the other hand, note that for the fixed values of n and m, all the sets above are finite and therefore all the problems can be solved mechanically. Our emphasis is on *efficiency*. To be more precise, let L be a large set of combinatorial structures (for example, all subsets of $\{1 \dots n\}$ of size m and all permutations of $[n]$) Each combinatorial problem requires enumerating, counting, or searching the subset of structures that satisfy a given property B. Call this set $L_B \subseteq L$. For example, in the problem (Q1), L is the set of all subsets of $[n]$ of size m and L_B is the set of all subsets of $[n]$ of size m that do not contain any consecutive numbers. For any fixed set of parameters m and n, the size of L is large but finite, enabling one to enumerate all possible structures and then to check each one of them for the property B. This approach results in an algorithm that requires time proportional to the size of the set L which is exponential in n (or m). We show a technique that provides answers to some combinatorial problems in polynomial time and for others, such as those involving enumeration, in time proportional to the size of L_B (and not L).

To explain the slicing technique, we use the term *small* to mean polynomial in n and m, and *large* to mean exponential in n or m. Thus, the set L is large. We first build a *small* structure P such that all elements of L can be generated by P. Second, we compute a *slice* of P with respect to B, denoted by P_B, such that P_B generates all elements of L_B. P_B is a small structure and can be efficiently analyzed to answer questions about L_B or enumerate all elements of L_B.

11.2   COUNTING IDEALS

For counting the number of elements in L and its sublattices, we use $N(P)$ to denote the number of ideals of the poset P. Since our interest is in efficient calculation of $N(P)$, we will restrict the *dimension* of the partial order generating the lattice. Determining whether a poset P with n points is 2-dimensional and isomorphism testing for 2-dimensional orders can be done in $O(n^2)$ time [Spi85]. All the posets used in this chapter are two dimensional. The following lemma shows that the number of ideals of a poset can be calculated efficiently for series–parallel posets (a special case of two-dimensional posets) [FLST86]. For generalization to counting ideals of two-dimensional posets, see Steiner [Ste84] and Chapter 13.

Lemma 11.1 (Counting Lemma)

1. *If Q is an extension of P then $N(Q) \leq N(P)$.*
2. *(Parallel) Let $P + Q$ be the disjoint union (or direct sum) of posets P and Q. Then, $N(P + Q) = N(P)N(Q)$.*
3. *Let $P \oplus Q$ be the ordinal sum of posets P and Q. Then, $N(P \oplus Q) = N(P) + N(Q) - 1$.*

4. *Assume that P can be decomposed into the least number of chains $C_1, C_2, \ldots C_n$.*
   Then

$$N(P) \le \prod_{i=1}^{n}(|C_i| + 1).$$

When each chain is at most m in length, we get that $N(P) \le (m + 1)^n$.

11.3   BOOLEAN ALGEBRA AND SET FAMILIES

Let X be a ground set on n elements. Assume that we are interested in the sets of subsets of X. By using $\subseteq$ as the order relation, we can view it as a distributive lattice L. This lattice has $n + 1$ levels and each level set of rank k in the Boolean lattice corresponds to $\binom{n}{k}$ sets of size k. L is generated by the directed graph in Figure 11.1(a). It is easy to verify that there is a bijection between nontrivial ideals of the graph and subsets of X.

Now consider all subsets of X such that if they include e_i then they also include e_j. To obtain the slice with respect to this predicate, we just need to add an edge from e_j to e_i. Figure 11.1(b) shows the slice with respect to the predicate "if e_3 is included then so is e_2." To ensure the condition that e_i is always included, we simply add an edge from e_i to $\perp$ and to ensure that e_i is never included in any subset, we add an edge from $\top$ to e_i. Figure 11.1(c) shows the slice that gives all subsets that always contain e_1, never contain e_4, and contain e_2 whenever they contain e_3.

As an application, we now solve some combinatorial problems. Let n be even. We are required to calculate the total number of subsets of $[n]$ which satisfy the property that if they contain any odd integer i, then they also contain $i + 1$ (or equivalently, compute the number of ways to select groups from $n/2$ couples such that a wife is always accompanied by her husband in the group although a husband may not be accompanied by his wife). Although this problem can be solved directly by a combinatorial argument, we will show how the slicing method can be applied. We first construct the poset that generates all the subsets of $[n]$. It is Figure 11.1(a) in the case of 4. We now define the subset of interest by a predicate B. For any subset G of $[n]$, we let $B(G)$ to be true if G contains $i + 1$ whenever it contains any odd integer i. From our discussion of regular predicates, it is clear that B is regular. To compute the slice, it is sufficient to have a predicate detection algorithm. Detecting the least ideal that satisfies B can be done efficiently because it satisfies the efficient advancement property: "If an ideal does not satisfy B, then there is some unaccompanied wife and therefore the element corresponding to the husband is crucial." By applying the predicate detection algorithm repeatedly, we can determine all the edges that need to be added to get the slice. In this example, it is sufficient to add an edge from e_{i+1} to e_i for odd i. The slice consists of $n/2$ chains each with exactly 2 elements (ignoring $\perp$ and $\top$). From the counting lemma (Lemma 11.1), it follows that the total number of ideals is $(2 + 1)^{n/2} = 3^{n/2}$. The reader should note that for any fixed value of n, the problem can be solved by a computer automatically and efficiently (because the slice results in a series-parallel poset).

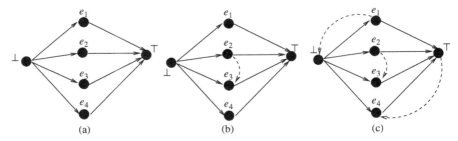

Figure 11.1   Graphs and slices for generating subsets of X when $|X| = 4$.

As another example, let us enumerate the subsets $\{a_1, \ldots, a_m\}$ of n such that for all i and j, a_i does not divide a_j.

We have the following result.

Lemma 11.2 *Consider the graph Q obtained from Figure 11.1(a) by adding an edge from i to j whenever i divides j. Then, Q can be used to enumerate all subsets of $[n]$ which do not contain any a_i and a_j such that a_i divides a_j.*

Proof: Define $B(G)$ as $\forall i, j : (i \neq j) \wedge (a_i \text{ divides } a_j) \wedge (a_j \in G) \Rightarrow (a_i \in G)$.

It is clear that B is a regular predicate and the resulting slice is acyclic. Each desired subset is simply the antichains of the poset so obtained. There is 1-1 correspondence between antichains and ideals.

∎

11.4   SET FAMILIES OF SIZE K

It is important to note that regularity of B is dependent on the lattice structure of L. For example, in many applications of set families, we are interested in sets of a fixed size k. The predicate B that the ideal is of size k is not regular. However, by considering alternative posets, this set family can still be analyzed. Here, the appropriate poset to use is the graph $\mathcal{K}(k, n - k)$ shown in Figure 10.3. As shown in Chapter 10, the set of ideals of $\mathcal{K}(k, n - k)$ are in 1-1 correspondence with all the subsets of $[n]$ of size k.

Note that by considering all possible choices made by P_k, this method gives an easy proof of the combinatorial identity

$$\binom{n}{k} = \sum_{m=k-1}^{n-1} \binom{m}{k-1}.$$

Let us now apply the slicing method to the first combinatorial problem (Q1) mentioned in the introduction. Assume that we are interested in counting all subsets of n of size k, which do not have any consecutive numbers. For (Q1), our interest is in

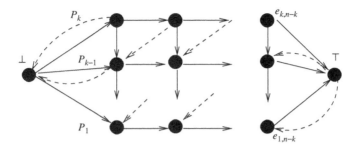

Figure 11.2   Slice for the predicate "does not contain consecutive numbers".

ideals that correspond to subsets without any consecutive numbers. It can be verified
that an ideal G satisfies B if whenever P_i has t elements in G, P_{i+1} has at least $t + 1$
elements in G. This condition is linear and we can use the algorithm in Figure 10.6
to compute the slice. Figure 11.2 shows the slice that includes precisely those subsets that do not contain consecutive numbers. By collapsing all strongly connected
components and by removing the transitively implied edges, we get a graph that is isomorphic to $\mathcal{K}(k, n - k - (k - 1))$ (i.e., the original graph when there are k chains and
each chain has only $n - k - (k - 1)$ elements). Therefore, the total number of order
ideals is $\binom{n-k+1}{k}$. Again one can come up with a combinatorial argument to solve the
problem (for example, see Theorem 13.1 and Example 13.1 in van Lint [vLW92]),
but it is easier to solve the problem using slicing.

   All the above-mentioned constructions can be generalized to multidimensional
grids to obtain results on multinomials instead of binomials.

11.5   INTEGER PARTITIONS

In this section, we apply slicing to integer partitions that have been studied by mathematicians for a long time.

Definition 11.3 $\lambda = (\lambda_1, ..., \lambda_k)$ *is an unordered partition of the integer n if*

   1. $\forall i \in [1, k - 1] : \lambda_i \geq \lambda_{i+1}$
   2. $\sum_{i=1}^{k} \lambda_i = n$

Definition 11.4 $p(n)$ *is the number of unordered partitions of the integer n.*

Definition 11.5 *A Ferrer's diagram for an integer partition* $\lambda = (\lambda_1, ..., \lambda_k)$ *of integer
n is a matrix of dots where the ith row contains* λ_i *dots (example Figure 11.3). Thus,
each row represents the size of a partition and the number of rows represents the
number of parts in the partition.*

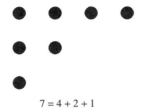

$$7 = 4 + 2 + 1$$

Figure 11.3   Ferrer's diagram for the integer partition $(4, 2, 1)$ for 7.

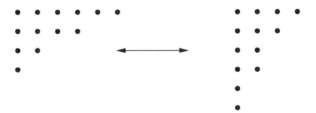

Figure 11.4   An Application of Ferrer's diagram.

As an application of Ferrer's diagram, we show that the number of partitions of n with k parts and the largest part equal to m is equal to the number of partitions of n with m parts and the largest part equal to k. The two numbers can be shown to be equal by noting that there exists a one-to-one correspondence between a partition λ of n with k parts such that the largest part is equal to m and a partition λ' of n with m parts such that the largest part is equal to k. This is because λ can be transformed to a partition of the latter type by rotating its Ferrer's diagram as shown in Figure 11.4.

We now define an order on the set of partitions. Given two partitions $\lambda = (\lambda_1, \lambda_2, \dots, \lambda_m), \delta = (\delta_1, \delta_2, \dots, \delta_n)$, we define

$$\lambda \geq \delta \equiv (m \geq n) \wedge (\forall i : 1 \leq i \leq n : \lambda_i \geq \delta_i).$$

This can also be viewed in terms of containment in the Ferrer's diagram i.e. $\lambda \geq \delta$ if the Ferrer's diagram for δ is contained in the Ferrer's diagram of λ. For example, $(4, 3, 2) \geq (2, 2, 2)$ as shown in figure 1.7.

Definition 11.6 (Young's Lattice)   *Given a partition λ,* **Young's lattice** *Y_λ is the lattice of all partitions that are less than or equal to λ.*

The Young's lattice for $(3, 3, 3)$ first introduced in Chapter 1 is shown in figure 11.5.

We claim that Y_λ is the set of ideals of the poset corresponding to the Ferrer's diagram of λ (an example of the poset for partition $(3, 3, 3)$ is shown in Figure 11.6). This claim holds because for any ideal δ of the Ferrer's diagram, the components satisfy $\forall i \geq j : \delta_i \geq \delta_j$. Since Young's lattice is a lattice of ideals, it is clearly distributive. One can see that the lattice of subsets of size k from the set of size n is a special case

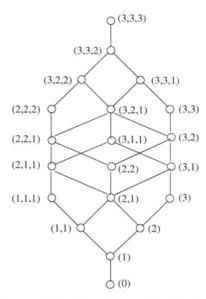

Figure 11.5   Young's lattice for $(3, 3, 3)$.

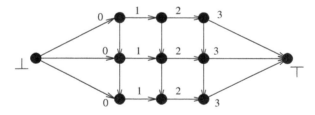

Figure 11.6   The poset corresponding to Ferrer's diagram of $(3, 3, 3)$.

of Young's lattice when all λ_i's are equal. Therefore, the number of integer partitions whose Ferrer's diagrams fit in a box of size k by $n - k$ is equal to $\binom{n}{k}$ (providing an alternate proof of Theorem 3.2 in Stanton and White [SW86]). Let $q(l, k, m)$ denote the number of partitions of l whose Ferrer's diagram fit in a box of size k by m. Since $p(n)$ has at most n parts and each part is at most n, it follows that the nth level of $Y_{(n,n,...,n)}$ contains all partitions of n. In Chapter 14, we use enumeration of the level

$$\underbrace{\phantom{Y_{(n,n,...,n)}}}_{n}$$

set of the ideal lattice to enumerate all partitions of n. An example of level sets can be seen in Figure 11.5. The third level has three partitions: 3, (2,1), and (1,1,1). This set corresponds to $p(3)$.

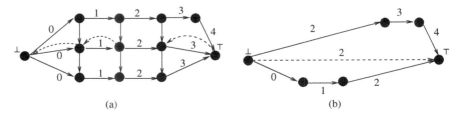

Figure 11.7   Slice for $\delta_2 = 2$.

By summing up the sizes of all level sets, it follows that

$$\binom{n}{k} = \sum_{l=0}^{k(n-k)} q(l, k, n - k).$$

Since the poset that generates the corresponding Young's lattice is symmetric with respect to k and m, we get that $q(l, k, m)$ equals $q(l, m, k)$; and since the poset is dual of itself (i.e., we get back the same poset when all arcs are reversed), we also get that $q(l, k, m)$ equals $q(mk - l, k, m)$. All these results are generally derived using Gaussian polynomials (see van Lint [vLW92]).

We now examine the partitions which have some additional conditions imposed on them. These additional conditions can then be viewed as predicates and the slicing method could be used to give us a graph which could generate all such partitions. Some very natural and interesting partitions are as follows:
All partitions that are less than or equal to λ

- with odd parts
- with distinct parts
- with even parts
- with ($\lambda_1 = \lambda_2$)
- with ($\lambda_k = 1$)

Interestingly, it turns out that all these predicates are regular! The reader is encouraged to prove that this is indeed true.

Assume that we are interested in all partitions less than or equal to $(4, 3, 3)$ such that their second component is some fixed value, say b. It is easy to verify that partitions $\delta \in Y_\lambda$ such that $\delta_2 = b$ form a sublattice, and therefore, the condition $\delta_2 = b$ is a regular predicate.

Figure 11.7(a) shows the slice of partitions in which $\delta_2 = 2$. Since the second part must be 2, additional edges ensure that the ideal of the graph has exactly two elements from P_2. On collapsing the strongly connected components and transitively reducing the graph, we get the series–parallel graph Figure 11.7(b). By applying counting lemma, we get that there are $(2 + 1)(2 + 1) = 9$ such partitions that can all be enumerated automatically using Figure 11.7(b). They are as follows:

$$\{220, 221, 222, 320, 321, 322, 420, 421, 422\}$$

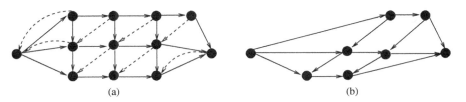

Figure 11.8   Slice for "distinct parts."

As another example assume that we are interested in all partitions less than $\lambda = (4, 3, 3)$, which have distinct parts. Figure 11.8(a) gives the slice and Figure 11.8(b) gives the graph after simplification. The graph is equivalent to that of subsets of size 3 from [5]. Hence, there are $\binom{5}{3}$ such partitions. These partitions can also be enumerated from the figure. They are as follows:

$$\{210, 310, 410, 320, 420, 430, 321, 421, 431, 432\}.$$

Some other subsets of partitions discussed in the literature are "partitions with odd number of parts," "partitions with distinct odd parts," "partitions with even number of parts," "kth part is at most h," etc. These are all regular predicates.

Now the reader may also see the solution for the second problem (Q2) mentioned in the introduction—enumerating all partitions in the Young's lattice Y_λ with the first part equal to the second part. We simply define the predicate B on a partition δ to be true when δ_1 equals δ_2. It is clear that the predicate is closed under joins and meets and is therefore a regular predicate. One can draw the slice and conclude that the number of partitions δ in Y_λ satisfying $\delta_1 = \delta_2$ is equal to the number of partitions in Y_δ where $\delta = (\lambda_2, \lambda_3, \ldots, \lambda_k)$. The slice can also be used to enumerate all required partitions.

11.6 PERMUTATIONS

We first show a poset such that its ideals can be mapped to all permutations of n symbols. Figure 11.9 shows the poset $T(n)$ that generates all permutations for $n = 5$. The poset $T(n)$ consists of $n - 1$ disjoint chains, $P_1, .., P_{n-1}$ where P_i has i elements. There are multiple ways to interpret a given ideal G. We use $G[i]$ to denote the number of elements from chain P_i included in the ideal G.

1. The simplest way is to view the permutation as a problem of putting n symbols into n places. $G[i]$ indicates the place for the symbol $i + 1$. We start with placing n and then go backward to 1. The symbol n has n choices for places. This we can determine from $G[n - 1]$, which is a number in $\{0..n - 1\}$. Given the place for symbol n, the symbol $n - 1$ has $n - 1$ choices of places, which is given by $G[n - 2]$ because one place is already occupied. This process is repeated till symbol 2 is placed. Finally, symbol 1 has no choice.

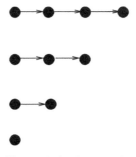

Figure 11.9 Poset $T(5)$.

2. Another method is to use the inversion table [Knu98]. The number of inversions of i in a permutation π is the number of symbols less than i that appear to the right of i in π. The way a permutation is generated from an ideal is as follows. We begin the permutation by writing 1. $G[1]$ decides where to insert the symbol 2. There are two choices. These choices correspond to number of *inversions* introduced by 2. If we place 2 after 1, then we introduce zero inversions; Otherwise, we introduce one inversion. Proceeding in this manner, we get that there is a bijection between the set of permutations and the set of ideals.

It is easy to show that the following predicates are regular. Further by computing the slice, we can also calculate the number of permutations satisfying B.

Lemma 11.7 *All the following properties of permutations are regular.*

1. *The symbol $m < n$ has at most j inversions (for $j < m$). The total number of such permutations is $\frac{n!(j+1)}{m}$.*
2. *$i \leq j$ implies that i has at most as many inversions as j. The total number of such permutations is same as the number of integer partitions less than $(n-1, n-2, \ldots, 1)$, which is equal to nth Catalan number.*

Proof: For the first part, note that it is sufficient to add an edge from $\top$ to element e_j in chain P_{m+1}. This ensures that the symbol m cannot have more than j inversions. Figure 11.10(a) shows the slice for set of permutations on [5] such that the symbol 4 has at most 1 inversion.

For the second part, we simple add an edge from element e_j on P_{i+1} to P_i for all j and i. Thus, P_i can execute j elements only if P_{i+1} has executed j or more elements. The claim then follows by comparing the poset with that corresponding to Young's lattice.

■

Note that the second part of Lemma 11.7 solves the problem (Q3) mentioned in the introduction.

The level set at rank k of the permutation lattice consists of all permutations with total number of inversions equal to k, and therefore, such permutations can be efficiently enumerated [Knu98, ER03].

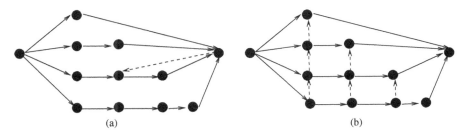

Figure 11.10   Slice for subsets of permutations.

11.7   PROBLEMS

11.1. Give an algorithm to enumerate the subsets $\{a_1, \ldots, a_m\}$ of n such that for all i and j, a_i does not divide a_j.

11.2. Compute the slice for a Catalan predicate that contains all n size subsets of $2n$ that are Catalan.

11.3. Consider the set of all n-tuples such that ith coordinate belongs to $[m_i]$. This set has $m_1 m_2 \ldots m_n$ elements and is the ideal lattice of disjoint union of n chains, $C_1, C_2, \ldots, C_n$ such that $|C_i| = m_i - 1$. This set reduces to the Boolean lattice when all m_i equal 2 and to the set of all permutations when $m_i = i$. Show that each of the following predicates is regular, and therefore, the subsets corresponding to them can be enumerated efficiently.

   (a) The set of all tuples $(a_1, a_2, \ldots, a_n)$ such that $\forall i, j : i \leq j \Rightarrow a_i \leq a_j$.

   (b) The set of all tuples $(a_1, a_2, \ldots, a_n)$ such that $a_i \geq c$ (or $a_i = c$, $a_i \neq c$ etc.) for some constant c.

   (c) The set of all tuples $(a_1, a_2, \ldots, a_n)$ such that $a_i = a_j$ for fixed i and j.

11.4. Consider the set of independent sets in a bipartite graph (X, Y, E). Every independent set S can be written as union of $S_X = S \cap X$ and $S_Y = S \cap Y$. Given two independent sets S and T, define

$$S \leq T \equiv S_X \subseteq T_X \wedge S_Y \supseteq T_Y.$$

(a) Show that the set of all independent sets forms a distributive lattice.

(b) Show that the set of independent sets that contain x only if they contain y forms a sublattice and that its slice can be computed for enumeration.

11.8   BIBLIOGRAPHIC REMARKS

The discussion on applications of slicing to combinatorics is taken from Garg [Gar06].

12

INTERVAL ORDERS

12.1 INTRODUCTION

This chapter covers weak orders (ranking), semiorders, and interval orders. All of these partial orders are "close" to a total order. The relationship between these orders is as follows. Every weak order is also a semiorder, and every semiorder is also an interval order.

12.2 WEAK ORDER

A weak order, also called ranking, is a slight generalization of a total order.

Definition 12.1 (Weak Order) *A poset* $(X, \leq)$ *is a* **weak order** *or a* **ranking** *if there exists a function* $f : X \rightarrow \mathbb{N}$ *such that* $\forall x, y \in X : x < y \equiv f(x) < f(y)$.

The term "weak order" is somewhat of a misnomer because a weak order has a lot of order. To allow for easy visualization of such orders, we will use the term "ranking" instead of the more accepted term "weak order." The set of elements in a ranking which have the same f value is called a **rank**. For example, the poset $(X, \leq)$ shown in Figure 12.1 is a ranking because we can assign $f(a) = 0, f(b) = f(c) = 1$, and $f(d) = 2$. Here, b and c are in the same rank. The difference between a chain and a ranking is that a chain requires existence of a *one-to-one* mapping such that $x < y$ iff $f(x) < f(y)$. For a ranking, we drop the requirement of the function to be *one-to-one*.

A chain is a ranking in which every rank is of size 1. An antichain is also a ranking with exactly one rank.

Introduction to Lattice Theory with Computer Science Applications, First Edition. Vijay K. Garg.
© 2015 John Wiley & Sons, Inc. Published 2015 by John Wiley & Sons, Inc.

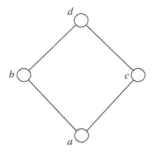

Figure 12.1   A poset that is a ranking.

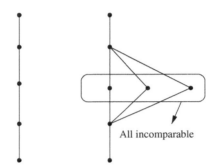

Figure 12.2   Examples of weak orders (or rankings.)

Rankings occur naturally in many applications. Any single scale of measurement provides us a ranking function. For example, in an election, if we order all candidates based on the number of votes they receive, the resulting order is a ranking. In a computer system, jobs are typically assigned a priority level (say a number between 1 and n) (Figure 12.2). This assignment imposes a ranking on all jobs.

An alternative characterization of rankings is as follows.

Theorem 12.2   *P is a ranking iff it does not have $\underline{1} + \underline{2}$ as a subposet.*

Proof: Left as an exercise.

∎

We now define the notion of *ranking extension* of a poset. Many applications, for example, task-scheduling with precedence constraints require that elements in a poset are processed in a order that does not violate precedence constraints. In general, a topological sort of a partial order that produces a linear extension of that partial order has been useful in such applications. Similar to a linear extension, we can define a ranking extension of a partial order as follows.

Definition 12.3   *A ranking s is a ranking extension of a partial order $P = (X, \leq)$ if $\forall x, y \in X : x <_P y \Rightarrow x <_s y.$*

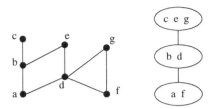

Figure 12.3   A poset and its normal ranking extension.

We call s a *normal ranking extension* of a poset P, if the length of s is equal to the height of the poset P. We have the following result.

Theorem 12.4 *For every poset P, there exists a normal ranking extension s.*

Proof: The ranking s can be constructed by the following algorithm (that is implicit in Dilworth's antichain covering theorem). Remove all the minimal elements of the partial order and put them in the lowest rank. Get the next set of minimal elements and put them as the next rank. By repeating this procedure till all elements in X are removed, we get the desired ranking. It can be easily verified that the ranking preserve order in P and has its length equal to the height of the poset. ■

For example, consider the poset in Figure 12.3. The normal ranking extension produced using the construction in Theorem 12.4 is

$$\{(a,f), (b,d), (c,e,g)\}$$

It is easily verified that the above-mentioned ranking preserves the partial order.

If the poset P denotes tasks, then a normal ranking extension represents a processing schedule (assuming that concurrent tasks can be executed in parallel). The length of the ranking corresponds to a critical path in P.

As another example, consider logical clocks frequently used in distributed systems for timestamping events. A logical clock is a function C from the set of events E to natural numbers such that

$$\forall e,f \in E : e < f \Rightarrow C(e) < C(f).$$

Thus, logical clocks are simply ranking extensions of the partial order of events in a distributed system.

12.3   SEMIORDER

A semiorder generalizes a ranking as follows.

Definition 12.5 (Semiorder) $P = (X, \leq)$ *is a semiorder if* $\exists f : X \rightarrow \mathbb{R}$ *and* $\delta \in \mathbb{R}, \delta \geq 0$ *such that*
$x < y$ *iff* $f(y) - f(x) > \delta.$

Note that every ranking is a semiorder, with $\delta = 0$. Also by scaling, if $\delta \neq 0$ we can always choose δ to be 1.

Examples

1. Load balancing:
   In a distributed system with multiple computers, it is often desirable to move jobs from one computer to the other if one is more heavily loaded than the other. Since moving jobs also incur some cost, it is not desirable to move jobs when the difference in the loads is not much. Therefore, from the perspective of a load balancing policy, the loads on the computers can be viewed as a semiorder. In this case, all processes have a rational number associated with the "load" on each process. The load of a computer is considered higher than that of the other computer's load only if it is bigger by at least δ.

2. Predicate detection (using Physical Time):
   Consider the problem of detecting whether certain "interesting" events can happen simultaneously in a distributed computation. Assume that the only information available to us is the sequence of events executed at each process along with the timestamp of the event assigned by the local clock at that process. Since physical clocks can be synchronized only approximately, we may define two events to be concurrent if they are at different processes and their clock values do not differ by some constant δ. If all interesting events within a process are separated by at least δ amount of time, we can define the order on the set of interesting events as follows:

$$e < f \equiv T(f) - T(e) > \delta$$

where $T(e)$ and $T(f)$ are the timestamps of events e and f, respectively. It can be verified that the set of interesting events forms a semiorder under $<$, and the problem of determining if k interesting events can happen simultaneously is equivalent to determining if there is an antichain of size k in this semiorder.

Semiorder has $2 + 2$ and $1 + 3$ as forbidden structures. Scott and Suppes' Theorem states that if a poset does not have $2 + 2$ or $1 + 3$ as subposets then it is a semiorder. The reader is referred to West [Wes04] for a proof of this theorem.

12.4 INTERVAL ORDER

Definition 12.6 (Interval Order) *$(X, \leq)$ is an interval order if every element $x \in X$ can be assigned a closed interval in real line denoted by $[x.lo, x.hi]$ such that for all $x, y \in X$ $x < y$ iff $x.hi < y.lo$.*

Lemma 12.7 *Every semiorder is an interval order.*

Proof: Consider the mapping: $x \mapsto [f(x) - \delta/2, f(x) + \delta/2]$. Thus, every semiorder can be mapped to an interval order.

■

Note that intervals $[0, 1]$ and $[1, 2]$ are concurrent because of the strict $<$ requirement in the definition. Interval orders have been discussed extensively in [Fis85].

Interval orders also occur naturally in computer science. In real-time systems, each activity has the beginning and the end time associated with it. Thus, the set of all activities forms an interval order.

We will later see that an interval order can be characterized using the forbidden poset $\underline{2} + \underline{2}$. The following lemma gives a characterization of $\underline{2} + \underline{2}$-free posets in terms of the upper holdings.

Theorem 12.8 $\forall x, y \in P : U(x) \subseteq U(y) \vee U(y) \subseteq U(x)$ *iff* P *does not contain* $\underline{2} + \underline{2}$.

Proof: LHS
$\equiv$
$$\forall x, y \in P : U(x) \subseteq U(y) \vee U(y) \subseteq U(x)$$
$\equiv \{$ trivially true when $x < y$ or $y < x$ $\}$
$$\forall x, y \in P : x \parallel y : U(x) \subseteq U(y) \vee U(y) \subseteq U(x)$$

Since the RHS does not contain $U(x)$ or $U(y)$, we eliminate them.
$\forall x, y \in P : x \parallel y : (\forall x' :: x < x' \Rightarrow y < x') \vee (\forall y' :: y < y' \Rightarrow x < y')$.

To prove the equivalence of the above-mentioned predicate and RHS, we show the inverse.
$\neg[\forall x, y \in P : x \parallel y : (\forall x' :: x < x' \Rightarrow y < x') \vee (\forall y' :: y < y' \Rightarrow x < y')]$.
$\equiv \{$ De Morgan's$\}$
$\exists x, y \in P : x \parallel y : (\exists x' :: x < x' \wedge y \not< x') \wedge (\exists y' :: y < y' \wedge x \not< y')$.
$\equiv \{$ predicate calculus $\}$
$\exists x, y \in P : x \parallel y : (\exists x', y' :: x < x' \wedge y \not< x' \wedge y < y' \wedge x \not< y')$.
$\equiv \{ y \not< x'$ replaced by $y \parallel x'$ because of $x' < y$ implies $x < y$ $\}$
$\exists x, y, x', y' \in P : x \parallel y \wedge x < x' \wedge y \parallel x' \wedge y < y' \wedge x \parallel y')$.

The above-mentioned predicate is equivalent to P does not contain $\underline{2} + \underline{2}$ because it is easy to verify that x, y, x', and y' are all distinct in the above-mentioned predicate (for example, $x \parallel y'$ and $y < y'$ implies that $x \neq y$).

■

From symmetry, we also get that P is $\underline{2} + \underline{2}$-free iff $\{D(x) \mid x \in P\}$ is a chain. We now have a characterization theorem for interval posets.

Theorem 12.9 *[Fis85] P is an interval order iff it does not contain $\underline{2} + \underline{2}$ as a subposet.*

Proof: [Bog93] We first show that if P contains $\underline{2} + \underline{2}$ then it is not an interval order. Let $a < b$ and $c < d$ be a subposet that is $\underline{2} + \underline{2}$. Assume if possible, P is an interval poset. By definition of interval order, we get that $a.hi < b.lo$. From $b \not> c$, we get that $b.lo \leq c.hi$. From the last two inequalities, we get that $a.hi < c.hi$. From symmetry of a and b with c and d, we also get that $c.hi < a.hi$, which is a contradiction. Thus, if a poset contains $\underline{2} + \underline{2}$, it cannot be an interval order.

Now we show that if P does not contain $\underline{2} + \underline{2}$ then it is an interval order. From Theorem 12.8, upper holdings and lower holdings form a chain. Problem 4 asks you

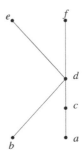

$D(a) = \{\ \}$	$U(a) = \{c,d,e,f\}$	$a = [0,0]$
$D(b) = \{\}$	$U(b) = \{d,e,f\}$	$b = [0,1]$
$D(c) = \{a\}$	$U(c) = \{d,e,f\}$	$c = [1,1]$
$D(d) = \{b,c,d\}$	$U(d) = \{f,e\}$	$d = [2,2]$
$D(f) = \{d,b,c,a\}$	$U(f) = \{\ \}$	$f = [3,3]$
$D(e) = \{d,b,c,a\}$	$U(e) = \{\ \}$	$e = [3,3]$

Figure 12.4   Mapping elements of poset to interval order.

to show that the total number of distinct nonempty upper holdings equals the total number of nonempty distinct lower holdings. Let this number be h. Now, we provide a function to map an element x of an interval order to a closed interval as

$$f(x) = [d(x), h - u(x)]$$

where $d(x)$ is the number of distinct sets of the form $D(y)$ properly contained in $D(x)$ and $u(x)$ is the number of distinct sets of the form $U(y)$ properly contained in $U(x)$. Problem 5 requires you to verify that $x < y$ iff $x.hi < y.lo$.

■

The table in Figure 12.4 shows the upper and lower holdings for all elements in the poset in Figure 12.4. In this example, there are three distinct nonempty upper (and lower) holdings.

The proof of Theorem 12.9 can readily be converted into an algorithm. Given a poset in adjacency list representation, one can topologically sort it in $O(n + e)$. This allows calculation of $d(x)$ and $u(x)$ for all elements in the poset in $O(n + e)$ time giving us an $O(n + e)$ algorithm to obtain interval representation. Table 12.1 gives the various orders and the corresponding forbidden structures for each order.

12.5   PROBLEMS

12.1. Prove Theorem 12.2.

12.2. How many nonisomorphic rankings are possible on a set of size n?

TABLE 12.1   Forbidden Structures for Various Orders

Order	Forbidden Structure
Chain	$\underline{1} + \underline{1}$
Weak Order	$\underline{1} + \underline{2}$
Semi Order	$\underline{2} + \underline{2}$ or $\underline{1} + \underline{3}$
Interval Order	$\underline{2} + \underline{2}$

12.3. Give a formula to compute the number of ideals and the number of linear extensions of a ranking.

12.4. Show that the number of distinct nonempty upper holdings is equal to the total number of nonempty distinct lower holdings for any $\underline{2} + \underline{2}$-free order.

12.5. Show that the interval assignment in the proof of Theorem 12.9 satisfies $x < y$ iff $x.hi < y.lo$.

12.6. Let P be any interval order with an element x such that $D(x)$ is the largest in size. Show that all elements that are incomparable to x are maximal.

12.6   BIBLIOGRAPHIC REMARKS

The reader will find details on interval order in the monograph by Fishburn [Fis85].

13

TRACTABLE POSETS

13.1 INTRODUCTION

So far, we have seen some efficient algorithms for determining characteristics of posets such as its width. However, there are no known efficient algorithms for some other important properties, such as the dimension, the number of ideals, and the number of linear extensions of a given poset. In these cases, we can study special classes of the poset for which there exist efficient algorithms for these computationally hard problems. In this chapter, we cover an important class of posets—two-dimensional posets and its special case series–parallel posets that arise frequently in computer science applications.

13.2 SERIES–PARALLEL POSETS

Traditional sequential programming languages provide a *series* operator ';' to compose two statement or functions in a serial manner. Thus, $s1; s2$ means that the statement $s2$ should be executed after the statement $s1$. The concurrent programming languages introduce an additional *parallel* operator ‖ to model parallel execution of activities. Consider the following programming expression:

$$(s1; s2)\|(s3; s4)$$

In this program, $s1$ is always executed before $s2$. However, the two branches formed by the parallel operator are executed independently of one another. The order of execution of statements in this program is a partial order of a special kind called series parallel order.

Introduction to Lattice Theory with Computer Science Applications, First Edition. Vijay K. Garg.
© 2015 John Wiley & Sons, Inc. Published 2015 by John Wiley & Sons, Inc.

We now give the definition of a *series parallel poset* (henceforth called *SP poset* or *SP order*).

Definition 13.1 (Series–Parallel Poset) *Any element by itself is an SP poset. Given two SP posets P_1 and P_2,*

1. *$P_1 * P_2$ is an SP order. The symbol $*$ is the sequencing operator. To form the new poset, take all maximal elements of P_1, and make each one less than every minimal element of P_2.*
2. *$P_1 + P_2$ is an SP order. The symbol $+$ is the parallel operator. To form the new poset, take the disjoint union of P_1 and P_2.*

We have used the symbols $*$ and $+$ instead of ; and $\|$ to keep the notation consistent with the standard lattice theory.

Figure 13.1 shows example series and parallel compositions for the SP posets P_1, P_2, and P_3 shown in (a–c).

SP orders can also be represented by an *SP tree*. In an SP tree, the leaves are the elements of the poset, and internal nodes are the series and parallel operators. Figure 13.2(a) shows an SP tree for the poset in Figure 13.1(e). A poset does not necessarily have a unique SP tree representation, since the parallel operator is symmetric.

We can form the *conjugate* of an SP tree by replacing all series operators with parallel and parallel with series. Note that conjugation is a self-inverse. Figure 13.2(b) shows the conjugate of the SP tree in Figure 13.2(a). Figure 13.2(c) shows the poset for the conjugate.

We now show that SP orders are special class of two-dimensional posets.

Theorem 13.2 *dim(SP order) ≤ 2.*

Proof: Recall that a poset Q is two-dimensional if there exists two linear orders such that their intersection is Q. For any SP order, we first perform a depth-first search (DFS) on the poset's SP tree. The order of traversal of the leaves gives us a linear order. We then perform a second DFS on the tree, this time visiting the children of P nodes (parallel operator) in the reverse order, to get the second linear order. It can be

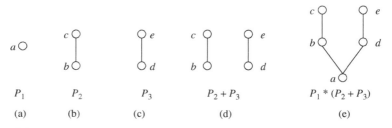

Figure 13.1 Example series and parallel compositions. (a–c) Posets. (d) Result of $P_2 + P_3$. (e) Result of $P_1 * (P_2 + P_3)$.

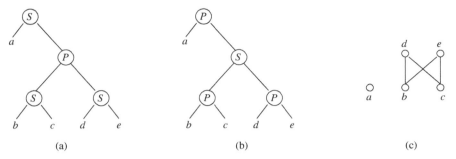

Figure 13.2 (a) An SP tree for the poset in Figure 13.1(e). (b) The conjugate SP tree. (c) The conjugate poset.

easily seen that both of these linear orders preserve the ordering of nodes under the S (series) operator and that their intersection is Q.

■

As an example, consider the SP tree from Figure 13.2(a). The first DFS yields the sequence ($abcde$), while the second gives ($adebc$). in both the linear orders b is less than c, as indeed is true in the poset. On the other hand, $b < d$ in the first linear order but $d < b$ is the second linear order, which gives us that b and d are incomparable which is indeed the case.

Another concept that is useful for series–parallel graph and, more generally, for two-dimensional posets is that of a *comparability graph*.

We begin with the definition of comparability.

Definition 13.3 (Comparable Relation) *Given a partial order $P = (X, \leq_P)$, we say $a \sim_P b$ (a is comparable to b) iff ($a \leq_P b$) $\vee$ ($b \leq_P a$).*

Definition 13.4 (Comparability Graph) *A comparability graph of a poset P is an undirected graph such that $(u, v) \in E$ iff u is comparable to v in P, i.e., $u \sim_P v$.*

The comparability graph can be obtained from either the SP poset or its SP tree:

- $G(P) =$ a graph with single vertex and no edge whenever P is a singleton.
- $G(P_1 * P_2) =$ add edges from all nodes in $G(P_1)$ to all nodes in $G(P_2)$.
- $G(P_1 + P_2) =$ simple union of $G(P_1)$ and $G(P_2)$.

We will return to comparability graphs later when we discuss two-dimensional posets.

Let us turn our attention to the question of the number of ideals of a poset. Let $i(P)$ denote the number of ideals of P. For SP orders, it is readily shown that the number of ideals can be computed as follows:

- $i(P) = 2$ whenever P is a singleton.

- $i(P_1 + P_2) = i(P_1).i(P_2)$
- $i(P_1 * P_2) = i(P_1) + i(P_2) - 1$.

13.3 TWO-DIMENSIONAL POSETS

In this section, we study properties of two-dimensional posets. A poset is two-dimensional if its dimension is 2 (defined in Chapters 2 and 16).

We first give another equivalent definition for two-dimensional posets: P is two-dimensional iff P has a conjugate poset Q. The notion of conjugate poset is defined in the following.

Definition 13.5 (Conjugate Poset) *A conjugate of partial order $P = (X, \leq_P)$ is a partial order $Q = (X, \leq_Q)$ such that $(a \sim_P b)$ iff $a \parallel_Q b$.*

Let G be the comparability graph, G^C its complement. The aforementioned states that for two-dimensional posets, G^C is guaranteed to also be a comparability graph.

As an example, Figure 13.3(a) shows a poset that is two dimensional. Figure 13.3(b) is the comparability graph G and Figure 13.3(c) shows G^C. Note that G^C is also a comparability graph. Figure 13.3(d) shows one valid conjugate for the original poset; it is not the only possible one.

Consider the poset shown in Figure 13.4. It is known as S_3 and has dimension equal to 3. This poset has no conjugate.

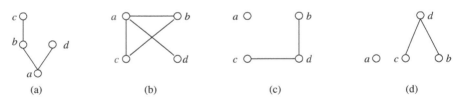

(a)   (b)   (c)   (d)

Figure 13.3   (a) A two-dimensional poset. (b) Its comparability graph G. (c) G^C. (d) A valid conjugate for the original poset.

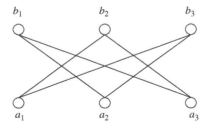

Figure 13.4   The poset S_3.

Yet, another characterization of two-dimensional posets is based on nonseparating linear extensions.

Definition 13.6 (Nonseparating Linear Extension) *A linear extension $L = (X, \leq_L)$ of a partial order $P = (X, \leq_P)$ is called a nonseparating linear extension (NSLE) if*

$$(u \leq_L w \leq_L v) \wedge (u \leq_P v) \Rightarrow (u \leq_P w) \vee (w \leq_P v).$$

Figure 13.5(a) shows an NSLE, and a poset (b) corresponding to it. The dotted lines show the possible relationships among u, v, and w. At least one of the dotted lines must represent a true edge in order for (a) to be an NSLE of Figure 13.5(b).

We now have the following result.

Theorem 13.7 *The following statements are equivalent:*

1. *P is two dimensional.*
2. *The incomparability graph of P is a valid comparability graph of some poset.*
3. *P has a conjugate Q.*
4. *P has an NSLE.*
5. *P can be identified with a permutation.*

We illustrate Theorem 13.7 with an example taken from Mohring [Moh89] and use this example to sketch the proof of the theorem. Consider the poset shown in Figure 13.6. The following two linear extensions are such that their intersection gives back the poset P.

$L1 = v_1 < v_4 < v_2 < v_5 < v_6 < v_3 < v_7$
$L2 = v_3 < v_2 < v_7 < v_1 < v_6 < v_4 < v_5.$

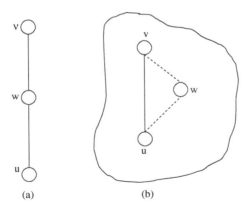

(a)   (b)

Figure 13.5 (a) is a non-separating linear extension of the partial order (b), when at least one of the dotted edges holds.

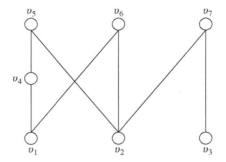

Figure 13.6 A two-dimensional Poset $P = (X, \leq_P)$.

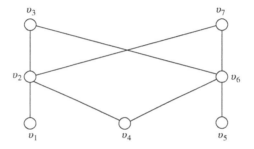

Figure 13.7 Conjugate $Q = L1 \cap L2^{-1}$ of the poset P.

$\{L1, L2\}$ is called *realizer* of P. Note that for every incomparable pair (a, b) in P, if $a < b$ in $L1$, then $b < a$ in $L2$.

We can derive the conjugate Q of P from $L1 \cap L2^{-1}$, where $L2^{-1}$ is the total order derived by reversing the order of the elements in $L2$.

$L2^{-1} = v_5 < v_4 < v_6 < v_1 < v_7 < v_2 < v_3$.

Figure 13.7 shows the poset Q that is the conjugate of P obtained from $L1 \cap L2^{-1}$. We now show that:

$$(x \sim_P y) \Leftrightarrow (x \,||_Q y)$$

Since $L1$ and $L2$ are linear extensions of P, we have

$$(x \leq_P y) \Rightarrow (x \leq_{L2} y) \wedge (x \leq_{L1} y).$$

Therefore,

$$y \leq_{L2^{-1}} x.$$

Since $Q = L1 \cap L2^{-1}$, we get $x \,||_Q y$. Similarly, if $y \leq_P x$, then $y \,||_Q x$.

Now, let $P = (X, \leq_P)$ be a two-dimensional poset with conjugate $Q = (X, \leq_Q)$. Then, $\leq_P \cup \leq_Q$ defines a total order on the elements of X.

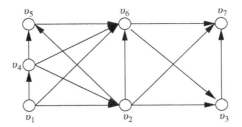

Figure 13.8   The order imposed by $\leq_P \cup \leq_Q$.

Lemma 13.8 $(X, \leq_P \cup \leq_Q)$ *is an NSLE of P.*

Proof: Left as an exercise.

∎

Continuing with our example, Figure 13.8 shows the order imposed by $(X, \leq_P \cup \leq_Q)$. Figure 13.8 uses directed edges to indicate the $\leq$ relation. The nonseparating linear extension consistent with the Figure is:

$v_1 < v_4 < v_2 < v_5 < v_6 < v_3 < v_7$.

Note that every linear extension of P is not an NSLE. For example, the following is a valid linear extension of P, but is not an NSLE:

$v_1 < v_3 < v_4 < v_2 < v_5 < v_6 < v_7$.

Finally, we show that every two-dimensional poset P can be identified with a permutation. Let $L1$ and $L2$ be the two linear extensions in a minimal realizer of P, where $|P| = n$. We can rename the elements of P in such a way that $L1$ is just $[v_1, v_2, v_3, ..., v_n]$. The position of these elements in the other linear extension, $L2$, then defines a permutation on $[n]$.

13.4   COUNTING IDEALS OF A TWO-DIMENSIONAL POSET

We now give an efficient algorithm to compute the number of order ideals of a two-dimensional poset. Assume that we are given the following:

- A two-dimensional poset $P = (V, \leq_P)$, and
- L: an NSLE of P

Let $L = [v_1, v_2, v_3, ..., v_n]$. We assign a label, $L(v_i)$, to each element v_i, as follows:

$$L(v_1) = 1$$
$$L(v_i) = 1 + \sum_{j < i,\ v_i || v_j} L(v_j).$$

Given the value of all labels, we can compute the number of nonempty order ideals of P as

$$N(P) = \sum_{i=1}^{n} L(v_i).$$

We illustrate the labeling scheme by means of an example. Consider the poset in Figure 13.9. Note that this poset is isomorphic to the one presented in Figure 13.6, but with a different numbering for the nodes. As noted in the figure, the following is an NSLE for the given poset:

$v_1 < v_2 < v_3 < v_4 < v_5 < v_6 < v_7$.

By our labeling scheme, we assign the following labels to the nodes in P.
$L(v_1) = 1$

$L(v_2) = 1 + 0 = 1$ {since $v_1 \nparallel v_2$ }
$L(v_3) = 1 + L(v_1) + L(v_2) = 3$ {since $v_1 \parallel v_3, v_2 \parallel v_3$}
$L(v_4) = 1 + 0 = 1$ {since $v_4 \nparallel \{v_1, v_2, v_3\}$}
$L(v_5) = 1 + L(v_4) + L(v_2) = 3$ {since $v_4 \parallel v_5, v_2 \parallel v_5$}
$L(v_6) = 1 + L(v_1) + L(v_2) + L(v_3) + L(v_4) + L(v_5)$
$\qquad = 10$ {since $\{v_1, v_2, v_3, v_4, v_5\} \parallel v_6$}
$L(v_7) = 1 + L(v_1) + L(v_2) + L(v_4) + L(v_5) = 7$ {since $\{v_1, v_2, v_4, v_5\} \parallel v_7$}

The following lemma is left as an exercise.

Lemma 13.9 $L(v_i)$ *is equal to the number of ideals containing v_i and possibly some elements v_j with $j < i$. $N(P)$ equals the number of nonempty ideals of P.*

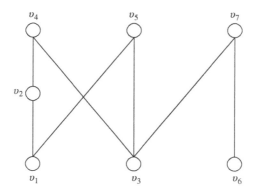

Figure 13.9   A partial order P that has a nonseparating linear extension.

13.5 PROBLEMS

13.1. Show that the problem of recognizing any special class of posets that can be characterized by a constant number of forbidden posets is in complexity class **NC**.

13.2. Give a (recursive) formula for $l(P)$, the number of linear extensions of an SP order P.

13.3. Prove Lemma 13.8.

13.4. Prove Lemma 13.9.

13.6 BIBLIOGRAPHIC REMARKS

The reader will find a more detailed discussion of computationally tractable posets in the survey paper by Möhring [Moh89].

14

ENUMERATION ALGORITHMS

14.1 INTRODUCTION

The number of ideals of a poset may be exponential in the size of the poset. We have already seen that the ideals of a poset form a distributive lattice under the $\subseteq$ relation. In this chapter, we explore different ways in which the lattice of ideals may be traversed, in order to enumerate all the ideals of a poset.

We explore the following three orders of enumeration:

- Breadth-first search(BFS): This order of enumeration corresponds to the BFS traversal of the lattice of ideals.
- Depth-first search(DFS): This order corresponds to the DFS traversal of the lattice of ideals.
- Lex order: This order corresponds to the "dictionary" order.

We first illustrate the above-mentioned three orders of enumeration by means of an example. Consider the poset shown in Figure 14.1(a). Figure 14.1(b) shows the lattice of ideals corresponding to this poset. In this figure, we have used the first digit and the second digit to indicate the number of events included in the ideal from the first chain and the second chain, respectively. For example, the ideal $\{e_1, e_2, f_1\}$ is denoted by 21.

We also give an efficient algorithm to enumerate lexally the level set of the ideal lattice for any given level. This algorithm takes time proportional to the number of elements in that level and not the entire lattice.

In Chapter 11, we have shown that many families of combinatorial objects can be mapped to the lattice of order ideals of appropriate posets. Thus, algorithms for lex

Introduction to Lattice Theory with Computer Science Applications, First Edition. Vijay K. Garg.
© 2015 John Wiley & Sons, Inc. Published 2015 by John Wiley & Sons, Inc.

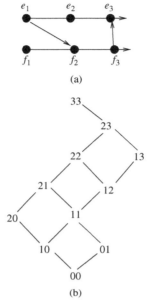

(a)

(b)

BFS: 00, 01, 10, 11, 20, 12, 21, 13, 22, 23, 33

DFS: 00, 10, 20, 21, 22, 23, 33, 11, 12, 13, 01

Lexical: 00, 01, 10, 11, 12, 13, 20, 21, 22, 23, 33

(c)

Figure 14.1 (a) A computation. (b) Its lattice of consistent global states. (c) Traversals of the lattice.

and BFS traversal discussed in the chapter can also be used to efficiently enumerate all subsets of $[n]$, all subsets of $[n]$ of size k, all permutations, all permutations with a given inversion number, all integer partitions less than a given partition, all integer partitions of a given number, and all n-tuples of a product space. Note that [SW86] gives different algorithms for these enumerations. Algorithms in this chapter are generic and by instantiating them with different posets all the above-mentioned combinatorial enumerations can be achieved.

14.2 BFS TRAVERSAL

We first present a naive algorithm for BFS traversal of the lattice of ideals. This algorithm uses the context of a distributed computation, i.e., the poset is given in chain-decomposed form, and each chain corresponds to a process in the distributed computation. We use E to denote the set of events in the computation and n to denote the number of processes. As we have seen earlier, ideals of the poset correspond to consistent global states(CGSs) in the distributed computation. Throughout this chapter, we use order ideals and CGSs interchangeably.

We keep two lists of CGSs: *last* and *current*. Initially, *current* has the initial CGS. To generate the next level of consistent global states, we set *last* to *current* and *current* to the set of global states that can be reached from *last* in one transition. Since a CGS can be reached from multiple global states, an implementation of this algorithm will result in either *current* holding multiple copies of a CGS or added complexity in the algorithm to ensure that a CGS is inserted in *current* only when it is not present. This problem occurs because the algorithm does not exploit the fact that the set of global states forms a distributive lattice.

We now show a method which ensures that a CGS is enumerated exactly once and that there is no overhead of checking that the CGS has already been enumerated (or inserted in the list). Our extension exploits the following observation.

Lemma 14.1 *If H is reachable from G by executing an event e and there exists an event $f \in H$ such that f is maximal in H, then there exists a CGS G' at the same level as G such that $G' = G - \{f\} + \{e\}$ and H is reachable from G'.*

Proof: Since f is a maximal event in H, it is also a maximal event in G. Since G is consistent and f is a maximal event in G, it follows that $G - \{f\}$ is a CGS. Since e and f are both maximal in H, they must be concurrent. If e is enabled at G and f is concurrent with e, then e is also enabled at $G - \{f\}$. Therefore, $G' = G - \{f\} + \{e\}$ is a CGS. H is reachable from G' on executing f.

∎

Let σ be a topological sort of all events E in the computation that maps every event e to $\sigma(e)$ a number from $1..|E|$. To avoid enumerating a global state H multiple times, it is sufficient to explore execution of events only in the order consistent with σ. Thus, an event e is explored from a global state G iff e is bigger than all the events in G. Let e be any enabled event in G. We explore execution of e on G iff

$$\forall f \in G : \sigma(f) < \sigma(e).$$

With this observation, our algorithm is shown in Figure 14.2. It keeps a queue Q of the CGS. At every iteration, it removes the CGS G at the head of the queue, visits G, and then inserts those successors of G that satisfy the above-mentioned rule.

We now show the correctness of the BFS enumeration algorithm.

Theorem 14.2 *Algorithm in Figure 14.2 enumerates every CGS exactly once.*

Proof: The proof is by induction on the size of the CGS. The base case holds because the empty global state is enumerated exactly once. Let H be any CGS with k events. Let e be the largest maximal event (in the order given by σ). Consider the CGS $G = H - \{e\}$. By induction, G is enumerated exactly once. Whenever G is enumerated, H is put in the queue Q because e is larger than all events in G.

```
var
    Q: set of CGS at the current level initially {(0, 0, … , 0)};
    σ: a topological sort of the poset P;

while (Q ≠ ∅) do
    G := remove_first(Q);
    enumerate(G);
    // generate CGS at the next level
    for all events e enabled in G do
        if (∀f ∈ maximal(G) : σ(f) < σ(e)) then
            H := G ∪ {e};
            append(Q, H);
    endfor;
endwhile;
```

Figure 14.2   BFS enumeration of CGS.

H cannot be enumerated more than once. Consider any CGS G' different from G but at the same level as G. It can be written as $H - \{f\}$ for some f different from e. G contains f and e is still explored; therefore $\sigma(f) < \sigma(e)$. However, this implies that we will not add H to the queue Q when exploring G' because f is smaller than the event e that exists in G'.

∎

We now give a more detailed implementation of the algorithm based on vector clocks which achieves the time complexity of $O(nM)$, where n is the number of processes (or width of the poset) and M is the number of ideals of the poset. In the implementation shown in Figure 14.3, a CGS is represented using the vector clock. For any global state G, we keep the following information.

1. *G.state*: the vector clock corresponding to the global state G. $G.state[i]$ equals the number of events executed on process P_i.
2. *G.pred*: the predecessor information for the next event on each process. $G.pred[i]$ equals the number of processes that must execute at least one event before the next event on P_i is enabled. The next event on P_i is enabled iff $G.pred[i]$ equals 0.
3. *G.admissible*: the subset of enabled events that can be explored so that no global state is reached twice. An index $i \in G.admissible$ iff the next event e on P_i is enabled and $\sigma(e)$ is greater than $\sigma(f)$ for any event that has been executed to reach G.

```
var
    Q: linked list of CGS at the current level initially empty;
    G: {state: integer vector, pred: integer vector, admissible: list of indices};
    ∀j : G.state[j] := 0;
    compute G.pred;
    G.admissible := {j|(G.pred[j] = 0)};
    Q.add(G);
    while (Q is not empty)
        G := remove_First(Q);
        enumerate(G.state);
        forall (k ∈ G.admissible)
            H := G;
            H.state[k] + +; // execute e_k, the admissible event on P_k
            forall (j : j ≠ k)
                // if the next event e_j on G[j] depends on e_k
                if (e_j.V[k] = H.state[k]) then
                    H.pred[j] := H.pred[j] − 1;
            endfor;
            f_k.V = vector clock of the next event on process k;
            forall (j : j ≠ k)
                if (f_k.V[j] > G[j]) then H.pred[k] + +;
            endfor;
            H.admissible := {j | (H.pred[j] = 0) ∧ (σ(e_j) > σ(e_k))};
            Q.append(H);
        endfor;
    endwhile;
```

Figure 14.3   A vector clock based BFS enumeration of CGS.

In the initial state, $G.state$ is a zero vector. We compute $G.pred[j]$ for each j by using the vector clock information for the next event on each process j. Initially, all enabled events are also admissible since G corresponds to the empty set of events executed so far.

In the **while** loop of the algorithm, we remove one global state G from Q and explore all admissible events from G. The new global state reached on executing the next event, e_k on P_k is called H. We then update $H.pred$ based on the vector clock of e_j for next events of all other processes P_j. We also set $H.admissible[j]$ to true iff $(H.pred[j] = 0)$ and $\sigma(e_j) > \sigma(e_k)$. Since we have executed e_k on P_k, the next event on P_k has changed and we recompute the value of $H.pred[k]$ by using the vector clock for the next event f_k (after e_k) on P_k. Now we have all the information for H, $H.state, H.pred$, and $H.admissible$, and we append it to Q for exploration.

We now analyze the time complexity of the above-mentioned algorithm. We determine the amount of work done before any global state H is inserted in Q. We need to update $H.state$, $H.pred$, and $H.admissible$ before inserting H. This update requires $O(n)$ time for every global state inserted in Q. Every CGS is inserted in Q exactly once giving us the overall time complexity of $O(nM)$.

We now compute the space complexity of the algorithm. The space required is mainly for the linked list Q. Let the width of the lattice of the CGS be w_L. Then, the number of CGS in Q at any time in the algorithm is proportional to w_L. Each CGS requires $O(n)$ storage giving us the overall space complexity of $O(nw_L)$ integers assuming that every component of the state vector can be represented by an integer.

The main disadvantage of the above-mentioned algorithm is that it requires space at least as large as the number of CGSs in the largest level set. Note that the largest level set is exponential in n and therefore when using this algorithm for a large system we may run out of memory.

14.3   DFS TRAVERSAL

We now show an algorithm that requires only $O(|E|)$ space. If we traverse ideals in the DFS order instead of the BFS order, then the number of CGS we have to store in the worst case is equal to the height of the lattice rather than the width of the lattice. This is a major advantage because the width of the ideal lattice may be exponentially bigger than its height. The height of the ideal lattice is always $|E|$, the number of events in the poset. In addition, when we traverse the lattice in the DFS order, we always consider global states G and H that differ by exactly one event. When we explore H from G by executing an event e_k on P_k, we can determine the new global state H by advancing along $G[k]$. When we are done exploring the global state H and are ready to return to the global state G from H, we can simply decrement $H[k]$ to get $G[k]$. This incremental feature allows us to avoid storing $G.state$, $G.pred$, and $G.admissible$ as required in the BFS algorithm.

To traverse in DFS manner, we show a recursive method in Figure 14.4. The procedure *dfsTraversal* is initially called with process indices of all events that are enabled at the initial global state. We keep the global state G and *pred* as global variables that are updated as we make the recursive call. We explore an admissible event e on process P_k from the global state G by calling *dfsTraversal(k)*. Since we are advancing on P_k, we recompute *pred[k]* with $O(n)$ complexity. Next, we decrement *pred[j]* for all P_j such that their next event e_j depends on e. Now, we recursively call *dfsTraversal(j)* on all j such that e_j is admissible. Once we are done with all the recursive calls, we restore the value of G and *pred*. This can also be done in $O(n)$ time. Since we take $O(n)$ time for each recursive call and there are M ideals, the time complexity of the algorithm is $O(nM)$. The total space requirement for DFS traversal is $O(|E|)$.

14.4   LEX TRAVERSAL

Lex traversal is the natural dictionary order used in many applications. It is important in many combinatorics applications where combinatorial structures (such as all subsets of $[n]$ of size k) are ordered in the lex order. Even in distributed computing

```
var
  G: array[1..n] of integer;
  pred: array[1..n] of integer;

procedure dfsTraversal(int k)
        let e be the event that is executed on P_k;
        G[k] + +;
        enumerate(G);

        //compute pred[j] for j ≠ k;
        forall (j : j ≠ k) with the next event e_j on P_j
             if e_j depends on e then pred[j] − −;

        //compute pred[k] using the vector clock for e_k, the next event on P_k;
        e_k.V = vector clock of the next event on process k;
        forall (j : j ≠ k)
             if (e_k.V[j] > G[j]) then pred[k] + +;

        forall (j) with next event e_j
             if (pred[j] = 0) and σ(e) < σ(e_j))
                 dfsTraversal(j);

        // restore values of G and pred
        forall (j : j ≠ k) with the next event e_j on P_j
             if e_j depends on e then pred[j] + +;
        G[k] − −;
        pred[k] = 0;
```

Figure 14.4   A vector clock based DFS enumeration of CGS.

applications, the user may be interested in the CGS that satisfies the predicate to be minimal with respect to some order. The lex order gives a total order on the set of CGS based on priorities given to processes and the CGS detected by this traversal gives the lexically smallest CGS.

It is useful to impose on the set of global states the *lex* or the dictionary order. We define the lex order ($<_l$) as follows. $G <_l H$ iff

$$\exists k : (\forall i : 1 \leq i \leq k - 1 : G[i] = H[i]) \wedge (G[k] < H[k]).$$

This imposes a total order on all global states by assigning higher priority to smaller numbered processes. For example, in Figure 14.1, global state $(01) <_l (10)$ because P_1 has executed more events in the global state (10) than in (01).

We use $\leq_l$ for the reflexive closure of the $<_l$ relation. Recall that we have earlier used the order $\subseteq$ on the set of global states, which is a partial order. The $\subseteq$ order shown in Figure 14.1(b) is equivalent to

$$G \subseteq H \equiv \forall i : G[i] \leq H[i].$$

Note that $01 \not\subseteq 10$ although $01 \leq_l 10$.

We now have two orders on the set of global states—the partial order based on containment ($\subseteq$) and the total order based on lex ordering ($\leq_l$). The relationship between the two orders defined is given by the following lemma.

Lemma 14.3 $\forall G, H : G \subseteq H \Rightarrow G \leq_l H.$

Proof: $G \subseteq H$ implies that $\forall i : G[i] \leq H[i]$. The lemma follows from the definition of the lex order.

∎

Since there are two orders defined on the set of global states, to avoid confusion we use the term *least* for infimum over $\subseteq$ order, and the term *lexically minimum* for infimum over the $\leq_l$ order.

Let *nextLex(G)* denote the CGS that is the successor of G in the lex order. For example, in Figure 14.1, *nextLex(01)* = 10 and *nextLex(13)* = 20. It is sufficient to implement *nextLex* function efficiently for enumeration of ideals in the lex order. One can set G to the initial CGS $\langle 0, 0, ..., 0 \rangle$ and then call the function *nextLex(G)* repeatedly. We implement the function *nextLex(G)* using two secondary functions *succ* and *leastConsistent* as described in the following.

We define *succ(G, k)* to be the global state obtained by advancing along P_k and resetting components for all processes greater than P_k to 0. Thus, *succ($\langle 7, 5, 8, 4 \rangle$, 2)* is $\langle 7, 6, 0, 0 \rangle$ and *succ($\langle 7, 5, 8, 4 \rangle$, 3)* is $\langle 7, 5, 9, 0 \rangle$. Note that *succ(G, k)* may not exist when there is no event along P_k, and even when it exists, it may not be consistent.

The second function is *leastConsistent(K)* that returns the least CGS greater than or equal to a given global state K in the $\subseteq$ order. This is well defined because the set of all consistent global states that are greater than or equal to K in the CGS lattice is a sublattice.

We now show how *nextLex(G)* can be computed.

Theorem 14.4 *Assume that G is a CGS such that it is not the greatest CGS. Then,*

$$nextLex(G) = leastConsistent(succ(G, k)),$$

where k is the index of the process with the smallest priority, which has an event enabled in G with respect to all higher priority processes.

Proof: We define the following global states for convenience:
$K := succ(G, k)$
$H := leastConsistent(K)$, and

$G' := nextLex(G)$.
Our goal is to prove that $G' = H$.

G' contains at least one event f that is not in G; otherwise $G' \subseteq G$ and therefore cannot be lexically bigger. Choose $f \in G' - G$ from the highest priority process possible.

Let e be the event in the smallest priority process enabled in G, i.e., e is on process P_k. Let $proc(e)$ and $proc(f)$ denote the process indices of e and f. We now do a case analysis.

Case 1: $proc(f) < proc(e)$
In this case, e is from a lower priority process than f. We show that this case implies that H is lexically smaller than G'. We first claim that $H \subseteq G \cup \{e\}$. This is because $G \cup \{e\}$ is a CGS containing K and H is the smallest CGS containing K. Now, since $H \subseteq G \cup \{e\}$ and G' contains an event $f \in G' - G$ from a higher priority process than e, it follows that H is lexically smaller than G', a contradiction.

Case 2: $proc(f) > proc(e)$
Recall that event e is on the process with the smallest priority that had any event enabled at G with respect to all higher priority processes. Therefore, existence of f in CGS G' implies existence of at least another event, say f' in $G' - G$ at a process with priority than at least equal to that of e (otherwise, we contradict the choice of e). However, existence of $f' \in G' - G$ contradicts choice of event f because, by definition, f is from the highest priority process in $G' - G$ and priority of f' is greater than priority of f.

Case 3: $proc(f) = proc(e)$.
Then, $K \subseteq G'$ because both G' and K have identical events on P_k and processes with higher priority and K has no events in lower priority processes. Since G' is a CGS and $K \subseteq G'$, we get that $H \subseteq G'$ by definition of H. From Lemma 14.3, it follows that $H \leq_l G'$. But G' is the next lexical state after G. Therefore, $H = G'$.

∎

The only task left in the design of the algorithm is to determine k and implement *leastConsistent* function. The following lemma follows from properties of vector clocks. First, we determine that an event e in enabled in a CGS G if all the components of the vector clock for other processes in e are less than or equal to the components of the vector clock in G. Secondly, to compute *leastConsistent(K)*, it is sufficient to take the component-wise maximum of the vector clock of all maximal events in K. Formally,

Lemma 14.5

1. *An event e on P_k is enabled in a CGS G iff $e.v[k] = G[k] + 1$ and*

$$\forall j : j \neq k : e.v[j] \leq G[j].$$

```
Lex()

Input: a poset P with any partition α into chains P₁,..Pₙ
Output: All ideals in lexical order
var
       G:array[1 ...n] of int initially ∀i : G[i] = 0; // current ideal
(1)    enumerate(G);
(2)    while (true)
(3)        for k := n down to 1 do
(4)            if (next element on Pₖ exists)
(5)                if (next element on Pₖ enabled for P₁..Pₖ₋₁) break;
(6)        if no such k, then return;// we have enumerated all tuples
(7)        G[k] := G[k] + 1;
(8)        for i := k + 1 to n do // reset lexically smaller components
(9)            G[i] := 0;
(10)       // ensure that G is an ideal
(11)       for i := 1 to k such that G[i] ≠ 0 do // include in G all
                    smaller elements
(12)           for j := k + 1 to n do
(13)               G[j] := max(G[i].V[j], G[j]);
(14)       enumerate(G);
(15) endwhile;
```

Figure 14.5   An algorithm for lexical traversal of all ideals of a poset with any chain partition.

2. *Let* $H = leastConsistent(K)$. *Then,*

$$\forall j : H[j] = max\{K[i].v[j] \mid 1 \le i \le n\}.$$

Incorporating these observations, we get the algorithm in Figure 14.5.

The algorithm in Figure 14.5 enumerates all ideals in the lexical order assuming that the poset P is in the chain partitioned form. Line (1) enumerates the least ideal in lexical order, which is always $(0, 0, ..0)$. The variable G is set to this value and enumerated at line (1). The *while* loop (lines (2) to (15)), enumerates the next lexically bigger ideal than G whenever possible. The *for* loop (lines (3)–(5)) finds the largest k such that the next element on P_k is such that all elements in $P_1..P_{k-1}$ smaller than that element are included in G. Formally, we say that element e is enabled in an ideal G iff

$$\forall f \in P : f < e \Rightarrow f \in G.$$

An element e is enabled in an ideal G with respect to P_i if

$$\forall f \in P_i : f < e \Rightarrow f \in G.$$

Therefore, e is enabled in G for $P_1..P_{k-1}$ iff

$$\forall i : 1 \leq i < k : e.V[i] \leq G[i].$$

If we do not find any k, then we must have enumerated all ideals and we break the *while* loop at line (6). We include the next element at P_k in G at line (7). We remove all elements in chains P_{k+1} to P_n at lines (8) and (9). Observe that G now contains elements only from chains P_1 to P_k. Lines (11)–(13) now ensure that G is an ideal by including sufficient elements from P_{k+1} to P_n. If $G[i]$ is not equal to zero for any $i \in \{1..k\}$, we include all elements in $G[i].V$.

For an example of this algorithm, consider the poset $L(3, 3)$ shown in Figure 14.6. Suppose that the last subset enumerated was $G = [1, 1, 0]$ also shown in the figure. For the next ideal, we start with P_3. The next element on P_3 (the element $e_{3,1}$) is considered for inclusion. It is enabled with respect to P_1 and P_2 because elements that are smaller than this element in P_1 and P_2 are already included in G. Hence, after line (9), G is $[1, 1, 1]$. Since k is 3, lines (10)–(13) do not change anything and the following subset enumerated is $[1, 1, 1]$. Now consider the next iteration of the *while* loop. We first check if the second element on P_3 is enabled. This is not the case since the second element on P_3 is greater than the second element on P_2, which is not included in G. Next, we try the second element on P_2. However, that element is also not enabled. Next, we try the second element on P_1 which is enabled. Hence, we get G as $[2, 1, 1]$. We now reset the components for processes with higher indices at lines (8) and (9). After the resetting of components, G is $[2, 0, 0]$ and is enumerated next. Note that even for this case, lines (10)–(13) do not change G. The algorithm continues to enumerate ideals as $[2, 1, 0]$, $[2, 1, 1]$, $[2, 2, 0]$, and so on.

Let us analyze the time complexity of Algorithm Lex. We compute the time required for enumeration of one ideal. Every iteration of the *while* loop enumerates one ideal. Line (4) requires determining if the next element on P_k in G exists and line (5) checks if that event is enabled for $P_1..P_{k-1}$. The next element on P_k exists iff $G[k]$ is less than the total number of elements in P_k, a condition that can be evaluated in $O(1)$ time. Let e be the next element on P_k in G. As mentioned earlier, it is enabled in G for $P_1..P_{k-1}$ iff

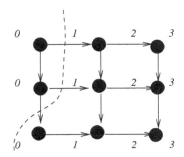

Figure 14.6 $L(3, 3)$ with example of an ideal.

$$\forall i : 1 \leq i < k : e.V[i] \leq G[i].$$

This condition can be evaluated in $O(k)$ time. Therefore, the Algorithm Lex requires $O(n^2)$ for enumeration of one ideal at line (5). Lines (11)–(13) also require $O(n^2)$ time giving us the overall complexity of $O(n^2)$ time per ideal.

14.5   UNIFLOW PARTITION OF POSETS

We describe in this section a special type of chain partition called *uniflow chain partition* that allows efficient enumeration of ideals and ideals *at a given level*. Every poset P has at least one such partition. Let n be the least number of chains in any uniflow chain partition of P. We present two algorithms in this section. The first algorithm enumerates all the ideals of a poset with a uniflow chain partition. It takes $O(n^2)$ time per ideal to enumerate the set of ideals of P. By considering special properties of the poset P, the time complexity can be reduced to $O(n)$ for many applications in combinatorics. The second algorithm enumerates all the ideals at a given level of a poset with a uniflow chain partition. This algorithm takes $O(n^3)$ time per ideal to enumerate the set of ideals of size k of poset P. Furthermore, the algorithm requires only $O(n)$ space in addition to the storage required for storing the poset.

A uniflow partition of a poset P is a partition of P into n chains $\{P_i \mid 1 \leq i \leq n\}$ such that no element in a higher numbered chain is smaller than any element in lower numbered chain. Formally, let $\alpha : P \rightarrow \mathbb{N}$ be a chain partition of P, i.e., α maps every element of P to a natural number such that

$$\forall x, y \in P : \alpha(x) = \alpha(y) \Rightarrow (x \leq y) \vee (y \leq x).$$

A chain partition α is *uniflow* for a poset if

$$\forall x, y \in P : \alpha(x) < \alpha(y) \Rightarrow \neg(y \leq x). \tag{14.1}$$

Figure 14.7(a) shows an example of the partitioned poset $L(n, m)$ with n chains each of m elements. In $L(n, m)$, element j of chain P_i is smaller than element j of all higher numbered chains. If chains are arranged from top to bottom such that the least numbered chain is at the top, then all edges across chains in a uniflow partition go in one direction. Figure 14.7(b) shows $L(3, 3)$. The dashed line shows an ideal of the poset. All the elements of the poset that are to the left of the dashed line are members of the ideal. In Figure 14.7(b), the ideal contains one element from P_1, one element from P_2, and no element from P_3. Each ideal of $L(3, 3)$ can be mapped to a subset of [6] of size 3 as follows. To choose a subset S of size 3, we use the number of elements of each chain included in the ideal. The number of elements included in P_1 dictates the largest number in S, the number of elements included in P_2 dictates the second largest number, and so on. If P_1 has k elements in the ideal, then we include $3 + k$ in S. Since the ideal in the figure includes one element from P_1, we include 4 in S.

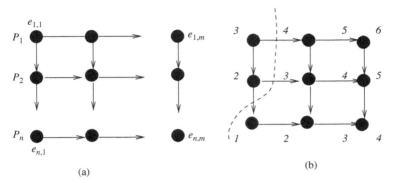

(a)   (b)

Figure 14.7 (a) Poset $L(n, m)$ with uniflow partition. (b) $L(3, 3)$ with an example of an ideal mapped to the subset $\{1, 3, 4\}$.

Similarly, we include 3 in S because one element from P_2 is included and include 1 in S because zero elements from P_3 are included. Thus, the ideal in the figure denotes the subset $\{1, 3, 4\}$ of [6]. We have labeled edges in Figure 14.7(b) to show the bijection between ideals and subsets of [6] of size 3.

Another example of a poset with uniflow partition is shown in Figure 14.8. The partitioned poset $D(n, m)$ consists of n disjoint chains each with m elements. Figure 14.8(b) shows $D(3, 3)$. For this example, the uniflow condition holds trivially because elements on distinct chains are incomparable. Each ideal of this poset corresponds to a tuple in the product space of 64 tuples from $(0, 0, 0)$ to $(3, 3, 3)$.

Figure 14.9(a) shows a chain partition that does not satisfy the uniflow property. The same poset can be partitioned into three chains with the uniflow property as shown in Figure 14.9(b). Note that every poset has at least one uniflow chain partition. Any linear extension can be transformed into a trivial uniflow chain partition by considering each element as a chain by itself.

In our definition of uniflow poset, we require that no element in a higher numbered chain be smaller than any element in a lower numbered chain. By renumbering the

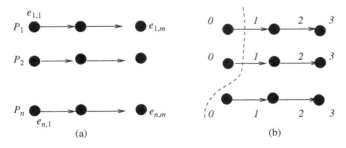

(a)   (b)

Figure 14.8 (a) Poset $D(n, m)$ with uniflow partition (b) $D(3, 3)$ with example of an ideal.

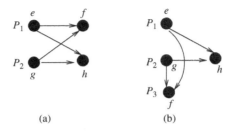

(a)   (b)

Figure 14.9   (a) Chain partition of a Poset that is not uniflow. (b) Uniflow chain partition of the same poset.

chains, any such poset also has a chain partition β with the dual property that

$$\forall x, y \in P \: : \: \beta(y) < \beta(x) \Rightarrow \neg(y \leq x). \tag{14.2}$$

We call a chain partition α that satisfies Equation 14.1, *positive* uniflow and a chain partition β that satisfies Equation 14.2, *negative* uniflow partition.

An advantage of uniflow chain partition is that it allows us to enumerate ideals from a given ideal efficiently as shown later.

Lemma 14.6 (Positive Uniflow Ideals Lemma) *Let G be any ideal of a poset P with a positive uniflow chain partition $\{P_i \mid 1 \leq i \leq n\}$. Any subset H_k of P for $1 \leq k \leq n$ that satisfies*

$$\forall i \: : \: 1 \leq i < k \: : \: H_k[i] = G[i]$$

and

$$\forall i \: : \: k \leq i \leq n \: : \: H_k[i] = 0$$

is also an ideal.

Proof: Follows from Equation 14.1.

∎

For example, in Figure 14.9(b), consider the ideal $G = \{e, f, g\}$ represented as $G = [1, 1, 1]$ in the uniflow partition. Then, Lemma 14.6 claims that the subsets of P represented by $[0, 0, 0]$, $[1, 0, 0]$, $[1, 1, 0]$ are also ideals. The claim may not hold if the chain partition does not have uniflow property. For example, in Figure 14.9(a), $G = \{e, f, g\}$ is represented as $G = [2, 1]$. However, the set $[2, 0]$ is not an ideal; it includes f but not g.

We get the following version of the Uniflow ideal lemma with a negative uniflow.

Lemma 14.7 (Negative Uniflow Ideals Lemma) *Let G be any ideal of a poset P with a negative uniflow chain partition $\{P_i \mid 1 \leq i \leq n\}$. Then, any subset H_k of P for $1 \leq k \leq n$ that satisfies*

$$\forall i \: : \: 1 \leq i \leq k \: : \: H_k[i] = G[i]$$

TABLE 14.1   Special cases of lex enumeration of ideals of a poset.

Enumeration	Ideals of the Poset
Product space	$D(n, m)$ (see Figure 14.8)
Subsets of $[n]$	$D(n, 1)$ (see Figure 14.8)
Subsets of $[m + n]$ of size n	$L(n, m)$ (see Figure 14.7)
Permutations of $1..n$	$T(n)$ (see Figure 14.12)
Integer partitions that fit in an n by m rectangle	$L(n, m)$ (see Figure 14.7)
Catalan subset of $[2n]$ of size n	$C(n)$ (see Figure 14.12)

and

$$\forall i : k + 1 \leq i \leq n : H_k[i] = |P_i|$$

is also an ideal.

Proof: Follows from Equation 14.2.

∎

We now simplify the algorithm for a positive uniflow chain partition. Owing to the positive uniflow property of the chain partition, if any element e belongs to the chain k, then any element smaller than e also belongs to a chain numbered k or lower. Hence, lines (10)–(13) in Algorithm Lex() in Figure 14.5 are not necessary owing to Positive Uniflow Ideals Lemma. Similarly, if the chain partition satisfies negative uniflow property then line (5) in Figure 14.5 is not necessary because for any element e on chain k, there is no element smaller than e in any chain numbered lower than k (Table 4.1).

14.6   ENUMERATING TUPLES OF PRODUCT SPACES

We first give the most straightforward application to enumeration of combinatorial objects. We show that we can derive efficient algorithms for many combinatorial objects such as all subsets of $[n]$, all subsets of $[n]$ of size k, all permutations, and all tuples of product spaces.

Consider a product space $(x_1, x_2, ..., x_n)$ such that each $x_i \in [0..m_i]$. It is clear that the product space has $\Pi_{i \in 1..n}(m_i + 1)$ tuples. We can view these tuples as ideals of the poset $D(n, m)$ with the chain partition shown in Figure 14.8. This partition satisfies positive as well as negative uniflow partitions; hence, we can apply both optimizations and get the algorithm shown in Figure 14.10.

It is clear that the above-mentioned algorithm produces a new tuple after at most $O(n)$ steps on account of two *for* loops at lines 3 and 6.

14.7   ENUMERATING ALL SUBSETS

We now consider the problem of enumerating all subsets of a given finite set. We show that there may be multiple posets such that the ideals of the poset are mapped

```
lexTraverseProductSpace()

Input: [m₁, m₂, ..., mₙ] // largest tuple of the product space
Output: All tuples in lex order
var
      G:array[1 ...n] of int initially ∀i : G[i] = 0; // current CGS
(1)   enumerate(G);
(2)   while (true)
(3)        for k := n down to 1 do
(4)             if (G[k] < mₖ) break;
(5)        if no such k, then return;// we have enumerated all tuples
(6)        G[k] := G[k] + 1;
(7)        for j := k + 1 to n do G[j] := 0;
(8)        enumerate(G);
(9)   endwhile;
```

Figure 14.10   An algorithm for traversal of product space in lex order.

in 1-1 manner with subsets. The first method of generating all subsets of the set $[n]$ is to view every subset as a binary string of size n. Enumerating all subsets is equivalent to enumerating all 2^n binary strings of size n. However, this is just a special case of enumerating the product space where each of m_k is 1. In this case, the product space corresponds to the ideals of the poset shown in Figure 14.11(a). Each process P_i executes a single event e_i. It is easy to verify that there is a bijection between every CGS of the computation and a subset of X. For example, when $n = 4$, the CGS $(0, 1, 0, 1)$ corresponds to the set $\{e_2, e_4\}$. The lex enumeration would correspond to enumeration of sets based on binary string representation. For n equal to 3, the enumeration would be $\{\}, \{1\}, \{2\}, \{1, 2\}, \{3\}, \{1, 3\}, \{2, 3\}, \{1, 2, 3\}$. Given any subset S, this enumeration corresponds to the following rule to generate the next subset after S: insert the smallest element j which is not in S and delete all elements smaller than j.

Figure 14.11(b) gives another computation that can also be used to enumerate all the subsets of $\{1..4\}$. In this example, the enumeration would result in the lex order (reversed). Each global state (or a cut) corresponds to a subset. For example, G corresponds to the subset $\{4, 2, 1\}$. We say that P_i has chosen element k if the cut (global state) goes through the label k for process P_i. In this computation, P_1 chooses the biggest element in the set. By the design of the computation, P_2 can only choose an element that is strictly smaller than the element chosen by P_1 for the global state to be consistent. For example, the global state H is not consistent because P_2 has also chosen 1, which is same as the element chosen by P_1. The choice of 0 by any

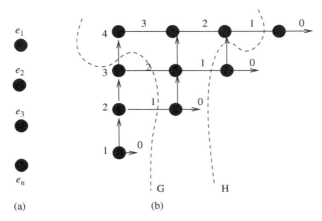

Figure 14.11   Posets for generating subsets of X.

P_i denotes that the process does not choose any element. It can be verified that if P_i chooses 0, then all higher numbered processes can only choose 0.

We leave it as an exercise for the reader to adapt the lex algorithm for traversing a poset with poset uniflow property to enumerate all subsets using the poset in Figure 14.11(b).

14.8   ENUMERATING ALL SUBSETS OF SIZE K

Figure 14.7 shows the poset $L(n, m)$ such that all the subsets of $[n + m]$ of size n are in 1-1 correspondence with its ideals. If $G[i]$ is j then we add $(j + (n - i + 1))$ to the set. For example, when $G = (1, 1, 0)$, i.e., $G[1] = 1$, $G[2] = 1$, and $G[3] = 0$, we get elements $1 + (3 - 1 + 1)$, $1 + (3 - 2 + 1)$, and $0 + (3 - 3 + 1)$. Thus, the subset corresponds to $\{4, 3, 1\}$. Figure 14.13 shows the algorithm to generate all ideals of $L(n, m)$. Since $L(n, m)$ satisfies positive uniflow property, once a suitable k is found at line (4), advancing along $G[k]$ and resetting $G[j]$ to 0 for all chains j numbered higher than k gives us the next lexically bigger ideal. Line (4) returns the element on highest numbered chain P_k, which is enabled with respect to $P_1, ... P_{k-1}$. The first few ideals enumerated for $L(3, 3)$ are

$$(0, 0, 0), (1, 0, 0), (1, 1, 0), (1, 1, 1), (2, 0, 0), ...$$

By mapping $G[i]$ to element $G[i] + (n - i + 1)$, we get the subsets

$$(3, 2, 1), (4, 2, 1), (4, 3, 1), (4, 3, 2), (5, 2, 1).$$

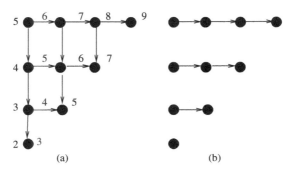

Figure 14.12   (a) Poset $C(5)$ with a uniflow partition (b) Poset $T(5)$ with a uniflow partition.

---

lexTraverseSubsetsOfGivenSize()

Input: n, m
Output: All subsets of $[n]$ of size m
var
        G:array$[1 \ldots n]$ of int initially $\forall i : G[i] = 0$; //
(1)   enumerate(G);
(2)   **while** (*true*)
(3)   **for** $k := n$ down to 1 do
(4)   if $((k == 1)\&\&(G[1] < m)) \,||\, ((k > 1)\&\&(G[k] < G[k-1])))$ then
(5)   break; // suitable k found
(5)   if no such k, then return;// we have enumerated all tuples
(6) $G[k] := G[k] + 1$;
(7)   **for** $j := k + 1$ to n do $G[j] := 0$;
(8)   enumerate(G);
(9)   **endwhile**;

Figure 14.13   An algorithm for traversal of all subsets of $[n]$ of size m in lex order.

14.9   ENUMERATING YOUNG'S LATTICE

Recall that the set of all partitions that are less than or equal to λ form the *Young's lattice* denoted by Y_λ. Figure 14.14 shows the poset for generating Young's lattice. By enumerating all ideals of the poset in lex order, we can enumerate all partitions that are less than or equal to λ.

Figure 14.15 gives the algorithm to enumerate Y_λ.

Now consider the Young Lattice for $\lambda = (N, N, \ldots N \ times)$. The Nth level set of this lattice corresponds to all integer partitions of N. By enumerating the Nth level

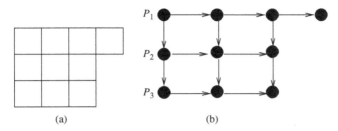

Figure 14.14   (a) A Ferrer's diagram. (b) A poset for generating Young's lattice.

---

lexTraverseYoungLattice()

Input: $\lambda = (\lambda_1, \ldots, \lambda_n)$
Output: All integer partitions less than or equal to λ
var
         G:array$[1 \ldots n]$ of int initially $\forall i : G[i] = 0$; //
(1)   enumerate(G);
(2)   **while** (*true*)
(3)   **for** $k := n$ down to 1 do
(4)   if $((k == 1)\&\&(G[1] < \lambda_1) \mid\mid ((k > 1)\&\&(G[k] < G[k-1])$
                    $\&\& (G[k] < \lambda_k)))$ then
(5)   break; // suitable k found
(5)   if no such k, then return;// we have enumerated all tuples
(6) $G[k] := G[k] + 1$;
(7)   **for** $j := k + 1$ to n do $G[j] := 0$;
(8)   enumerate(G);
(9)   **endwhile**;

Figure 14.15   An algorithm for traversal of all integer partitions in Y_λ in lex order.

set, we can enumerate all integer partitions of N. We discuss algorithms to enumerate
level sets in the following section.

14.10   ENUMERATING PERMUTATIONS

Finally, we show that our algorithms can also be used to enumerate permutations. We
first show a poset such that its ideals can be mapped to all permutations of n symbols.
Figure 14.12(b) shows the poset $T(n)$ for $n = 5$. The poset consists of $n - 1$ chains.
We use the inversion table[Knu98] to map an ideal to a permutation. The number of
inversions of i in a permutation π is the number of symbols less than i that appear to
the right of i in π. The way a permutation is generated from an ideal is as follows. We

begin the permutation by writing 1. P_1 decides where to insert the symbol 2. There are two choices. These choices correspond to number of *inversions* introduced by 2. If we place 2 after 1, then we introduce zero inversions; Otherwise, we introduce one inversion. Proceeding in this manner, we get that there is a bijection between the set of permutations and the ideals. By using the algorithm to generate all ideals of the product space and converting the ideal viewed as a tuple of inversion number to corresponding permutation, we get an algorithm to generate all permutations.

In many applications, we are interested in subsets of combinatorial families. For example, we may be interested in enumerating all permutations of 1..7 in which 7 has at most three inversions. By using methods of slicing, one can compute posets such that its ideals correspond to precisely this subset. Now we can use the algorithm for lex order traversal to enumerate all such permutations.

14.11 LEXICAL ENUMERATION OF ALL ORDER IDEALS OF A GIVEN RANK

Many combinatorial objects have bijections with ideals of a given rank rather than all ideals. For example, all subsets of $[n]$ of size r can be mapped to level r of the Boolean lattice, which is simply ideals of $D(n, 1)$. As another example, consider the ideals of $L(n, n)$. It is easy to see that all integer partitions of n have bijection with the set of ideals of rank n. In this section, we give an efficient algorithm to generate all ideals of a given rank. In this section, we assume that the poset is decomposed using a *negative* uniflow chain partition. Figure 14.17(a) shows a poset $NL(n, m)$ with a negative uniflow chain partition. Figure 14.17(b) shows a poset $NL(3, 3)$ such that all ideals at rank 3 correspond to integer partitions of 3. There are three integer partitions for 3

$$3, 2 + 1, 1 + 1 + 1.$$

These partitions correspond to the following ideals in the lexical order.

$$[0, 0, 3], [0, 1, 2], [1, 1, 1].$$

Note that the indices of the chains are in the reversed order of the conventional way of writing integer parts from the greatest to the smallest. The algorithm in Figure 14.16 enumerates these partitions in the above-mentioned order.

The algorithm works as follows. We first find the lexically smallest ideal at the required level r. This step is performed by the method $getSmallest(G, r)$ (shown in Figure 14.18), which returns the lexically smallest ideal of P bigger than G at level r. For example, in Figure 14.17, $getSmallest([0, 0, 0], 3)$ returns the lexically smallest ideal $[0, 0, 3]$. Given an ideal G at level r, we repeatedly find the next lexically bigger ideal at level r using the algorithm $getSucc(G, r)$ shown in Figure 14.19. For example, in Figure 14.17, $getSucc([0, 0, 3], 3)$ returns the next lexically smallest ideal $[0, 1, 2]$.

The method $getSmallest(G, r)$ on poset P assumes that the rank of G is at most r and that G is an ideal of the poset P. It first computes d as the difference between

```
LevelTraverse()

Input: P: a poset partitioned into uniflow chains P₁,..Pₙ
       r: integer; // a level number
Output: All ideals of P at level r in the lexical order
var
       G: array[1 ...n] of int initially ∀i : G[i] = 0; // least ideal
(1)  G := getSmallest(G, r);
(2)  while (G ≠ null)
(3)      enumerate(G);
(4)      G := getSucc(G, r);
(5)  endwhile;
```

Figure 14.16   An algorithm for traversal of a level set in lexical order.

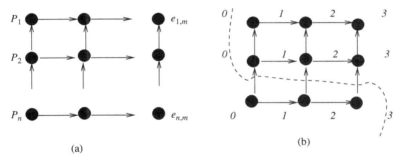

(a)   (b)

Figure 14.17   (a) Poset $NL(n, m)$ with a negative uniflow partition. (b) $NL(3, 3)$ with example of an ideal.

r and the rank of G. We need to add d elements to G to find the smallest ideal at rank r. We exploit the negative Uniflow Ideal Lemma (Lemma 14.7) by adding as many elements from the largest numbered chain as possible. If all the elements from the largest numbered chain are already in G, then we continue with the second largest numbered chain, and so on. For our example in Figure 14.17, consider finding smallest ideal at level 3 starting from $G = [0, 0, 0]$. In this case, we are done by adding all three elements from P_3 to get the answer as $[0, 0, 3]$.

The following lemma shows that the resulting set is the smallest ideal of rank r and which is greater than or equal to G.

Lemma 14.8 *Let G be any ideal of rank at most r. Then, getSmallest(G, r) is lexically the smallest ideal of rank r greater than or equal to G.*

Proof: Let H be the set returned by *getSmallest(G, r)*. We first show that H is an ideal. H is initialized to G which is an ideal. We show that H continues to be an ideal

```
getSmallest(G,r)

Input: P: a poset partitioned into negative uniflow chains P₁, ..Pₙ;
       r: integer; // a level number
       G: an ideal;
Output: H: lexically smallest ideal at level r greater than or equal to G
var
       H:array[1..n] of int initially ∀i : H[i] = G[i];
(1)   int d := r − rank(G);
(2)   for j := n down to 1 do
(3)       if (d ≤ |Pⱼ| − G[j])
(4)           H[j] := G[j] + d;
(5)           return H;
(6)       else
(7)           H[j] := |Pⱼ|;
(8)           d := d − (|Pⱼ| − G[j]);
(9)   endfor;
```

Figure 14.18   An algorithm to find the lexically smallest ideal at level r greater than G.

after every iteration of the *for* loop. At iteration j, we add to H elements from chain $n − j + 1$. Since all elements from higher numbered chains are already part of H, and all elements from lower numbered chains cannot be smaller than any of the newly added element, we get that H continues to be an ideal.

By construction of our algorithm, it is clear that rank of H is exactly r. We now show that H is the lexically smallest ideal at rank r greater than or equal to G. If not, let W different from H be the lexically smallest ideal at rank r greater than or equal to G. Since $W <_l H$, let k be the smallest index such that $W[k] < H[k]$. Since $G ≤_l W$, k is one of the indices for which we have added elements. Because rank of W equals rank of H, there must be an index k' higher than k such that $W[k'] > H[k']$. However, by the property of H for any index k' higher than k, $H[k']$ equals $|P_{k'}|$. Hence, $W[k']$ cannot be greater than $H[k']$.

∎

We now discuss the method *getSucc*(G, r) shown in Figure 14.19. To find the next lexical ideal of G at level r, we proceed as follows. The *for* loop (lines (1)–(11)) searches for an appropriate element z not in G such that on addition of z, the resulting ideal K is guaranteed to be greater than G. The search for z is started from chain n down to 1 so that we choose the lexically smallest z that is not in G. Line (2) checks if there is any element in P_k. If all elements from P_k are already included in G, we go to the next value of k. Otherwise, in lines (3)–(4), we include in K all elements in

---

getSucc(G, r)

Input: G: Any ideal at level r
  r: integer; // a level number
Output: Lexical successor of G at level r
var
  K:array[1 ...n] of int initially $\forall i : K[i] = 0$;;
(1) **for** $k := n$ down to 1 **do**
(2)   **if** (the next element z on P_k exists)
(3)   **for** $i := 1$ to $k - 1$: // include in K all elements
      from G from P_1 to P_{k-1}
(4) $K[i] := G[i]$;
(5) $K[k] := G[k] + 1$;// include the element z
(6)   // include in K all elements required to make it an ideal
(7)   **for** $i := 1$ to k:
(8)   **for** $j := k + 1$ to n:
(9) $K[j] := max(K[j], G[i].V[j])$;
(10)   **if** ($rank(K) \le r$) break ;// found suitable K
(11) **endfor**;
(12) **if** no suitable K then return null;// we have enumerated all tuples
(13) **else** return getSmallest(K, r);

Figure 14.19 An Algorithm to find the next bigger ideal in a level set.

G from chains 1 to $k - 1$. Line (5) includes in K all elements in G from P_k and z. To ensure that K is an ideal, for every element y in K, we add $D[y]$ to K at lines (7)–(9). At line (10), we check whether the resulting ideal is at level r or less. If $rank(K)$ is at most r, then we have found a suitable K that can be used to find the next lexically bigger ideal than G and we break the *for* loop to go to line (13). If we have tried all values of k and did not find a suitable K, then G is the largest ideal at level r and we return null.

For our example in Figure 14.17, consider the call of *getSucc* from the ideal [0, 0, 3] for rank 3. Since there is no next element in P_3, we consider the next element in P_2. At line (5), the value of K is [0, 1, 0]. Lines (7)–(9) make K an ideal resulting in K to be [0, 1, 1] at line (10). Since $rank(K)$ is 2, we break the *for* loop and call *getSmallest*(K, r) to find the smallest ideal at level r that contains K. For our example, we call *getSmallest*([0, 1, 1], 3) at line (13). The resulting ideal is the lexical successor of G at level r. For our example, this ideal corresponds to [0, 1, 2].

We now show the correctness of the method *getSucc*(G, r).

Lemma 14.9 *Let G be any ideal of rank at most r. Then, getSucc(G, r) returns the least ideal at rank r that is lexically greater than G.*

TABLE 14.2   Special cases of lex enumeration of level sets of the ideal lattice of a poset

Enumeration	Poset	Level number
Subsets of $[n]$ of size k	$D(n, 1)$ (see Figure 14.8)	k
Integer partitions of n	$L(n, n)$ (see Figure 14.7)	n
All compositions of n with k parts	$D(k, n - k)$ (see Figure 14.8)	$n - k$
Permutations of $1..n$ with k inversions	$T(n)$ (see Figure 14.12)	k

Proof: Let W be the ideal returned by $getSucc(G, r)$. We consider two cases. Suppose that W is null. This means that for all values of k, either all elements in P_k are already included in G or on inclusion of the next element in P_k, z, the smallest ideal that includes z has rank greater than r. Hence, G is lexically biggest ideal at level r.

Now consider the case when W is the ideal returned at line (13) by $getSmallest(K, r)$. We first observe that K after executing line (9) is the next lexical ideal (at *any* level) after G. If $rank(K)$ is at most r, then $getSmallest(K, r)$ returns the smallest lexical ideal greater than or equal to K at level r. If $rank(K)$ is greater than r, then there is no ideal at level r such that $\forall i : 1 \leq i \leq k - 1 : K[i] = G[i]$ and $K[k] > G[k]$ and $rank(K) \leq r$. Thus, at line (13), we use the largest possible value of k for which there exists an ideal lexically bigger than G at level r.

■

The algorithm $getSucc(G, r)$ takes $O(n^3)$ time in the worst case because of nested for loops. We now apply the level enumeration algorithm to various combinatorial families given in Table 14.2.

Theorem 14.10 *All subsets of $[n]$, all integer partitions, all compositions of n with k parts, and all permutations with k inversions can be generated in $O(n^3)$ time per enumeration by using the LevelTraverse algorithm shown in Figure 14.16.*

Proof: It is easy to verify that the level sets of the ideals of the posets listed in Table 14.2 correspond to the combinatorial family listed in column 1 of Table 14.2

■

14.12   PROBLEMS

1. Show that in the algorithm shown in Figure 14.2, if H is inserted as the first element in Q, rather than the last element, then the algorithm traverses the lattice in the depth-first-search order.

2. Show that in the algorithm shown in Figure 14.2, we can replace the condition for exploring e by

$$\forall f \in maximal(H) : \sigma(f) < \sigma(e).$$

3. Give a nonrecursive version of the Algorithm in Figure 14.4 for DFS traversal of ideals.

4. Show that H at line (12) in Figure 14.5 is indeed the next lexical state after G.

5. Show that in Figure 14.5, it is sufficient to take the maximum of G, and the vector $K[k]$ to compute H whenever the value of k in the current iteration is greater than or equal to the one in the previous iteration instead of lines (9)–(12).

6. Give an algorithm to generate all partitions of n with at most k parts.

7. Give an algorithm to generate all the subsets of $[n]$ of size k in lexical order which do not contain any consecutive numbers.

14.13   BIBLIOGRAPHIC REMARKS

The first algorithm for BFS traversal of the lattice of global states is from Cooper and Marzullo [CM91]. The second algorithm for BFS traversal is taken from Garg [Gar03]. The algorithm for DFS traversal of the lattice is due to Alagar and Venkatesan [AV01]. The algorithm for Lexical traversal of the lattice is taken from Ganter and Reuter [GR91] and Garg [Gar03]. The notion of uniflow partition of posets and the algorithm for enumerating level sets of the ideal lattice are from Garg [Gar14].

15

LATTICE OF MAXIMAL ANTICHAINS

15.1 INTRODUCTION

Given any poset, there are three important distinct lattices associated with it: the lattice of ideals, the lattice of normal cuts, and the lattice of maximal antichains. The lattice of ideals captures the notion of consistent cuts in a distributed computation and is discussed in Chapter 14. For a poset P, its completion by normal cuts is the smallest lattice that has P as its suborder and is discussed in Chapter 6. In this chapter, we discuss the lattice of maximal antichains with applications to global predicate detection.

Recall that an antichain A is *maximal* if there does not exist any event that can be added to the set without violating the antichain property. The *lattice of maximal antichains*, denoted by $L_{MA}(P)$ is the set of all maximal antichains under the order consistent with the order on the lattice of consistent cuts.

The lattice of maximal antichains captures all maximal sets of concurrent events and has applications in detection of global predicates because it is usually much smaller than the lattice of consistent cuts. In the extreme case, the lattice of consistent cuts may be exponentially bigger in size than the lattice of maximal antichains. We show in this Chapter that some global predicates can be detected on the lattice of maximal antichains instead of consistent cuts, thereby providing an exponential reduction in the complexity of detecting them. Figure 15.1(a) shows a poset corresponding to a distributed computation. Its lattices of consistent cuts and maximal antichains are shown in Figure 15.1(b) and (c), respectively.

Introduction to Lattice Theory with Computer Science Applications, First Edition. Vijay K. Garg.
© 2015 John Wiley & Sons, Inc. Published 2015 by John Wiley & Sons, Inc.

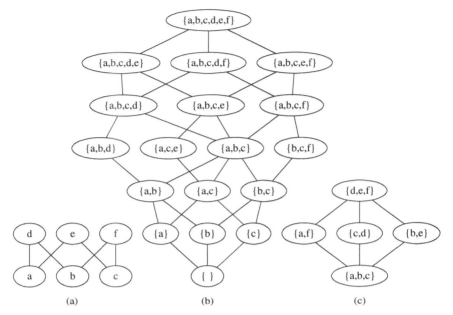

Figure 15.1 (a) The original poset. (b) Its lattice of ideals (consistent cuts). (c) Its lattice of maximal antichains.

In this chapter, we discuss algorithms for computing L_{MA} for a finite poset P with implicit representation (i.e., represented using vector clocks). Incremental algorithms assume that we are given a poset P and its lattice of maximal antichains L and we are required to construct L_{MA} of the poset P' corresponding to P extended with an element x. These algorithms store the entire lattice L_{MA}. Our first algorithm called incremental algorithm for lattice of maximal antichains (ILMAs) is a simple modification of the algorithm by Nourine and Raynoud [NR99, NR02] based on vector clocks. The algorithm requires $O(wm \log m)$ time and $O(wm \log n)$ space, where w is the width of the poset P, n is the size of the poset P, and m is the size of $L_{MA}(P)$. The second algorithm called online algorithm for lattice of maximal antichains (OLMAs) does not require lattice $L_{MA}(P)$ to compute elements of the new lattice. Let M be the set of new elements generated due to x. The time complexity of OLMA is dependent on the size of M independent of the size of the lattice $L_{MA}(P)$.

Even though the OLMA algorithm has lower space complexity than ILMA, in the worst case, the size of M can be exponential in the number of processes. If the goal is to not *construct*, but simply *enumerate* (or check for some global predicate) all the elements of L_{MA}, then we can also use BFS, depth first search (DFS), and lexical enumeration of lattice of maximal antichains. It is important to note that algorithms for BFS and DFS enumeration of lattices are different from the standard graph-based BFS and DFS enumeration because lattice enumeration algorithms cannot store the explicit graph corresponding to the lattice due to high space complexity. Hence, the

TABLE 15.1   Incremental Construction of the Lattice of Maximal Antichains of a poset P extended with x.

Incremental Algorithm	Time Complexity	Space Complexity
Algorithm ILMA	$O(wm \log m)$	$O(mw \log n)$
Algorithm OLMA	$O(m_x w^2 \log m_x))$	$O(m_x w \log n)$

TABLE 15.2   Algorithms for Lattice Enumeration of Maximal Antichains

Offline Algorithm	Time Complexity	Space Complexity
BFS-MA	$O(mw^2 \log m)$	$O(w_L w \log n)$
DFS-MA	$O(mw^4)$	$O(nw \log n)$
Lexical	$O(mn^3)$	$O(n \log n)$

TABLE 15.3   The Notation Used in this Chapter

Symbol	Definition	Symbol	Definition
n	Size of the poset P	m	Size of the maximal antichains lattice L
w	Width of the poset P	m_x	number of strict ideals $\geq D(x)$
w_L	Width of the lattice L		

usual technique of marking the visited nodes is not applicable. These algorithms for BFS, DFS, and lexical enumeration can be generalized to enumeration of any family of closed sets.

Tables 15.1 and 15.2 summarize the time and space complexity for construction and enumeration algorithms for the lattice of maximal antichains with the notation in Table 15.3.

15.2   MAXIMAL ANTICHAIN LATTICE

We first define three different but isomorphic lattices: the lattice of maximal antichain ideals, the lattice of maximal antichains, and the lattice of strict ideals. Besides, giving an insight in the structure of the lattice of maximal antichains, these lattices have different closure properties making them useful in different contexts. The lattice of strict ideals is closed under union and is used in the incremental algorithms such as ILMA and OLMA algorithms. The lattice of maximal ideals is closed under intersection and is used in the DFS-MA algorithm.

Definition 15.1 (Maximal Antichain) *An antichain A is maximal in a poset $P = (X, \leq)$ if every element in $X - A$ is comparable to some element in A.*

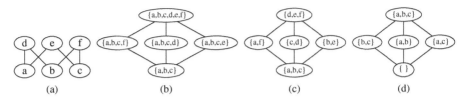

Figure 15.2   (a) The original poset. (b) Its lattice of maximal ideals. (c) Its lattice of maximal antichains. (d) Its lattice of strict ideals.

In Figure 15.2(a), the set $\{d, e\}$ is an antichain but not a maximal antichain because f is incomparable to both d and e. The set $\{d, e, f\}$ is a maximal antichain. It is easy to see that A is a maximal antichain iff $D(A) \cup U[A] = X$.

Definition 15.2 (Maximal Ideal) *An ideal Q of a poset $P = (X, \leq)$ is a maximal antichain ideal (or, maximal ideal) if the set of its maximal elements, denoted by maximal(Q), is a maximal antichain.*

The set of maximal ideals is closed under intersection but not union. In Figure 15.2(b), the ideals $\{a, b, c, d\}$ and $\{a, b, c, e\}$ are maximal ideals, but their union $\{a, b, c, d, e\}$ is not a maximal ideal.

Definition 15.3 (Lattice of Maximal Ideals of a Poset) *For a given poset $P = (X, \leq)$, its lattice of maximal ideals is the poset formed with the set of all the maximal ideals of P under the set inclusion order. Formally,*

$$L_{MA}(P) = (\{A \subseteq X : A \text{ is a maximal ideal of } P\}, \subseteq).$$

For the poset in Figure 15.2(a), the set of all maximal ideals is
$$\{\{a, b, c\}, \{a, b, c, d\}, \{a, b, c, e\}, \{a, b, c, f\}, \{a, b, c, d, e, f\}\}.$$
The poset formed by these sets under the $\subseteq$ relation is shown in Figure 15.2(c). This poset is a lattice with the meet as the intersection.

A lattice isomorphic to the lattice of maximal ideals is that of the maximal antichains.

Definition 15.4 (Lattice of Maximal Antichains of a Poset) *For a given poset $P = (X, \leq)$, its lattice of maximal antichains is the poset formed with the set of all the maximal antichains of P with the order $A \preceq B$ iff $D[A] \subseteq D[B]$.*

In Section 15.3, we discuss incremental algorithms for lattice construction. In these algorithms, we have the lattice $L_{MA}(P)$ for a poset P, and our goal is to construct $L_{MA}(P \cup \{x\})$, where x is a new event that is not less than any event in P. It would be desirable if all the elements of $L_{MA}(P)$ continue to be elements of $L_{MA}(P')$. However, this is not the case for maximal antichains. An antichain that is maximal in P may not be maximal in $P \cup \{x\}$. For example, in Figure 15.2, suppose that f arrives last. The set $\{d, e\}$ is a maximal antichain before the arrival of f, but not after. Some algorithms explicitly determine the maximal antichains that get changed when a new event arrives. In this chapter, the problem is circumvented by building the lattice of strict ideals instead of the lattice of maximal antichains. If S is a strict ideal of P, then it continues to be one on arrival of x so long as x is a maximal element of $P \cup \{x\}$. The lattice of strict ideals is isomorphic to the lattice of maximal antichains but easier to implement via an incremental algorithm.

Definition 15.5 (Strict Ideal) *A set Y is a strict ideal of a poset $P = (X, \leq)$, if there exists an antichain $A \subseteq X$ such that $D(A) = Y$.*

Definition 15.6 (Lattice of Strict Ideals of a Poset) *For a given poset $P = (X, \leq)$, its lattice of strict ideals is the poset formed with the set of all the strict ideals of P under the set inclusion order.*

Figure 15.2 shows a poset with the three isomorphic lattices: the lattice of maximal ideals, the lattice of maximal antichains, and the lattice of strict ideals. To go from the lattice of maximal ideals to the lattice of maximal antichains, a maximal ideal Q is mapped to the antichain $maximal(Q)$. Conversely, a maximal antichain A is mapped to the maximal ideal $D[A]$. To go from the lattice of antichains to the lattice of strict ideals, a maximal antichain A is mapped to the set $D(A)$. Conversely, a strict ideal Z is mapped to an antichain as the minimal elements in Z^c, the complement of Z. For example, when Z equals $\{b, c\}$, its complement is $\{a, d, e, f\}$. The set of the minimal elements of the set $\{a, d, e, f\}$ is $\{a, f\}$, which is the antichain corresponding to $\{b, c\}$. The correctness of this mapping is shown in the proof of correctness of ILMA algorithm (Theorem 15.7).

15.3   AN INCREMENTAL ALGORITHM BASED ON UNION CLOSURE

We now give an incremental algorithm to compute the lattice of maximal antichains. The ILMA algorithm is a modification of the algorithm given by Nourine and Raynaud [NR99] based on computing the lattice of strict ideals.

The ILMA algorithm, shown in Figure 15.3, is based on computing closure under union of strict ideals. It takes as input the poset P, an element x, and the lattice of maximal antichains of P. The poset and the lattice are assumed to be represented using vector clocks. It outputs the lattice of maximal antichains of $P' = P \cup \{x\}$. At step 1, we compute the vector clock corresponding to the set $D(x)$. The vector clock for x, V corresponds to $D[x]$. By removing x from the set $D[x]$, we get $D(x)$. The removal of x is accomplished by decrementing $S[i]$ in step 1. At step 2, we add S to L and make L closed under union.

The above-mentioned algorithm can also be used to compute the lattice of maximal antichains of any poset in an offline manner by repeatedly invoking the algorithm with elements of the poset in any total order consistent with the poset. To start the algorithm, the initial poset P would be a minimal element of P and the corresponding lattice L would be a singleton element corresponding to the empty strict downset.

We now show the correctness of the algorithm.

Input: P: a finite poset as a list of vector clocks
$\qquad$ L: lattice of maximal antichains as a balanced binary tree of vector
$\qquad$ clocks
$\qquad$ x: new element
Output: L' := Lattice of maximal antichains of $P \cup \{x\}$ initially L

//Step 1: Compute the set $S := D(x)$
Let V be the vector clock for x on process P_i;
$S := V$;
$S[i] := S[i] - 1$;

//Step 2: Add S and take closure with respect to union
if $S \notin L$ **then**
$\qquad$ $L' := L' \cup \{S\}$;
$\qquad$ **forall** vectors $W \in L$ **do**
$\qquad\qquad$ **if** $max(W, S) \notin L$ **then** $L' := L' \cup max(W, S)$;

Figure 15.3   The algorithm ILMA for construction of lattice of maximal antichains.

Theorem 15.7 *The lattice L' constructed by ILMA algorithm is isomorphic to the lattice of maximal antichains of P'.*

Proof: It is easy to verify that every vector in L' is a strict ideal I of the poset $P' = P \cup \{x\}$. By induction, we can assume that L contains all the strict ideals of P. Step (1) adds the strict ideal for $D(x)$ and step (2) takes its union with all existing strict ideals. Since *max* is an idempotent operation, it is sufficient to iterate over L once.

The bijection from L' to the set of maximal antichains is as follows. Let I be a strict ideal in L', i.e., there exists an antichain A such that $D(A) = I$. Let I^c denote the complement of I, and let B equal to the set of the minimal elements of I^c. Thus, $B = minimal(I^c)$. B is an antichain because it contains minimal elements of I^c.

It can be shown that B is a unique antichain for every strict ideal I. To show that B is a maximal antichain, it is sufficient to show that $D(B) \cup U[B] = X$. Since $U[minimal(I^c)] = I^c$, we get that $U[B] = I^c$ by definition of B. We now show that $D(B) \supseteq I$ from which our claim will follow because $I \cup I^c = X$. Since $A \subseteq minimal(I^c)$, we get that $A \subseteq B$ by definition of B. Since $D(A) = I$, we get $D(B) \supseteq I$. Hence, $D(B) \cup U[B] = X$.

∎

The time complexity of ILMA is dominated by step 2. Checking if the vector is in L requires $O(w \log m)$ time if L is kept as a balanced binary search tree of vector clocks. Thus, the time complexity of step 2 is $O(wm \log m)$. By repeatedly invoking ILMA algorithm for a maximal element, we can construct DM completion of a poset with n elements in $O(nwm \log m)$ time. The space complexity is dominated by storage requirements for L. With implicit representation, we have to store m elements where each element is stored as a vector of dimension w of coordinates each of size $O(\log n)$. Hence, the overall space complexity is $O(mw \log n)$.

15.4   AN INCREMENTAL ALGORITHM BASED ON BFS

In the ILMA algorithm, we traverse the lattice L for every element x. It requires us to maintain the lattice L, which may be exponentially bigger than poset P, making the algorithm impractical for large posets. We now show an online algorithm OLMA, which does not require the lattice L but only uses the poset P. Let M be the set of new elements (strict ideals) generated due to x. The time complexity of OLMA is dependent on the size of M independent of the size of the lattice L.

The incremental online algorithm OLMA is shown in Figure 15.4. At lines (1) and (2), we compute the vector S for the set $D(x)$. At line (4), we check if S is already in $L_{MA}(P)$. Note that we do not store the lattice $L_{MA}(P)$. The check at line (4) is done by checking if S is a strict ideal of P. If this is the case, we are done and M is an empty set. Otherwise, we need to enumerate all strict ideals that are reachable from S in the lattice $L_{MA}(P')$. We do so in lines (5)–(15) by traversing the strict ideals greater than or equal to S in the BFS order. The set $\mathcal{T}$ consists of strict ideals that have not been explored yet. At line (7), we remove the smallest strict ideal H and enumerate it at line (8). To find the set of strict ideals that are reachable by taking union with one additional event e, we explore the next event e after the ideal H along every process. There are two cases to consider.

If $(D(e) \subseteq H)$, then the smallest event on process k that will generate new strict ideal by taking union with H is the successor of e on process k, $succ(e)$, if it exists. Since $D(succ(e))$ contains e which is not in H, we are guaranteed that $max(H, D(succ(e)))$ is strictly greater than H. It is also a strict ideal because it corresponds to union of two strict ideals, H and $D(succ(e))$.

If $(D(e) \nsubseteq H)$, then the smallest event on process k that will generate new strict ideal by taking union with H is e. We add to $\mathcal{T}$ the strict ideal $max(H, D(e))$.

It is left as an exercise to show that this method of BFS traversal is guaranteed to explore all strict ideals greater than or equal to $D(x)$ (see Exercise 1).

The function $levelCompare$ in 15.4 provides a total order on all vectors. The vector H deleted is the smallest in $\mathcal{T}$. Any vector that we add due to H is strictly greater than H (either at line (11) or line (13)). Hence, once a vector has been deleted from $\mathcal{T}$, it can never be added back again.

We now analyze the time and space complexity of the algorithm OLMA. Lines (7)–(15) are executed for every strict ideal in M. Suppose that the number of strict ideals greater than or equal to $D(x)$ is m_x. The foreach loop at line (9) is executed w times. Computing max of two vectors at lines (11) and (13) take $O(w)$ time. Adding it to the set $\mathcal{T}$ takes $O(w \log w_L)$ time if $\mathcal{T}$ is maintained as a balanced binary tree of the vectors, where w_L is the maximum size of $\mathcal{T}$. Hence, the total time complexity for enumerating M is $O(m_x w^2 \log w_L)$. Recall that the ILMA algorithm traversed over the entire lattice when adding a new element resulting in $O(wm \log m)$ complexity for incremental construction.

Input: a finite poset P, x maximal element in $P' = P \cup \{x\}$
Output: enumerate M such that $L_{MA}(P') = L_{MA}(P) \cup M$

(1) $S :=$ the vector clock for x on process P_i;
(2) $S[i] := S[i] - 1$;
(3)   **if** S is not a strict ideal of P **then**
(4)   // BFS(S): Do Breadth-First-Search traversal of M
(5) $\mathcal{T} :=$ set of vectors initially $\{S\}$;
(6)   **while** $\mathcal{T}$ is nonempty **do**
(7) $H :=$ delete the smallest vector from $\mathcal{T}$ in the levelCompare order;
(8)   enumerate H;
(9)   **foreach** process k with next event e **do**
(10)   **if** $(D(e) \subseteq H)$ **then**
(11)   **if** $succ(e)$ exists **then** $\mathcal{T} := \mathcal{T} \cup \{max(H, D(succ(e)))\}$;
(12)   **else**
(13) $\mathcal{T} := \mathcal{T} \cup \{max(H, D(e))\}$;
(14)   **endfor**;
(15)   **endwhile**;
(16)   **endif**;

         int levelCompare(VectorClock a, VectorClock b)
(1)   **if** $(a.\text{sum}() > b.\text{sum}())$ return 1; // $a > b$
(2)   **else if** $(a.\text{sum}() < b.\text{sum}())$ return -1; // $a < b$
(3)   **for** (int $i = 0$; i $<$ $a.\text{size}()$; i++)
(4)   **if** $(a[i] > b[i])$ return 1;
(5)   **if** $(a[i] < b[i])$ return -1;
(6)   **return** 0; // $a = b$

Figure 15.4   The algorithm OLMA for construction of lattice of strict ideals.

We now compute the complexity of the OLMA algorithm to build the lattice for the entire poset. For simplicity, we bound m_x by m. Since the OLMA algorithm would be called n times, the time complexity is $O(nmw^2 \log w_L)$.

The space complexity of the OLMA algorithm is $O(w_L w \log n)$ bits to store the set $\mathcal{T}$ where w_L is the maximum size that $\mathcal{T}$ will take during BFS enumeration.

15.5   TRAVERSAL OF THE LATTICE OF MAXIMAL ANTICHAINS

In some applications (such as global predicate detection discussed in Section 15.6), we may not be interested in storing L_{MA} but simply enumerating all its elements (or storing only those elements that satisfy given property). Recall that the size of $L_{MA}(P)$

may be exponential in the size of the poset P in the worst case. In this section, we consider the problem of enumerating all the maximal antichains of a computation in an offline manner. In the OLMA algorithm, we enumerated all strict ideals greater than or equal to $D(x)$, when x arrives. We can use the OLMA algorithm in an offline manner as well. We simply use $BFS(\{\})$ instead of $BFS(D(x))$ that enumerates all the strict ideals. We call this algorithm BFS-MA.

We now show that the space complexity can be further reduced by using DFS enumeration of L_{MA}. The DFS enumeration requires storage proportional to the height of L_{MA}, which is at most n.

In the previous section, we had used the lattice of strict ideals instead of lattice of maximal ideals. In this section, we use the lattice of maximal ideals because the lattice of maximal ideals is closed under intersection, which allows us to find the smallest maximal ideal that contains a given set (at line (3) in 15.5).

One of the main difficulties is to ensure that we do not visit the same maximal antichain ideal twice because we do not store all the nodes of the lattice explicitly and hence cannot use the standard technique of marking a node visited during traversal. The solution we use is similar to that used for the lattice of ideals [AV01] and the lattice of normal cuts [Gar12]. Let $pred(H)$ be the set of all maximal ideals that are covered by H in the lattice. We use the total order $levelOrder$ on the set $pred(H)$. We make a recursive call on H from the maximal ideal G iff G is the biggest maximal ideal in $pred(K)$ in the total order given by $levelOrder$. To find $pred(H)$, we first note that every maximal antichain of a poset P is also a maximal antichain of its dual P^d. Hence, the lattice of maximal antichains of P is isomorphic to the lattice of maximal antichains of P^d. Traversing $L_{MA}(P)$ in the upward direction (in the Hasse diagram) is equivalent to traversing $L_{MA}(P^d)$ in the backward direction.

The algorithm for DFS enumeration is shown in Figure 15.5. From any maximal ideal G, we explore all enabled events to find maximal ideals with at least one additional event. There are at most w enabled events and for each event it takes $O(w^2)$ time to compute the smallest maximal ideal K at line (3). At line (4), we check if K covers G using the characterization provided by Reuter [Reu91] as follows. A maximal ideal K covers the maximal ideal G in the lattice of maximal ideals iff $(K - G) \cup (U[Maximal(G)] - U[Maximal(K)])$ induces a complete height-one subposet of P with $(K - G)$ as the maximal elements and $(U[Maximal(G)] - U[Maximal(K)])$ as minimal element. This check can be performed in $O(w^2)$ time. In line (5), we traverse K using recursive DFS call only if M equals G. Since there can be w predecessor for K and it takes $O(w^2)$ time to compute each predecessor; the total time complexity to determine whether K can be inserted is $O(w^3)$. Computing M requires $O(w^3)$ time. Hence, the overall time complexity of the algorithm is $O(mw^4)$.

The main space requirement of the DFS algorithm is the stack used for recursion. Every time the recursion level is increases, the size of the maximal ideal increases by at least 1. Hence, the maximum depth of the recursion is n. Therefore, the space requirement is $O(nw \log n)$ bits because we only need to store vectors of dimension w at each recursion level.

Algorithm DFS-MaximalIdeals(G)
Input: a finite poset P, starting state G
Output: DFS Enumeration of all maximal ideals of P
(1)   enumerate(G);
(2)   **foreach** event e enabled in G do
(3) K := smallest maximal ideal containing $Q := G \cup \{e\}$;
(4)   **if** K does not cover G then go to the next event;
(5) M := get-Max-predecessor(K) ;
(6)   **if** $M = G$ then
(7)   DFS-MaximalIdeals(K);

function VectorClock **get-Max-predecessor**(K)
//returns the predecessor that is the biggest in the levelCompare order

(1) H = maximal ideal in P^d that has the same maximal antichain as K
(2)   // find the maximal predecessor using maximal ideals in the dual poset
(3)   **foreach** event e enabled in the cut H in P^d do
(4)   *temp* := advance along event e in P^d from cut H;
(5)   // get the set of maximal ideals reachable in P^d
(6)   *pred*(e) := smallest maximal ideal containing *temp* that covers H
(7)   **return** the biggest *pred*(e) in the levelCompare order;

Figure 15.5   Algorithm DFS-MA for DFS enumeration of lattice of maximal antichains.

15.6   APPLICATION: DETECTING ANTICHAIN-CONSISTENT PREDICATES

Global predicate detection problem has applications in distributed debugging, testing, and software fault-tolerance. The problem can be stated as follows. Given a distributed computation (either in an online manner or in an offline manner), and a global predicate B (a Boolean function on the lattice of consistent global states), determine if there exists a consistent global state that satisfies B. The global predicate detection problem is NP-complete [CG98] even for the restricted case when the predicate B is a singular 2CNF formula of local predicates [MG01a]. The key problem is that the lattice of consistent global states may be exponential in the size of the poset. Given the importance of the problem in software testing and monitoring of distributed systems, there is strong motivation to find classes of predicates for which the underlying space of consistent global states can be traversed efficiently. In this section, we describe an approach in which we construct the lattice of maximal antichains L_{MA} instead of the lattice of consistent global states L_I. The lattice L_{MA} is usually much smaller (even exponentially smaller) than L_I. We describe a class called *antichain* predicate that satisfies the property that they hold on the lattice L_I iff they hold on the lattice L_{MA}. We give several examples of predicates that occur in practice which belong to this class.

We first define the class of antichain-consistent predicates. A global predicate B is an *antichain-consistent* predicate if its evaluation depends only on maximal events of a consistent global state and if it is true on a subset of processes, then presence of additional processes does not falsify the predicate. Formally,

Definition 15.8 (Antichain-Consistent Predicate) *A global predicate B defined on L_I is an antichain-consistent predicate if for all consistent global states G and H:*

$$(maximal(G) \subseteq maximal(H)) \land B(G) \Rightarrow B(H)$$

We now give several examples of antichain-consistent predicate.

- *Violation of resource usage*: The predicate, B, "there are more than k concurrent activation of certain service," is antichain-consistent.
- *Global control point*: The predicate, B, "process P_1 is at line 35 and P_2 is at line 23 concurrently," is also antichain-consistent.

We can now show the following result.

Theorem 15.9 *There exists a consistent global state that satisfies an antichain-consistent predicate B iff there exists a maximal ideal that satisfies B.*

Proof: Let G be a consistent global state that satisfies B. If G is a maximal ideal, we are done. Otherwise, consider G^c. Since G is not a maximal ideal, there exists $y \in minimal(G^c)$ such that y is incomparable to all elements in $maximal(G)$. It is easy to see that $G_1 = G \cup \{y\}$ is also a consistent global state which is contained in H. Furthermore, $maximal(G) \subseteq maximal(G_1)$. Since B is antichain-consistent, it is also true in G_1. If G_1 is a maximal ideal, we are done. Otherwise, by repeating this procedure, we obtain H such that $maximal(G) \subseteq maximal(H)$, and H is a maximal ideal. From the definition of antichain-consistent, we get that $B(H)$.

The converse is obvious because every maximal ideal is also an ideal.

■

Hence, instead of constructing the lattice of ideals, we can use algorithms in Sections 15.3 and 15.5 to detect an antichain-consistent global predicate resulting in significant, possibly exponential, reduction in time complexity.

15.7   CONSTRUCTION AND ENUMERATION OF WIDTH ANTICHAIN LATTICE

For many global predicates, we are interested in the last event executed at all processes. For example, consider a set of processes that execute three kinds of events: internal, send event, and *blocking receive* event. The blocking receive event blocks the process until it receives a message from some process. It is clear that if there are no in-transit messages and the last event executed at all processes is a receive event, then the system has a communication deadlock. In this example, we require that the last event at each process be blocking receive. Even if one process is left out, that process could send messages to all other processes unblocking them. This example motivates the following definition.

Definition 15.10 (Width Antichain) *An antichain A is a width antichain of poset P if its size is equal to the width of the poset.*

Clearly, the set of all width antichains is contained in the set of all maximal antichains, which in turn is contained in the set of all antichains. It is left as an exercise to show that the set of all width antichains (or maximum-sized antichains) form a distributive lattice [Dil50, Koh83], a sublattice of the lattice of all antichains.

On the basis of width antichains, we can define

Definition 15.11 (Width Ideal) *An ideal Q of a poset $P = (X, \leq)$ is a width ideal if maximal(Q) is a width antichain.*

Definition 15.12 (Width Predicate) *A global predicate B defined on L_I of a distributed computation on w processes is a width predicate if $B(G) \Rightarrow |maximal(G)| = w$.*

We now give some examples of width predicate.

- *Barrier synchronization*: The predicate, B, "Every process has made a call to the method `barrier`," is a width predicate.
- *Deadlock for dining philosophers*: The predicate, B, "Every philosopher has picked up a fork," is also a width predicate.

Clearly, to detect a width antichain predicate, it is sufficient to construct or traverse the lattice of the width ideals. Here, we simply give the ideas behind the algorithm to construct or traverse the lattice.

Theorem 15.13 *Given any finite poset P, there exists an algorithm to enumerate all its width antichains in $O(w^2 m)$ time where w is the width of the poset P and m is the size of the lattice of width antichains.*

Proof:
The width ideal lattice is a sublattice of the lattice of ideals with the same join and meet operations. Since the lattice of ideals is distributive, so is the width ideal lattice. Owing to its distributive property, this lattice is completely characterized by its join-irreducible elements. The join-irreducible elements of $L_{WA}(P)$ are given by

$$J(L_{WA}(P)) = \{\text{the least width ideal that contains } e \mid e \in P\}$$

Given $J(L_{WA}(P))$, the poset formed by the join-irreducibles, one can construct the distributive lattice of all ideals by using algorithms to enumerate all ideals. There is

TABLE 15.4   Summary of Lattices Based on Antichains

Lattice	Antichain Property	Meet	Join	Distributive
Ideals	All antichains	Intersection	Union	Yes
Maximal Ideals	Maximal Antichains	Intersection	Based on meet	No
Width Ideals	Antichains of size width	Intersection	Union	Yes

1-1 correspondence between width ideals of P and ideals of $J(L_{WA}(P))$. Hence, it is sufficient to give an algorithm to construct $J(L_{WA}(P))$. To this end, define a predicate B to be true on an ideal G iff $maximal(G)$ forms a width antichain. The predicate B is a regular predicate with an efficient advancement property, and therefore, we can compute the slice (the set of all join-irreducibles) of P with respect to B in $w^2 n$ time where n is the size of the poset P. Once we have the slice for B, we can enumerate all its ideals in $w^2 m$ time using the algorithms to enumerate ideals provided in Chapter 14 where m is the number of width ideals of P (or, equivalently the number of ideals of the slice for B).

■

Table 15.4 gives a summary of the three lattices discussed in the chapter. The lattice of ideals has 1-1 correspondence with the lattice of all antichains. Given an ideal G, the set $maximal(G)$ is an antichain. Given an antichain, A, $D[A]$ is an ideal. In this lattice, the meet and join of two elements correspond to the intersection and the union of ideals. The lattice of maximal ideals has 1-1 correspondence with the lattice of all maximal antichains. The meet in this lattice is the set intersection, but the join is not union. It is defined based on the meets in the following standard manner: the join of two maximal ideals G and H is the meet of all maximal ideals that contain both G and H. The lattice of width ideals is in 1-1 correspondence with the antichains of size width. This lattice is a sublattice of the lattice of ideals with the meet and the join operations corresponding to the intersection and the union operations.

15.8   LEXICAL ENUMERATION OF CLOSED SETS

In this section, we give an algorithm to enumerate all the elements of the lattice of maximal antichains. The algorithm, due to Ganter and Reuter [GR91], is general enough to enumerate any lattice that is a subset of the Boolean lattice (or a product space) and is defined using a closure operator as defined in Chapter 6.

The algorithm in Figure 15.6 is a generalization of the algorithm to enumerate all ideals in the lex order presented in Figure 14.5. At line (8), we compute H as the closure of the set K. If H contains any new event from chains $P_1..P_{k-1}$, we go to the next iteration of the *for* loop; otherwise, H is the next lexically bigger closed set as shown by the following lemma.

```
lexTraverseClosedSets(P)

Input: a poset P
Output: All Closed sets in lex order
var
        G:array[1 …w] of int initially ∀i : G[i] = 0; // current closed set
        K:array[1 …w] of int; // K = succ(G, k)
        H:array[1 …w] of int; // H = closure(K)
(1)     if G is closed enumerate(G);
(2)     while (G ≠ top) do // where top is the largest closed set
(3)         for k := w down to 1 do
(4)             if (there is no next event on Pₖ) continue;
                // compute K := succ(G, k)
(5)             K := G;
(6)             K[k] := K[k] + 1; // advance on Pₖ
(7)             for j := k + 1 to w do K[j] := 0;
                // compute closure(K); and determine if it is next in the lex
                  order
(8)             H := closure(K)
(9)             if (∃j : 1 ≤ j ≤ k − 1 : H[j] > G[j]) continue;
(10)            G := H;
(11)        endfor
(12)        enumerate(G);
(13)    endwhile;
```

Figure 15.6   An algorithm for traversal of closed sets in lex order.

Theorem 15.14 *The set H at line (10) is the next closed set in the lexical order after G.*

Proof: H is a closed set because it is equal to $closure(K)$. We only need to show that it is the next closed set in the lexical order. Since K is lexically bigger than G, so is $closure(K)$. Hence, H is a closed set bigger than G. We only need to show that there is no closed set bigger than G and smaller than H. Suppose, if possible, there is another closed set F bigger than G and smaller than H. Let f be the smallest index such that $F[f] > G[f]$. If $f < k$, then we get that $F > H$ because due to line (9), for all j smaller than k, $H[j] = G[j]$. If $f = k$, then F is at least as big as K because K has $K[j]$ equal to 0 for $j > k$. Hence, $closure(F) \supseteq closure(K) = H$. If $f > k$, then we would have tried F or a set smaller than F as K because at line (3), we try k in decreasing order. However, no index bigger than k was found.

■

TABLE 15.5   Definition of Closure Operators for Lattices

Lattice	Closure (the condition for Y to be a closed set)
Ideals	$ideal(Y) \equiv (f \in Y) \wedge (e \leq f) \Rightarrow e \in Y$
Normal cuts	$Y^{ul} = Y$
Maximal ideals	$ideal(Y) \wedge (f \notin Y \Rightarrow \exists e \in max(Y) : e \leq f)$
Maximum antichains	$ideal(Y) \wedge (|max(Y)| = width(P))$

Assuming that the closure of the set can be done in $O(w^2)$ time, we get the overall complexity of the algorithm as $O(w^3 C)$, where C is the number of closed sets.

Note that this algorithm allows us to enumerate all the following sets as shown in Table 15.5.

1. *The set of all ideals*: An ideal of a poset $P = (X, \leq)$ is a simply a subset of X that is closed under $\leq$. A set $Y \subseteq X$ is an ideal iff it satisfies the following condition:

$$(f \in Y) \wedge (e \leq f) \Rightarrow e \in Y.$$

However, for this case, we have already seen a more efficient algorithm in Chapter 14 with time complexity $O(w^2 M)$ instead of $O(w^3 M)$ where M is the number of ideals and w is the number of chains in P. There, we had to apply exactly one closure operator before getting the next lexically bigger closed set.

2. *The set of all Normal cuts*: A normal cut of $P = (X, \leq)$ is simply a subset Y of X such that $Y^{ul} = Y$. It was shown in Chapter 6 that ul is a closure operator.

3. *The set of all maximal ideals (or, the set of maximal antichains)*: The lattice of all maximal antichains is isomorphic to the lattice of all maximal ideals as shown earlier. An ideal Y for a poset $(X, \leq)$ is a maximal ideal iff it satisfies the following condition:

$$f \notin Y \Rightarrow \exists e \in max(Y) : e \leq f.$$

We leave it as an exercise to show that the definition satisfies properties for closure.

4. *The set of all width ideals (or, the antichains of size width)*. It is easy to show that if G and H are width ideals, then so is $G \cap H$. For any poset, $P = (X, \leq)$, if $max(X)$ is a width ideal then, the set of all width ideals forms a topped intersection-closed family. Hence, for any subset Y of X, there is a smallest ideal, Z, such that its maximal elements form an antichain of size equal to the width of the poset. The set Z is closure of X. We leave this claim also as an exercise.

TABLE 15.6   Generation of Lattices based on Unions

Lattice	Basis	Notation for Basis Elements
Ideals	Principal ideals	$D[x]$ for all $x \in X$
Normal Cuts	Co-principal ideals	$X - D[x]$ for all $x \in X$
Maximal Antichain Ideals	Strict principal ideals	$D(x)$ for all $x \in X$
Width Ideals	Least width-sized antichain ideals	$J(L_{WA}(P))$

15.9   CONSTRUCTION OF LATTICES BASED ON UNION CLOSURE

In this section, we show that all four lattices—the lattice of ideals, normal cuts, maximal ideals, and width ideals—can also be constructed using union closures. In Figure 15.3, we presented an algorithm to construct the lattice of maximum antichain ideals based on union closure of strict principal ideals. Similar algorithms can be designed to construct the lattice of ideals, the lattice of normal cuts, and the lattice of width ideals based on the union closure.

Table 15.6 shows the basis elements for union closure for various lattices corresponding to a poset $(X \leq)$. The notation $J(L_{WA}(P))$ corresponds to the join-irreducible elements of the lattice of width antichains of P.

15.10   PROBLEMS

15.1. Show that the algorithm OLMA enumerates all strict ideals greater than or equal to $D(x)$.

15.2. Give an algorithm for incremental construction of the lattice of maximal antichains based on DFS traversal.

15.3. Give parallel algorithms for online and offline construction of the lattice of maximal antichains.

15.4. Show that if G and H are maximal ideals, then so is $G \cap H$.

15.5. Show that if G and H are width ideals, then so is $G \cap H$.

15.6. Show that all four predicates on Y defined in Table 15.5 define closed families of subsets.

15.7. Give algorithms to compute closure of any set Y for all closure operators defined in Table 15.5.

15.8. Show that the basis elements shown in Table 15.6 indeed generate the corresponding lattices.

15.11 BIBLIOGRAPHIC REMARKS

Some earlier incremental algorithms for the lattice of maximal antichains are by Jourdan, Rampon, and Jard [JRJ94] and Nourine and Raynaud [NR99, NR02]. The discussion of ILMA and OLMA algorithms is taken from [Gar13]. The discussion of lexical enumeration is taken from [GR91] and [Gar03]. Construction of lattices based on union and intersection closure is also discussed in Nourine and Raynaud [NR99, NR02].

16

DIMENSION THEORY

16.1 INTRODUCTION

The notion of dimension of a poset was introduced in a seminal paper by Dushnik and Miller [DM41]. The dimension of a poset, roughly speaking, is the dimension of the Euclidean space in which the poset can be embedded. The dimension of a poset reveals important information about the poset. For example, many problems that are algorithmically hard for general posets, such as counting the number of ideals, are easy for posets of dimension less than or equal to two. As we saw in Chapter 2, the concept of dimension also lets us represent the order relation of a poset in an implicit manner. The dimension theory of ordered sets has been an active area of research and the reader will find a good survey of results in the book by Trotter[Tro92]. In this chapter, we cover only the most basic results and their applications.

We begin with the classical dimension theory based on notion of chain realizers. A chain realizer shows how a poset with n elements and dimension d can be represented using d-dimensional vectors of coordinates from $0..n - 1$. In Section 16.7, we discuss string realizers that also use d coordinates but each coordinate may use fewer bits. Finally, in Section 16.8, we discuss rectangle realizers that always require less or equal number of coordinates, with each coordinate requiring possibly fewer bits than required by the chain realizers.

16.2 CHAIN REALIZERS

Theorem 2.1 in Chapter 2 shows that every poset has a linear extension. In dimension theory, we study if a poset can equivalently be represented using a small number of its linear extensions. Let the operation of intersection of partial orders on the same ground set be defined as the intersection of the partial order relations. It is easy to verify that intersection of two partial orders is a partial order. Further, every finite poset P is the intersection of all linear extensions of P. However, we may need only a subset of these linear extensions to obtain P, which brings us to the following definition.

Definition 16.1 (Realizer) *A family $R = \{L_1, L_2, \ldots, L_t\}$ of linear orders on X is called a realizer of a partial order $P = (X, \leq)$ if $P = \cap_{L_i \in R} L_i$.*

Definition 16.2 (Dimension) *The dimension of $P = (X, \leq)$, denoted by dim(P), is the size of the smallest realizer.*

As a simple example consider the poset P defined on $X = \{a, b, c\}$ with $\leq$ relation defined as

$$\leq = \{(a, b), (a, c)\}$$

The linear order $L_1 = \{(a, b), (b, c), (a, c)\}$ orders b less than c. The linear order $L_2 = \{(a, c), (c, b), (a, b)\}$ orders c less than b. It is easy to verify that when we take the intersection of L_1 and L_2, we get $\{(a, b), (a, c)\}$. Hence, $\{L_1, L_2\}$ is a realizer of P.

For the poset $P = (X, \leq)$ shown in Figure 16.1, there are five linear extensions. The reader can verify that the intersection of these orders is exactly P. Clearly, $dim(X, \leq) \geq 2$ since it is not a chain. On the other hand, $dim(X, \leq) \leq 2$ since $R = \{L_4, L_5\}$ is a realizer of P.

The reader should note the following facts. First, if $x \leq y$, then x is less than y in all linear orders L_i, because each of L_i is a linear extension of P. If $x||y$ in P, then the realizer of P must have at least one linear extension in which x is less than y and another linear extension in which y is less than x.

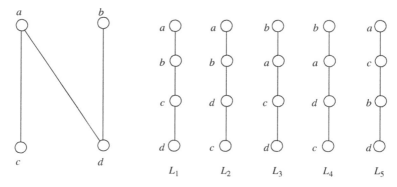

Figure 16.1 An example of a realizer.

16.3   STANDARD EXAMPLES OF DIMENSION THEORY

The following family of examples is quite useful in studying dimension theory. For $n \geq 3$, let $S_n = (X, \leq)$ be the height two poset with $X = \{a_1, a_2, \ldots, a_n\} \cup \{b_1, b_2, \ldots, b_n\}$. The $<$ relation is defined as follows. $\forall a_i, b_j \in X$, $a_i < b_j$ in S_n iff $i \neq j$. The poset S_n is called the *standard example* of an n-dimensional poset. An example is shown in Figure 16.2 for n equal to 5.

The standard example shows that the dimension of a poset can be large.

Theorem 16.3 (Dushnik-Miller [DM41]) $dim(S_n) = n.$

Proof:

- $dim(S_n) \leq n$:
  For each $i = 1, 2, \ldots, n$, define a linear order L_i on X by
  $L_i = [a_1, a_2, \ldots, a_{i-1}, a_{i+1}, \ldots, a_n, b_i, a_i, b_1, b_2, \ldots, b_{i-1}, b_{i+1}, \ldots, b_n]$. Then $R = \{L_1, L_2, \ldots, L_n\}$ is a realizer, so $dim(S_n) \leq n$. Note that a_i is less than b_i in all linear orders except L_i.

- $dim(S_n) \geq n$:
  Let $R = \{L_1, L_2, \ldots, L_t\}$ be any realizer of S_n. Suppose, if possible, $t < n$. Since $a_i || b_i$ in P, there exists at least one linear order L in R in which b_i is less than a_i. We will say that L *reverses* the pair (a_i, b_i) if b_i is less than a_i in L. Since there are n pairs (a_i, b_i) and t linear orders where $t < n$, by pigeonhole principle, there exists at least one linear order L_s which reverses at least two pairs. Let the two pairs that it reverses be (a_i, b_i) and (a_j, b_j). Then $b_i < a_i$ and $b_j < a_j$ in L_s. However, $a_j < b_i$ and $a_i < b_j$ in P, so $a_j < b_i$ and $a_i < b_j$ in L_s. Thus, $a_i < b_j < a_j < b_i < a_i$ in L_s which is clearly false. Therefore, $t \geq n$. Hence, $dim(S_n) \geq n$.

∎

We now show the relationship between the dimension of a poset and the Euclidean dimension. Let $P = (X, \leq_P)$ and $Q = (Y, \leq_Q)$ be two posets. A map f from X to Y is called an *embedding* if for any $x, x' \in P$

$$x \leq_P x' \equiv f(x) \leq_Q f(x').$$

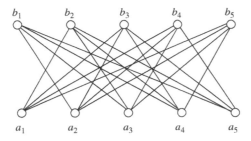

Figure 16.2   Standard example S_5.

Clearly, if a poset P has dimension n, then there exists an embedding of P in $\mathcal{R}^n$. Every element $x \in P$ is mapped into a vector of dimension n such that the coordinate i of the vector equals the position of x in L_i of a minimum realizer of P.

16.4   RELATIONSHIP BETWEEN THE DIMENSION AND THE WIDTH OF A POSET

In this section, we show that the dimension of a poset is always less than or equal to the width of the poset. To prove this result, we first show a lemma due to Hiraguchi, which shows existence of a linear order with a special property for any given chain.

Lemma 16.4 (Hiraguchi [Hir55]) *Let* $P = (X, \leq)$ *be a poset and let* $C \subseteq X$ *be a chain. Then, there exist linear extensions* L_1, L_2 *of P such that*

1. $y < x$ in L_1 for every $x, y \in X$ with $x \in C$ and $x||y$ in P.
2. $y > x$ in L_2 for every $x, y \in X$ with $x \in C$ and $x||y$ in P.

Proof: We give a constructive proof of the first claim. The second claim is similar. We use induction on the size of C. When C is empty, the claim is vacuously true. Let z be the maximum element of the chain C. We partition the poset into two sets: $U[z]$, the set of all elements that are greater than or equal to z and $X - U[z]$. In the subposet $(X - U[z], \leq)$, the size of C has decreased by one; hence, by induction, there exists a linear extension L_d such that for all $x \in C - \{z\}$ and $y \in X - U[z]$ such that $x||y$, $y < x$ in L_d. Let L_u be any linear extension of the subposet $(U[z], \leq)$. We claim that $L_d < L_u$ is a linear extension of P such that for any $x \in C$ and y incomparable to x, $y < x$. The claim clearly holds for z because all incomparable elements to z appear in L_d and $z \in L_u$. It also holds for all elements of $C - \{z\}$ because if $x \in C - \{z\}$ and $y||x$, then $y \in X - U[z]$.   ∎

Let $P = (X, \leq)$ be a poset with A and B as any two subsets of X. If L is any linear order of P, we say that A is *over* B, denoted by A/B, if

$$\forall a \in A, b \in B : a||b \Rightarrow a > b \text{ in } L$$

Thus, Hiraguchi's lemma claims shows that there exists L_1 that satisfies C/X and L_2 that satisfies X/C. Moreover, it is easy to convert the proof into an efficient algorithm for constructing the linear order.

Theorem 16.5 (Dilworth [Dil50]) *Let* $P = (X, \leq)$ *be a poset. Then* $dim(P) \leq width(P)$.

Proof: We show this theorem by giving a realizer of size $n = width(P)$. By Dilworth's chain partitioning theorem, there exists a partition $X = C_1 \cup C_2 \cup \cdots \cup C_n$, where C_i is a chain for $i = 1, 2, \ldots, n$. We construct a realizer $R = \{L_1, L_2, \ldots, L_n\}$ of P as follows. For each C_i, we construct a linear extension L_i of P such that C_i/X in L_i using the procedure in Lemma 16.4. To show that R is a realizer of the poset, it suffices to show that for every incomparable x and y in P, there exist a linear order in which $x < y$. If $y \in C_i$, then L_i gives us this property.

■

We later show a stronger result that $dim(P) \le width(J(P))$.

A lower bound on the $dim(P)$ can be provided using the width of the subposet of dissectors of P. Let $Dis(P)$ be the subposet formed by dissectors of a finite poset P.

Theorem 16.6 (Reading [Rea02]) *Let $P = (X, \le)$ be a poset. Then $width(Dis((P)) \le dim(P)$.*

We leave its proof as an exercise.

16.5 REMOVAL THEOREMS FOR DIMENSION

In this section, we show that the dimension of a poset does not decrease abruptly when a chain or an element is removed from the poset. The first theorem shows that when a chain is removed, the dimension cannot decrease by more than 2.

Theorem 16.7 (Hiraguchi Chain Removal Theorem [Hir55]) *Let $P = (X, \le)$ be a poset and let $C \subsetneq X$. Then*

$$dim(X, \le) \le 2 + dim(X - C, \le).$$

Proof: Let Q be the poset after removal of the chain C. Let R_Q be any realizer for Q of size t. We show that there exists a realizer of P of size $t + 2$. We first note that any linear order L of Q can be extended to L' such that L' is a linear order of P (see Problem 3). We construct a realizer R_P as follows. It contains t linear orders of R_Q extended for P and two additional linear orders that satisfy C/X and X/C, respectively. Given any pair of incomparable elements $x, y \in X$, we need to show that there exists a linear order in R_P in which $x < y$. If both x and y belong to Q, then one of the linear orders in R_Q puts x before y. If x belongs to C, then the linear order satisfying X/C satisfies $x < y$. If y belongs to C, then the linear order satisfying C/X satisfies $x < y$.

■

The following theorem shows that when a point is removed from the poset, the dimension cannot decrease by more than one.

Theorem 16.8 (Hiraguchi Point Removal Theorem [Hir55]) *Let $P = (X, \le)$ be a poset with $|X| \ge 2$, and $x \in X$. Then*

$$dim(X, \le) \le 1 + dim(X - \{x\}, \le).$$

Proof: Let Q be the poset after removal of the point x. Let R_Q be the realizer of size t for Q. Our goal is to construct a realizer of size $t + 1$ for P. We have to ensure that for every element y incomparable to x, there is one linear order that puts x below y and another one that puts y below x. For R_P, we use first $t - 1$ linear orders from R_Q extended for P. From the last linear order of R_Q, we construct two linear orders L_u and L_d as follows. Let $inc(x)$ be the set of elements incomparable to x. The linear order L_u keeps x above $inc(x)$ and L_d keeps x below $inc(x)$. L_u is given by the order $L_t(D(x) \cup inc(x)) < x < L_t(U(x))$, where the notation $L_t(Z)$ represents the linear order L_t restricted to the set Z. Similarly, L_d is given by the order $L_t(D(x)) < x < L_t(inc(x) \cup U(x))$. To show that R_P is indeed a realizer for P, it is sufficient to show that if $a < b$ in L_t for incomparable a and b, then $a < b$ either in L_u or L_d. If $a < b$ in L_t but not in L_u, then $a \in U(x)$. Similarly, If $a < b$ in L_t but not in L_d, then $b \in D(x)$. However, $a \in U(x)$ and $b \in D(x)$ implies that $b < a$ in P, a contradiction.

■

The previous theorem allows us to remove any point in the poset without decreasing the dimension by more than one. Can we remove two points from the poset such that the dimension does not decrease by more than one? It is clear that we cannot remove any two arbitrary elements (consider the standard example), but are there any two points that we can remove without decreasing the dimension by more than one. This leads us to a famous open problem in dimension theory.

Conjecture: For all posets $P = (X, \leq)$ such that $|X| \geq 4$, there exist $x, y \in X$:

$$dim(X, \leq) \leq 1 + dim(X - \{x, y\}, \leq).$$

Here is an example of a two-point removal theorem (under certain conditions).

Theorem 16.9 *Let x and y be two distinct maximal elements of a poset P such that $D(x) \subseteq D(y)$. Then removal of x and y from P does not decrease the dimension by more than one.*

Proof: Let Q be the poset after removal of x and y. Let R_Q be a realizer for Q. We construct realizer for P as follows. For each linear order L in R_Q, we have the linear order $L < y < x$ in R_P. In addition, to R_P, we add a linear order $D(x) < x < D(y) - D(x) < y < (X - D(y) - \{x, y\})$. It is easy to verify that R_P is a realizer for P.

■

16.6   CRITICAL PAIRS IN THE POSET

We have seen that a crucial property of a realizer of a poset P is that for every incomparable pair (x, y), there exists a linear order in the realizer that reverses the pair. We now introduce the notion of critical pairs which allows us to restrict our attention to a subset of incomparable pairs.

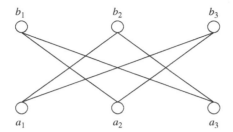

Figure 16.3   Example of a critical pair: (a_1, b_1).

Definition 16.10 (Critical Pair) *Let $P = (X, \leq)$ be a poset with incomparable elements x and y. The ordered pair (x, y) is called a* critical pair *in P if:*

1. *$D(x) \subseteq D(y)$, and*
2. *$U(y) \subseteq U(x)$.*

Observe that if $x < y$, the above-mentioned statements hold trivially. In Figure 16.3, while (a_1, b_1) is a critical pair, (b_1, a_1) is not. In Figure 16.1, (c, b) is a critical pair.

Theorem 16.11 (Rabinovitch and Rival [RR79]) *Let $P = (X, \leq)$ be a poset and R be a family of linear extensions of P. Then, the following statements are equivalent.*

1. *R is a realizer of P.*
2. *For every critical pair (y, x), there is some $L \in R$ for which $x < y$ in L.*

Proof: Let (y, x) be any incomparable pair. We show that there exists a linear order in R that puts $x < y$. It is sufficient to show that there exists a critical pair (y', x') and that any linear order that reverses (y', x') also reverses (y, x). If (y, x) is a critical pair, then we are done with $y' = y$ and $x' = x$. Otherwise, either $\neg(D(y) \subseteq D(x))$ or $\neg(U(x) \subseteq U(y))$. First, suppose $\neg(D(y) \subseteq D(x))$. This implies that there exists z, which is in $D(y)$ but not in $D(x)$. Of all possible z, we choose a minimal element y' in $D(y)$ but not in $D(x)$. The element y' cannot be in $U(x)$ because x and y are incomparable. Hence, x and y' are incomparable. Furthermore, $D(y') \subseteq D(x)$ by minimality of y' in $D(y)$. Moreover, any linear order that puts x below y' also puts x below y. If (y', x) is a critical pair, we are done. Otherwise, from $\neg(U(x) \subseteq U(y'))$, we get that there exists a maximal $x' > x$ in P such that x' and y are incomparable. It is easy to verify that (y', x') is a critical pair and any linear order that reverses (y', x') must have $x \leq x' < y \leq y'$ and hence reverses (y, x).   ∎

16.7   STRING REALIZERS

If a poset P with n elements has dimension d, then we can assign an implicit code to each element $x \in P$ such that the order relation between any two elements $x, y \in P$ can be determined using their code. The code of any element x is a d-dimensional vector v_x where $v_x[i]$ equals the rank of x in the linear order L_i of the realizer for P. By the definition of the realizer, we have that

$$x < y \equiv \forall i : v_x[i] < v_y[i].$$

In this scheme, each element in x requires $d \log n$ bits. In this section, we look at an alternative way of encoding posets that requires fewer bits.

As a motivating example, consider A_n, the poset on n elements that form an antichain of size n. Intuitively, this poset has no asymmetry and should require least number of bits to encode. The binary relation corresponding to A_n is the empty set. However, when we use a chain realizer for encoding this poset, we end up using $2n \log n$ bits for encoding the poset—$2 \log n$ bits for each element because the dimension of A_n is two. In the encoding scheme proposed in this section, we will use just n bits to encode this poset. If we require that the code of any element be at least one bit, this is clearly the best possible encoding for an antichain. We use a type of poset called strings that are generalization of both chains and antichains as the building block for realizers to reduce the number of bits required to encode a poset. We first give the definition of a *string*.

Definition 16.12 (string) *A poset $P = (X, \leq)$ is a string if and only if $\exists f : X \to \mathcal{N}$ such that $\forall x, y \in X : x < y$ iff $f(x) < f(y)$*

The set of elements in a string which have the same f value is called a *rank*. For example, a poset $(X, \leq)$ where $X = \{a, b, c, d\}$ and $\leq = \{(a, b), (a, c), (a, d), (b, d), (c, d)\}$ is a string because we can assign $f(a) = 0$, $f(b) = f(c) = 1$, and $f(d) = 2$. We call $f(x)$, the rank of element x. Here, b and c are in the same rank with rank equal to 1. The difference between a chain and a string is that a chain requires existence of a *one-to-one* mapping such that $x < y$ iff $f(x) < f(y)$. For strings, we drop the requirement of the function to be *one-to-one*. We represent a finite string by the sequence of ranks in the string. Thus, P is equivalent to the string $\{(a), (b, c), (d)\}$. Note that in Chapter 13, we used the term ranking for these posets. We have used the term string in this chapter to be consistent with the papers that analyzed this method of encoding [GS01, RT10].

A chain is a string in which every rank is of size 1. An antichain is also a string with exactly one rank. Thus, a string generalizes both chains and antichains.

Observe that a string can be encoded very efficiently. Given the ranks of any two elements, one can easily determine the order between them. Therefore, if all labels of a string map to consecutive numbers, then the maximum number of bits required is $\lceil \log_2 r \rceil$, where r is the number of ranks in the poset. Note that this encoding drops the distinction between elements that have the same order relationship with all other elements. Thus, two elements x and y have the same code $f(x) = f(y)$ iff for any element z, (1) $x < z$ iff $y < z$ and (2) $z < x$ iff $z < y$.

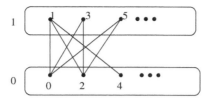

Figure 16.4   Encoding an infinite poset with strings.

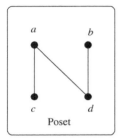
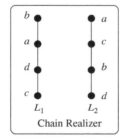
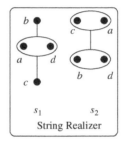

Figure 16.5   A poset with a chain realizer and a string realizer.

This technique allows more efficient encoding of the partial order than the use of chains as in dimension theory. At an extreme, the range of f may be finite even when the domain of f is infinite. For example, the order in Figure 16.4 where { all even numbers } < { all odd numbers } on natural numbers can be encoded by assigning 0 to all even numbers and 1 to all odd numbers. Such a poset cannot be assigned codes using the classical dimension theory.

The following definition is useful in understanding the number of bits required to encode a poset.

Definition 16.13 *Let* $P = (X, \leq)$ *be any poset. For* $x, y \in X$, *we say that* x *is order-equivalent to* y *(denoted by* $x \sim y$) *iff* x *is incomparable to* y *and for all* $z \in X : x < z \equiv y < z$ *and for all* $z \in X : z < x \equiv z < y$

We also say that two elements x and y have *duplicate holdings* if they are order-equivalent. Let *numeq*(P) denote the number of equivalence classes of the relation $\sim$. It is clear that the number of bits required to encode a poset is at least $\log numeq(P)$. In the poset of Figure 16.4, there are only two equivalence classes and hence we were able to encode each class with a single bit.
We write $x \leq_s y$ if $x \leq y$ in string s and $x <_s y$ if $x < y$ in string s.

Definition 16.14 (String Realizer) *For any poset* $P = (X, \leq)$, *a set of strings* S *is called a string realizer iff* $\forall x, y \in X : x < y$ *in* P *if and only if*

1. $\forall s \in S : x \leq_s y$, *and*
2. $\exists t \in S : x <_t y$.

The definition of less-than relation between two elements in the poset based on the strings is identical to the less-than relation as used in vector clocks. This is one of the motivation for defining string realizer in the above-mentioned manner. In a distributed system where the code of elements is determined in a decentralized manner, the relationship between two events may not be known globally. Thus, if event e happened before f, this relationship may be known only to a single process. From the perspective of other processes, e and f may be indistinguishable, for example, when both are internal to the process. This order is more easily captured where a vector u is deemed as smaller than vector v even when u is smaller than v in just one component and identical in all the other components.

A string realizer for the poset in Figure 16.5 is given by two strings:

$$s_1 = \{(c), (d, a), (b)\} \quad s_2 = \{(d, b), (c, a)\}$$

There are two important differences between definitions of string realizers and chain realizers. First, if $\mathcal{R}$ is a chain realizer of a poset P, then P is simply the intersection of linear extensions in $\mathcal{R}$. This is not true for a string realizer (see Figure 16.5). Secondly, all the total orders in $\mathcal{R}$ preserve P, i.e., $x < y$ in P implies that $x < y$ in all chains in $\mathcal{R}$. This is not true for string realizer. For example, $d < a$ in poset P of Figure 16.5, but (d, a) appears as a rank in the string s_1. We are only guaranteed that a will not appear lower than d in any string.

Now, analogous to the dimension we define

Definition 16.15 (String Dimension) *For any poset $(X, \leq)$, the string dimension of $(X, \leq)$, denoted by $sdim(X, \leq)$, is the size of the set S with the least number of strings such that S is a string realizer for $(X, \leq)$.*

Example 16.16 *Consider the standard example S_m. The following function f can be used to create a string realizer of S_m. For all $k, i = 1, 2, \ldots, m$,*

$$f_k(a_i) = \begin{cases} 0 & \text{if } k \neq i \\ 1 & \text{otherwise} \end{cases}$$

$$f_k(b_i) = \begin{cases} 0 & \text{if } k = i \\ 1 & \text{otherwise} \end{cases}$$

For example,

$$a_1 = (1, 0, 0, \ldots, 0), \quad b_1 = (0, 1, 1, \ldots, 1)$$
$$a_2 = (0, 1, 0, \ldots, 0), \quad b_2 = (1, 0, 1, \ldots, 1).$$

In this example, the length of each string is 2 and thus each element requires only m bits for encoding. If we use classical dimension based on total orders, each element would require $m * \log m$ bits.

Example 16.17 *Consider the poset* $(X, \leq)$ *as follows.*
$X = \{\emptyset, \{a\}, \{b\}, \{a, b\}, \{a, c\}, \{a, b, c\}\}$
$P = \{(A, B) \in X \times X : A \subseteq B\}.$
    A string realizer for the poset can be obtained as follows. For each set $A \in X$, *we use a bit vector representation of the set* A. *Thus,* $\{a, c\}$ *is represented by* $(1, 0, 1)$ *and the set* $\{a, b\}$ *is represented by* $(1, 1, 0)$. *This representation gives us a string realizer with three strings such that every string has exactly two ranks. This example can be easily generalized to get a string realizer of size n for any poset* P *that is a subposet of the Boolean lattice on n elements.*

The following lemma is easy to show.

Lemma 16.18

1. *Every set of strings on a set* X *defines a partial order.*
2. *A poset* P *is embeddable in* $\mathcal{N}^k$ *iff there is a string realizer of size k.*

We now establish the relationship between string dimension and chain dimension. It may appear, at first, that the string dimension of a poset may be much smaller than the chain dimension. However, this is not the case as shown by the following result.

Theorem 16.19 (Equivalence Theorem) *For any poset* $P = (X, \leq)$ *such that* $sdim(P) \geq 2$,
$$sdim(P) = dim(P).$$

Proof: We first show that $sdim(P) \leq dim(P)$. It is sufficient to show that for any chain realizer of size k, there exists a string realizer of equal or smaller size. Given a chain realizer C, we construct the string realizer as follows. Each chain is simply viewed as a string. Our obligation is to show that the order generated from the string realizer is the same as the one based on chain realizer (recall that the definition of *less than* for string realizer is different from *less than* in a chain realizer.) If x is less than y, then it appears below x in all chains; and therefore, in all strings. Hence, x is less than y in the string realizer as well. If x and y are incomparable, then there is at least one chain that puts x below y and another chain that puts y below x. The same holds for strings; and, therefore, x and y are incomparable in the string realizer as well.
    We now show that $dim(P) \leq sdim(P)$, whenever $sdim(P) \geq 2$.
    Given a string realizer of P, S, we construct the corresponding chain realizer. We achieve this by imposing an appropriate linear order on all nodes in the same rank of the string to form a chain.
    First consider the case when a set of elements G belong to the same rank in all strings. This means that all these elements are order-equivalent and incomparable to each other. We will combine all these elements into one element say z. After finding the chain realizer of the new set, we replace z with any total order on G in one of the chains and the dual of the total order in another chain. Observe that we can do this because there are at least two chains due to our assumption of $sdim(P) \geq 2$.

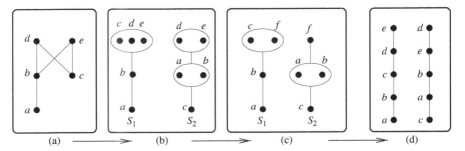

Figure 16.6   An example of converting a string realizer to a chain realizer.

Now assume that there are no two elements that are always in the same rank. Suppose that $\{x_1, x_2, \ldots, x_m\}$ have the same rank r in any string s. For any pair of elements, x_i and x_j, we have two cases. If whenever x_i appears in different rank than x_j, it appears below x_j, then we know that $x_i < x_j$. If in one string x_i appears below x_j and in another string it appears above x_j, then x_i is incomparable with x_j. It is sufficient to do a topological sort of all elements in rank r since the topological sort preserves $<$ order. By repeating this process for other ranks, we obtain a chain for the string s such that the resulting string realizer also realizes the same poset. We apply this operation to all strings to get a chain realizer.

■

Figure 16.6 shows an example of converting a string realizer into a chain realizer. Since d and e appear in the same rank in all strings, we first combine d and e into one element f. As a result, we get strings in Figure 16.6(c). We then untie the rank (c, f) by keeping c less than f in s_1 and untie the rank (a, b) in s_2 by keeping a less than b. We now have the chain order. Now we replace f by d and e, keeping d less than e in s_1 and e less than d in s_2 to get the chains in Figure 16.6(d).

The concept of string realizer has the advantage over chain realizer that it generally requires less number of bits to encode a partial order by using strings than by using chains. Using dimension theory, if a partial order has dimension k, then it can be encoded using $k * log(n)$ bits. String realizers result in a lower number of bits for encoding. Let $sbits(P)$ denote the minimum number of bits required to code an element using a string realizer. Formally,

$$sbits(P) = \min_S \sum_{s \in S} \lceil \log(height(s)) \rceil,$$

where S ranges over all string realizers of P. In other words, we consider all string realizers and use the one which results in the least number of bits.

The number of bits used by a string realizer is always less than or equal to that used by a chain realizer, i.e.,

Theorem 16.20 *For all posets $P = (X, \leq)$ with n elements and dimension k,*

$$sbits(P) \leq k \log n.$$

Proof: From Theorem 16.19, $sdim(P) \leq dim(P)$ for all P. To encode a string of length l, we require $\lceil \log l \rceil$ bits. The length of each string is clearly less than or equal to $n = |X|$.

∎

Note that for any nonstring poset, given a string realizer with k strings, there is also a chain realizer with k chains. However, since chains are "longer" than strings in general, it takes more bits to encode position in the chain. For the *standard example*, encoding using chain realizer takes $n/2 * \log n$ bits per element.

Another popular method to encode a partial order is to use "adjacency matrix" representation discussed in Chapter 2. Any partial order can be coded using $log(n) + n$ bits per element using "adjacency matrix" type representation. For every element, we store a binary array of size n. Further, each element is assigned a unique index into the array. Let $index(x)$ be the index of x in $1..n$ and $x.v$ be the n bit array for element x. We set $x.v[index(y)]$ to 1 if $x < y$ and to 0 otherwise. It is easy to determine the relationship between x and y given $index(x)$, $x.v$, $index(y)$, and $y.v$. We now show that string-based encoding is always better than adjacency matrix- based coding.

Theorem 16.21 *For all posets $P = (X, \leq)$, we have*

$$sbits(P) \leq n.$$

Proof: We show a string realizer of n strings with each string of size 2. Let $X = \{x_1, x_2, ..., x_n\}$. We construct a string s_i for each x_i, $1 \leq i \leq n$. Every string s_i has two ranks. The upper rank consists of x_i and all elements greater than x_i. The lower rank consists of all elements smaller than x_i and all elements that are incomparable to x_i.

We now show that this is a proper string realizer of P. Consider any two elements x_i and x_j. By symmetry, there are only two cases:

Case 1: $x_i < x_j$
In this case, x_i is less than x_j in string s_j. In all other strings, x_i appears either in the same rank or in the lower rank as x_j. Note that if x_i appears in the upper rank for string s_k for any k, then x_j also appears in the upper rank.

Case 2: $x_i||x_j$
In this case, x_i is less than x_j in string s_j, but x_j is less than x_i in string s_i.

∎

Note that we could have used a "dual" string realizer in the proof of Theorem 16.21 in which each string s_i has two ranks as follows. The upper rank consists of all elements bigger than x_i and all elements that are incomparable to x_i. The lower rank consists of x_i and all elements smaller than x_i. It can be easily verified that this leads to a proper string realizer.

We can improve the bound for $sbits(P)$ for bipartite posets.

Theorem 16.22 *For all bipartite posets $P = (L, U, \leq)$,*

$$sbits(P) \leq n/2 + \log n.$$

Proof: Assume without loss of generality that $|L| \leq n/2$. We can use dual constructions when $|U| \leq n/2$. We also assume that there are no nodes with duplicated holdings. If there are nodes with duplicated holdings, then we first combine them and later split them as in the proof of Theorem 16.19.

For each $x \in L$, we construct a string s_x as in the proof for Theorem 16.21. These strings give information about any pair of elements such that either both are in L or one is in L and the other is in U. For the poset in Figure 16.7, these strings are shown as the first three in Figure 16.8.

We create one more string t that will allow us to infer relationship for other types of pairs. The lowest rank in t consists of all elements in L. The upper part of t is constructed as follows. We first derive the poset Q on the set U, which is given by the string realizer formed by strings $\{s_x | x \in L\}$. For our example, the poset Q on $\{b1, b2, b3\}$ is simply $\{(b1, b2)\}$. Now we consider any chain consistent with dual of

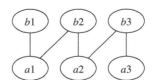

Figure 16.7   A bipartite poset.

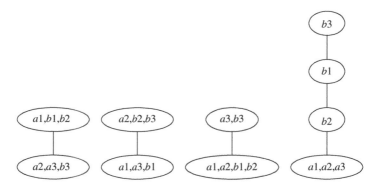

Figure 16.8   String realizer for the bipartite poset in Figure 16.7.

the poset Q. For our example, a chain consistent with the dual of Q is $b2 < b1 < b3$. This string is the upper part of the string t and the lowest rank of t is all elements in L. The length of the string t is at most $\log n$. For our example, t is the last string in Figure 16.8.

We show that this construction gives a string realizer for $(L, U, \leq)$. There are two cases.

Case 1: $x_i < x_j$

This case implies that $x_i \in L$ and $x_j \in U$. By our construction, x_i is less than x_j in string t. x_i appears in the upper rank in exactly one string s_i, but in that string x_j is also in the upper rank.

Case 2: $x_i || x_j$

If both x_i and x_j are in L, then we know that x_i is less than x_j in string s_j and x_j is less than x_i in string s_i.

If both of them are in U, we have the following cases. If x_i is less than x_j in first $|L|$ strings, then by our construction of t, it is greater than x_j in string t. Otherwise, we know that in one of the strings among L strings x_i is less than x_j and in some other string x_j is less than x_i.

The last case is when x_i is in L and x_j is in U (or vice versa). In this case, x_j is less than x_i in string s_i and x_i is less than x_j in string t.

■

Our constructions of string realizers so far were dependent on the number of elements. We now discuss a method that may result in a more efficient construction when the width of the poset is small.

Theorem 16.23 *Every partial order $P = (X, \leq)$ on $n \geq 2$ elements can be encoded using a string realizer in at most $\log(height(P) + 1) * width(P)$ bits.*

Proof: For convenience, let $w = width(P)$. We use Dilworth's chain covering theorem which states that $(X, \leq)$ can be partitioned into w chains $C_1, C_2, ..., C_w$. We then use the transitively reduced diagram of $(X, \leq)$ with w processes as given by the chain decomposition. Further, we use Fidge and Mattern's algorithm to assign vector timestamp for each event when the poset diagram is viewed as a computation. These vector timestamps determine a string realizer with w coordinates such that no coordinate is greater than $height(P) + 1$.

■

As an example, we show the encoding of the poset in Figure 16.7. Using this technique, we use six bits to encode each element as the number of coordinates (width) is three and each coordinate requires two bits for encoding (Figure 16.9).

We can tighten the above-mentioned result by focusing on the subposet of join-irreducibles of P. Let $J(P)$ denote the subposet formed by the join-irreducibles of P.

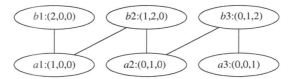

Figure 16.9   Encoding for the bipartite poset in Figure 16.7.

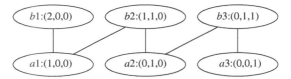

Figure 16.10   Another Encoding for the bipartite poset in Figure 16.7.

Theorem 16.24 *Every partial order $P = (X, \leq)$ on $n \geq 2$ elements can be encoded using a string realizer in at most $\log(height(J(P)) + 1) * width(J(P)$ bits.*

Proof: For convenience, let $w = width(J(P)) \leq width(P)$. Let $J(P)$ be partitioned into $width(J(P))$ chains $D_1, D_2, ..., D_w$ chains. For every element $x \in X$, we assign the code for x as follows. For each $i \in \{1..w\}$, let

$$v_x[i] = |\{z \in D_i | z \leq x\}.|$$

It is easy to verify that $x \leq y$ iff $v_x \leq v_y$. This code gives us the required string realizer.

■

Continuing with our example, we find that $b2$ and $b3$ are not join-irreducible. Hence, we get the code assignment as shown in Figure 16.10. We now use only 4 bits to encode any element. The first coordinate requires 2 bits and the other two coordinates require only 1 bit each.

We now define the notion of string length to derive a lower bound on dimension of any poset. The length of a realizer S for the poset P, denoted by $slength(P, S)$, is defined as the length of the longest string in the string realizer S of P. Let $slength(P)$ denote the length of the longest string in the string realizer with the minimum number of strings. The following lemma shows the relationship among $dim(P)$, $slength(P)$, and $numeq(P)$.

Lemma 16.25 $dim(P) \geq \log(numeq(P)) / \log(slength(P))$.

Proof: The proof follows from the fact that the total number of codes is at most $slength(P)^{dim(P)}$. Further, two elements in different equivalence classes cannot have the identical code. This implies that $slength(P)^{dim(P)} \geq numeq(P)$.

■

16.8   RECTANGLE REALIZERS

We have seen how we can represent a poset using chains and strings. Both methods allowed us to encode elements of the posets with vectors of integers. We showed that using vectors based on strings was more economical because we needed fewer bits to represent each coordinate in the vector. We now discuss an alternate approach in which our goal is to reduce the number of coordinates in the vector. In this approach, we use posets with dimension at most two—called *two-dimensional posets*—as "building blocks" for realizing a given poset. For convenience, we refer to two-dimensional posets as *rectangles*. An element x is less than another element y in the given partial order if and only if x is less than y in at least one of the rectangular orders and y is not less than x in any of the rectangular orders. The set of rectangular orders that realizes a given partial order constitutes its *rectangular realizer*. In addition, the *rectangular dimension* of a poset is the least number of rectangular orders needed to realize the corresponding partial order. Clearly, by definition, the rectangular dimension of a poset is one if and only if its dimension is at most two. Trivially, the rectangular dimension of a poset is upper bounded by its dimension.

It turns out that there are posets with arbitrarily high dimension but only constant rectangular dimension. As an illustration, consider the family of *standard examples*. The dimension of $\mathbf{S}_n$ is given by n for each $n \geq 3$. This implies that $O(n \log n)$ bits per element are required to encode $\mathbf{S}_n$ using the dimension theory. We show in this section that the rectangular dimension of $\mathbf{S}_n$ is two for each $n \geq 3$ and thus each rectangle can be encoded using $O(\log n)$ bits. Therefore, using rectangles leads to a much more efficient representation of $\mathbf{S}_n$.

We now formally define the notions of rectangle, rectangular realizer, and rectangular dimension of a poset.

Definition 16.26 (rectangle)   *A rectangle is a two-dimensional poset.*

When a poset $\mathbf{P} = (X, \leq)$ is a rectangle, we call P as a *rectangular order*. For a rectangular order R, we use $R.1$ and $R.2$ to refer to the two total orders that realize R. In case the dimension of R is one, both $R.1$ and $R.2$ refer to the same total order. Clearly, $R = R.1 \cap R.2$. A chain as well as an antichain is a rectangle.

Definition 16.27 (rectangular realizer)   *Let* $\mathbf{P} = (X, \leq)$ *be a poset. A family* $\mathcal{R} = \{R_1, R_2, \ldots, R_t\}$ *of rectangular orders on* X *is called a* realizer *of* P *on* X *(also,* $\mathcal{R}$ realizes $\mathbf{P}$*) if for every* $x, y \in X$, $x < y$ *in* P *if and only if* $y \not< x$ *in* R_i *for each* $i \in [1, t]$ *and* $x < y$ *in* R_j *for some* $j \in [1, t]$.

If $x \parallel y$ in P, then in a rectangular realizer $\mathcal{R}$ of P, two cases are possible. Either $x \parallel y$ in all rectangular orders in $\mathcal{R}$ or $x < y$ in some rectangular order in $\mathcal{R}$ and $y < x$ in some other rectangular order in $\mathcal{R}$. On the other hand, if $x < y$ in P, then $x < y$ in some rectangular order in $\mathcal{R}$ and $x < y$ or $x \parallel y$ in all other rectangular orders in $\mathcal{R}$. The notion of rectangular dimension can now be defined as follows:

Definition 16.28 (rectangular dimension)   *The   rectangular   dimension   of   a poset* $\mathbf{P} = (X, \leq)$, *denoted by* $\mathrm{rdim}(X, \leq)$ *(or* $\mathrm{rdim}(\mathbf{P})$*), is the least positive integer* t

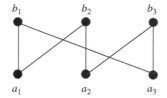

Figure 16.11   An example of a poset with rectangular dimension two.

for which there exists a family $\mathcal{R} = \{R_1, R_2, \ldots, R_t\}$ *of t rectangular orders on X so that* $\mathcal{R}$ *realizes* **P**.

As an example, the rectangular dimension of the poset depicted in Figure 16.11 is two. The two rectangular orders realizing it are given by $\{(a_1 < a_2 < a_3 < b_1 < b_2 < b_3), (a_3 < a_2 < a_1 < b_3 < b_2 < b_1)\}$ and $\{(b_1 < a_2 < b_2 < a_3 < b_3 < a_1), (b_3 < a_1 < b_2 < a_3 < b_1 < a_2)\}$.

We now show the result mentioned in the introduction.

Theorem 16.29   *The rectangular dimension of* S_n *is two for any* $n \geq 3$.

Proof: It is clear that the rectangular dimension of S_n is at least two because the chain dimension of S_n is $n \geq 3$. We show a rectangular realizer with two rectangles. The first rectangle, R_1, encodes the complete bipartite poset in which all a's are concurrent, all b's are concurrent, and all a's are less than all b's. The second rectangle, R_2, encodes n disjoint chains $b_i < a_i$ for $i = 1..n$. It is easy to verify that $\{R_1, R_2\}$ is a rectangular realizer for S_n. Given any distinct a_i, a_j, they are concurrent in both the rectangles and therefore $a_i \parallel a_j$ in the realized poset. The same holds for b_i and b_j. Now consider a_i and b_j for $i \neq j$. In R_1, $a_i < b_j$ and in R_2, $a_i \parallel b_j$; therefore, $a_i < b_j$ in the realized poset. Finally, $a_i < b_i$ in R_1 but $b_i < a_i$ in R_2; therefore, $a_i \parallel b_i$ in the realized poset.

∎

The rectangular dimension of a poset and its dual are identical because the dual of a two-dimensional poset is again a two-dimensional poset.

The notions of rectangular realizer and rectangular dimension defined for a poset can be generalized to any (acyclic) relation on a ground set. For a collection of rectangular orders $\mathcal{R} = \{R_1, R_2, \ldots, R_t\}$, let $\text{rel}(\mathcal{R})$ denote the relation realized by $\mathcal{R}$. For example, consider the rectangular orders $\{(a < b < c), (c < a < b)\}$ and $\{(a < b < c), (b < c < a)\}$. The relation realized by the two orders collectively is given by $\{(a, b), (b, c)\}$. Note that the relation is not transitive because it does not contain the ordered pair (a, c).

16.9   ORDER DECOMPOSITION METHOD AND ITS APPLICATIONS

In this section, we give a method to construct rectangular realizers for a poset. In our construction of rectangular realizers, we often use *non-interfering* rectangles.

Definition 16.30 (non-interference) *A rectangular order R is said to be* non-interfering *with a partial order P if $R \subseteq P$.*

In addition, a rectangular realizer is *non-interfering* with a partial order if every rectangular order in the realizer is non-interfering with the partial order. In other words, if two elements are incomparable in the partial order, they are also incomparable in all rectangular orders in the realizer. In that case, the partial order is given by the union of all rectangular orders in the realizer. Trivially, every partial order (even a relation) has a non-interfering rectangular realizer.

The main idea of the order decomposition method is as follows. Given a poset $\mathbf{P} = (X, \leq)$, we first decompose the partial order P into t suborders P_i for $i = 1, 2, \ldots, t$. It is not necessary for the suborders to be disjoint. We next compute a rectangular realizer $\mathcal{R}_i$ for each subposet $(P, \leq)$ such that $\mathcal{R}_i$ is non-interfering with P. Then, the collection of rectangular orders $\mathcal{R} = \mathcal{R}_1 \cup \mathcal{R}_2 \cup \cdots \cup \mathcal{R}_t$ constitutes a rectangular realizer of P on X. When we specify a decomposition of a partial order into suborders, we do not enumerate the reflexive pairs which can always be added later.

Suppose the Hasse diagram (or covering graph) of a poset $\mathbf{P} = (X, \leq)$ is such that every element in the graph has at most one outgoing edge. In this case, the covering graph resembles a forest of trees. In particular, for every element $x \in X$, $U(x)$ forms a chain in P. Such a poset belongs to the class of *series–parallel* posets. The dimension of a series–parallel poset is at most two and hence its rectangular dimension is at most one. Similarly, a poset whose Hasse diagram is such that every element has at most one incoming edge also has rectangular dimension of one.

A natural question to ask is what other posets have "small" rectangular dimension? In this section, we show that posets with "low" indegree have "small" rectangular dimension.

For a poset $\mathbf{P} = (X, \leq)$ and an element $x \in X$, let *indegree* of x in P be defined as the number of elements less than x in P. The *outdegree* of an element can be dually defined.

Theorem 16.31 *Let $\mathbf{P} = (X, \leq)$ be a poset with the maximum value of in-degree for any node at most k where $k \geq 1$. Then,*

$$\mathrm{rdim}(X, \leq) \leq k$$

Proof: The central idea is to decompose the partial order into at most k suborders such that the subposet induced by each suborder is a rectangle. For each element $x \in X$, number all elements in $D(x)$ from 1 to $|D(x)|$. The ith suborder P_i for $i = 1, 2, \ldots, k$ is given by the reflexive transitive closure of the set $\{(x, y) \mid x \in X$ and y is the ith element in $D(x)$, if it exists$\}$. Clearly, each element has at most one incoming edge in the Hasse diagram of $(X, \leq)$. Hence, $(X, \leq)$ is a series–parallel poset, which implies that P_i is a rectangular order. Since $P_i \subseteq P$, P_i is non-interfering with P. Therefore, it follows that the set $\{P_1, P_2, \ldots, P_k\}$ constitutes a rectangular realizer of P on X.

■

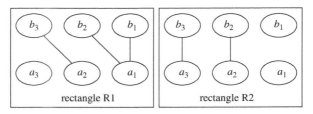

Figure 16.12   An example of decomposing a poset into series-parallel posets.

As an example of the construction in Theorem 16.31, consider the poset in Figure 16.11. The poset can be decomposed into two subposets shown in Figure 16.12 each with rectangular dimension one. The reader is referred to Mittal and Garg [MG04] for more details on the rectangular dimension.

16.10   PROBLEMS

16.1. Show that if P is a subposet of Q, then $dim(P) \leq dim(Q)$.

16.2. Show that all proper subposets of S_n have smaller dimension than n.

16.3. Let $P = (X, \leq)$ be a poset and Q be a subposet of P. Let L be a linear extension of Q. Show that there exists a linear extension of P which restricted to Q is identical to L. Give an efficient algorithm to construct such a linear extension.

16.4. Show that for every n, there exists an interval order with dimension greater than n.

16.5. Let C and D be two disjoint chains in P such that every element of chain C is incomparable to every element in chain D. Show that removal of chains C and D does not decrease the dimension by more than two.

16.6. ([Hir55] Let $P = (X, \leq)$ be a poset with $|X| \geq 4$. Then

$$dim(X, \leq) \leq \frac{|X|}{2}.$$

(Hint: Use Theorem 16.9 and Problem 5.)

16.7. Let $J(P)$ be the subposet formed by the join-irreducibles and $Dis(P)$ be the subposet formed by dissectors of a finite poset P. Show that

$$width(Dis(P)) \leq dim(P).$$

(Hint: Show that P has the standard example of size equal to $width(Dis(P))$ as a subposet.)

16.8. [MG04] A subposet $(Y, \leq)$ is called a *critical subposet* of the poset $(X, \leq)$ if for every incomparable pair (x, y) from Y either (x, y) or (y, x) forms a critical pair in the subposet $(X \setminus Y, \leq)$. Show that

$$\text{rdim}(X, \leq) \leq 1 + \max \{\text{rdim}(X \setminus Y, \leq), \dim(Y, \leq)\}.$$

16.9. [MG04] Let $P = (X, \leq) = (L, U, \leq)$ be a bipartite poset with nonempty L and U. Show that
$$\text{rdim}((X, \leq)) \leq \min\{\lceil |L|/2 \rceil, \lceil |U|/2 \rceil\}.$$

16.10. [MG04] Let $P = (X, \leq)$ be a poset such that for every element $x \in X$, either $\deg_D(x) \leq k$ or $\deg_D(x) \geq |X| - k$ where $k \geq 1$. Show that

$$\text{rdim}(X, \leq) \leq \lceil 3k/2 \rceil + 1$$

16.11 BIBLIOGRAPHIC REMARKS

There is an excellent detailed treatment of dimension theory in the book by Trotter [Tro92]. The discussion of string realizer is from Garg and Skawratananond [GS01] and rectangular realizer is from Mittal and Garg [MG04].

17

FIXED POINT THEORY

In this chapter, we introduce the notion of fixed points of a function defined over ordered sets. The theory of fixed points allows us to obtain extremal solutions of equations involving operations over lattices. For example, given any function f with suitable properties, we can find x the least element in the lattice such that $f(x)$ equals x. In computer science applications, we can use fixed point theory to define the meaning of recursion when functions are defined over lattices (or complete partial orders). We illustrate these notions by defining probabilistic version of formal languages.

We begin by defining complete partial orders because they are weaker than complete lattices but still allow computation of fixed points. We then give Knaster–Tarski fixed point theorem that shows existence of least and greatest fixed points for monotone functions. If the function is *continuous* (a stronger property than monotonicity), then we show how one can give an explicit construction of the least fixed point. Section 17.3 gives applications of these results.

17.1 COMPLETE PARTIAL ORDERS

The completeness of a lattice is a strong property of posets and the given structure may not always satisfy it. We consider a weaker requirement on a poset than that of a complete lattice.

Introduction to Lattice Theory with Computer Science Applications, First Edition. Vijay K. Garg.
© 2015 John Wiley & Sons, Inc. Published 2015 by John Wiley & Sons, Inc.

Definition 17.1 *A poset* $(X, \leq)$ *is called a* complete partial order (cpo) *if*

- inf X *exists, and*
- *the least upper bound exists for any increasing chain of* X.

Note that a complete lattice is always a cpo. The set of natural numbers with the natural ordering is an example of a lattice which is not a cpo.

We are now ready to define properties of f. Recall that a function f is *monotone* iff

$$\forall x, y \in X : x \leq y \Rightarrow f(x) \leq f(y)$$

A stronger property is *continuity*.

Definition 17.2 *A function* $f : X \to X$ *is called* continuous *or* sup-continuous *iff for all chains* $\{x_i\}$,

$$f(\bigsqcup_i x_i) = \bigsqcup_i f(x_i)$$

It can be easily shown that every continuous operator is monotone.

17.2   KNASTER–TARSKI THEOREM

The following fixed point theorem is due to Knaster and Tarski [Tar55].

Theorem 17.3 *Let* $L = (X, \leq)$ *be a complete lattice and* $f : X \to X$ *be a monotone function on* L. *Then,*
(a) The least fixed point of f exists and is given by

$$z = \inf \{x \mid f(x) \leq x\}$$

(b) The greatest fixed point of f exists and is given by

$$z = \sup \{x \mid x \leq f(x)\}$$

Proof: We prove part (a) and leave part (b) as an exercise. For convenience define $Z = \{x \mid f(x) \leq x\}$. We first observe that since X is a complete lattice, the biggest element $\top$ exists. Since $f(\top) \leq \top$, Z is nonempty. Completeness of X implies that $z = \inf Z$ exists. Hence, z is well defined.
We now show that $f(z) \leq z$.

$$\begin{aligned}
&\text{true} \\
\Rightarrow \quad &\{ z \text{ is inf of } Z \} \\
&\forall y \in Z : z \leq y \\
\Rightarrow \quad &\{ f \text{ monotone} \} \\
&\forall y \in Z : f(z) \leq f(y) \\
\Rightarrow \quad &\{ f(y) \leq y \} \\
&\forall y \in Z : f(z) \leq y \\
\Rightarrow \quad &\{ z \text{ is the } greatest \text{ lower bound} \} \\
&f(z) \leq z
\end{aligned}$$

We now show that $z \leq f(z)$
From above,

$\quad f(z) \leq z$
$\Rightarrow \quad \{ f \text{ monotone } \}$
$\quad f(f(z)) \leq f(z)$
$\Rightarrow \quad \{ \text{ definition of } Z \}$
$\quad f(z) \in Z$
$\Rightarrow \quad \{ z \text{ is inf of } Z \}$
$\quad z \leq f(z)$

We have shown that z is a fixed point. It is easy to see that it is the least fixed point because all fixed points are also in Z.

∎

It follows from Theorem 17.3 that a monotone function defined over a complete lattice always has an infimal and a supremal fixed point. It lets us deduce the existence of a fixed point but does not give us any method of computing it. The following theorem gives a method of computing fixed points under stronger conditions.

Theorem 17.4 Let f be a continuous function defined on a complete lattice. Let $z = sup\{f^i(\bot)|0 \leq i\}$. Then, z is the smallest fixed point.

Proof: We first show that z is a fixed point.

$\quad f(z)$
$=$
$\quad f(sup\{f^i(\bot)|0 \leq i\})$
$= \quad \{ f \text{ continuous} \}$
$\quad sup\{f^{i+1}(\bot)|0 \leq i\}$
$= \quad \{ \text{composition of } f \}$
$\quad sup\{f^i(\bot)|1 \leq i\}$
$= \quad \{ \bot \text{ is the smallest element} \}$
$\quad sup\{f^i(\bot)|0 \leq i\}$
$= \quad \{ \text{ definition of } z \}$
$\quad z$

We now show that it is the smallest fixed point. Let y be any other fixed point. Since $\bot$ is the least element, $\bot \leq y$. As f is monotone, we deduce that $\forall i : f^i(\bot) \leq f^i(y)$. This means that $\forall i : f^i(\bot) \leq y$ as y is a fixed point. From this, we deduce that $z \leq y$ from the definition of z.

∎

In the first part of Theorem 17.4, since $\{f^i(\inf X), i \geq 0\}$ is an increasing chain, $f^*(\inf X)$ exists under the weaker condition that $(X, \leq)$ is a cpo. Thus it is possible to compute the infimal fixed point of a sup-continuous function whenever it is defined over a cpo.

17.3   APPLICATION: DEFINING RECURSION USING FIXED POINTS

In this section, we show an application of fixed point theory to define probabilistic languages over a finite set of events. We also define operators under which the set of probabilistic languages (p-languages) is closed, thus forming an algebra of p-languages. We show that this set is a complete partial order and our operators are continuous in it. Hence, recursive equations may be defined in this algebra using fixed points of continuous functions.

Definition 17.5 *A p-language L over alphabet A is defined as $L : A^* \to [0, 1]$ with the constraint that*
(C1) $L(\epsilon) = 1$
(C2)   *for all s :* $\sum_{a \in A} L(sa) \leq L(s)$

The interpretation of $L(s)$ is taken as the probability that s occurs in the system. (C1) says that the null string (ϵ) is always possible in the system. (C2) captures the property that if a system executes sa, then it must have executed s. Thus, the combined probability $\sum_a L(sa)$ must not be greater than $L(s)$. (C2) also implies that if s is a prefix of t, then $L(s)$ is greater than or equal to $L(t)$.

On the basis of L, we can define a probability density function C_L on the set A^*.

$$C_L(s) = L(s) - \sum_a L(sa) \quad \text{for } s \in A^*. \tag{17.1}$$

The interpretation of $C_L(s)$ is that it is the probability that the system does s and stops, that is, it does not do anything afterward. We will drop the subscript L, when clear from the context. As $\sum_a L(sa) \leq L(s)$, $C(s)$ is always greater than or equal to zero. Since $L(s)$ is less than or equal to 1, so is $C(s)$ for any s. Thus, $C(s)$ always lies between 0 and 1.

Example 17.6 Let L be defined as: $L(\epsilon) = 1, L(a) = 0.4, L(ab) = 0.2, L(b) = 0.6, L(ac) = 0.1$ and $L(s) = 0$ for all other strings s. Then, it is easy to see that L satisfies required properties. Hence, it is a p-language. Further, C for this p-language is $C(a) = 0.1, C(ab) = 0.2, C(ac) = 0.1, C(b) = 0.6$.

Example 17.7 The nil language I is defined as $I(\epsilon) = 1, I(s) = 0$ for $s \neq \epsilon$. For this language, $C_I(\epsilon) = 1, C_I(s) = 0$ for $s \neq \epsilon$.

Example 17.8 Consider a Bernoulli process. Every experiment has two outcomes a or b, with probability p and $(1 - p)$, respectively. Here, our alphabet $A = \{a, b\}$, and $L(s) = p^{\#(a,s)}(1 - p)^{\#(b,s)}$ for any $s \in A^*$, where $\#(x, s)$ represents the number of occurrences of x in the string s. It is easy to check that this language satisfies (C1) and (C2). Also note that $C(s) = 0$ for any s.

We note that both p-languages and completion probability are functions defined from A^* to $[0, 1]$. We call them language functions or simply functions. Let $\mathcal{F}$ be the set of all functions. We define a function $\Lambda : \mathcal{F} \to \mathcal{F}$ as follows:

$$\text{For any } s, \quad \Lambda(f)(s) = \sum_a f(sa)$$

Thus, if f is a p-language, then $\Lambda(f)$ gives the probability that the system will execute something after s. It is easy to check that Λ is a linear functional. With this notation, the constraint (C2) on f is

$$\Lambda(f) \leq f.$$

Similarly, for any p-language K, its corresponding completion probability density function (pdf) is easily derived as

$$C_K = K - \Lambda(K)$$

Now we make the following observations:

Lemma 17.9 (a) $\sum_s C(s) \leq 1$
(b) For any s : $L(s) = \sum_t C(st)$ iff $\lim_{k \to \infty} \sum_{|t|=k} L(st) = 0$
(c) $\sum_s C(s) = 1$ iff $\lim_{k \to \infty} \sum_{|t|=k} L(t) = 0$

Proof: *Proof (a)* : We first show that $\sum_{|s|=n} L(s) \leq 1$. This can be shown using induction on n. It is trivially true for $n = 0$. Assume that it is true for $n = k$. Then,

$\sum_{|s|=k+1} L(s)$
$= \{\ s = ta\ \}$
$\quad \sum_{|t|=k} \sum_a L(ta)$
$\leq \{\ (C2)\ \}$
$\quad \sum_{|t|=k} L(t)$
$\leq \{$ Induction hypothesis $\}$
$\quad 1$

We now show that $\sum_{s \in A^*} C(s) \leq 1$
Let

$$S(n) = \sum_{|s| \leq n} C(s)$$

Then $\sum_s C(s) = \lim_{n \to \infty} S(n)$ It is easy to show by induction that $S(n) = 1 - \sum_{|s|=n+1} L(s)$.
Therefore, $0 \leq S(n) \leq 1$. Since $\{S(n)\}$ is a monotone increasing sequence bounded above by 1, the limit exists and is at most 1.

Proof (b): From equation (17.1), we get that

$$L(s) = C(s) + \sum_a L(sa)$$

Therefore, by repeated application of this equation, we get,
$L(s) = \sum_{|t| < k} C(st) + \sum_{|t|=k} L(st)$ for all $k \geq 1$
$= \lim_{k \to \infty} \sum_{|t| < k} C(st) + \lim_{k \to \infty} \sum_{|t|=k} L(st)$
$= \sum_t C(st) + \lim_{k \to \infty} \sum_{|t|=k} L(st)$

The lemma follows.

Proof (c): By substituting ϵ for s in part (b).

∎

The first part of the above-mentioned proposition justifies the use of probability density function for completion. The second part of the above-mentioned lemma indicates that given any pdf, we can also view it as completion probability of a system.

We call a system terminating if $\sum C(s) = 1$. From now on, we will assume that all our systems are terminating. This assumption is only for simplicity, as the theory we develop can be easily extended to the case when there is a nonzero probability that the system does not terminate.

We can now define an ordering between p-languages. We use $\mathcal{L}_A$ (or simply $\mathcal{L}$) to denote the set of all p-languages defined over the set A.

Definition 17.10 *Let $K, L \in \mathcal{L}$. Then,*
$K \preceq L$ *if and only if* $\forall s : K(s) \leq L(s)$

Example 17.11 Let $K, L, U \in \mathcal{L}$ be defined as : $K(a) = 0.4, K(ab) = 0.3$
$L(a) = 0.5, L(b) = 0.4, L(ab) = 0.3$
$U(a) = 0.4, U(b) = 0.5, U(ab) = 0.4$
Then, $K \preceq L$, and $K \preceq U$, while L and U are incomparable.

Lemmas 17.12 and 17.13 describe the properties of this order.

Lemma 17.12 $(\mathcal{L}, \preceq)$ *is an* inf *semi-lattice.*

Proof: Let $K, L \in \mathcal{L}$. Then their least upper bound (if it exists) is denoted by $K \sqcup L$, and the greatest lower bound by $K \sqcap L$. They can be obtained as
$\quad K \sqcup L(s) = \sup(K(s), L(s))$
$\quad K \sqcap L(s) = \inf(K(s), L(s))$
Let $K, L \in \mathcal{L}$ and $V = K \sqcap L$. It is easy to see that V is also a function from A^* to $[0, 1]$, and that $V(\epsilon) = 1$. We now show that
for all s : $\quad \sum_a V(sa) \leq V(s)$.
For any s
$\quad \sum_a V(sa)$
$= \{$definition $\sqcap \}$
$\quad \sum_a \inf(K(sa), L(sa))$
$\leq \{$ arithmetic, using induction $\}$
$\quad inf(\sum_a K(sa), \sum_a L(sa))$
$\leq \{ K, L \in \mathcal{L} \}$
$\quad inf(K(s), L(s))$
$= \{$definition $\sqcap \}$
$\quad V(s)$.

∎

In Example 17.11, $V = L \sqcap U$ is defined as $V(a) = 0.4, V(b) = 0.4, V(ab) = 0.3$. However, $K \sqcup L$ may not exist for all K, L. As an example consider the following:

$K(\epsilon) = 1, K(a) = 0.6\ L(\epsilon) = 1, L(b) = 0.7$ Then $K \sqcup L$ is not defined (does not belong to $\mathcal{L}$). Even though $\sqcup$ may not exist for any set of p-languages, it exists for any chain of p-languages, i.e., a family of p-languages $\{L_i \mid i = 0, 1..\}$ such that $L_i \leq L_{i+1}$ for all i.

Lemma 17.13 $\leq$ *is a complete partial order(cpo) on the set* $\mathcal{L}$. I *is the least element in this cpo.*

Proof: It is easy to verify that $\leq$ is reflexive, antisymmetric, and transitive. Thus, it is a partial order. We just need to show that if L_i is a chain of p-languages, then its least upper bound exists. We define $\bigsqcup L_i(s) = \sup_i L_i(s)$. This is well defined because $L_i(s)$ is a monotonic sequence bounded above by 1. We also write it as $\lim_{n \to \infty} L_i(s)$. It is easy to see that $\bigsqcup L_i$ is also a function from A^* to $[0, 1]$ and that $\bigsqcup L_i(\epsilon) = 1$. We now show that

for all s : $\qquad \sum_a \bigsqcup L_i(sa) \leq \bigsqcup L_i(s)$.

For any s,

$\qquad \sum_a \bigsqcup L_i(sa)$
$= \{\text{definition } \sqcup \}$
$\qquad \sum_a \sup_i L_i(sa))$
$= \{ L_i \text{ monotone } \}$
$\qquad \sum_a \lim_{i \to \infty} L_i(sa))$
$= \{ \text{ finite sum } \}$
$\qquad \lim_{i \to \infty} \sum_a L_i(sa))$
$\leq \{ L_i \in \mathcal{L} \}$
$\qquad \lim_{i \to \infty} L_i(s))$
$= \{\text{definition } \bigsqcup \}$
$\qquad \bigsqcup L_i(s)$. ∎

As a result of the above-mentioned lemma, we can easily compute fixed points of continuous functions.

We now define some operations between various languages. These operators are useful in describing a complex system as a combination of many simple systems.

The **choice** operator denoted by $+_e$ captures nondeterministic choice between two systems. Given two p-languages L_1 and L_2, and a real number e between 0 and 1, the combined system is denoted $L_1 +_e L_2$ for e in $[0, 1]$. We use $\hat{e}$ to be equal to $1 - e$.

Definition 17.14 $L_1 +_e L_2 = eL_1 + \hat{e}L_2$

The interpretation of the above-mentioned definition is: do L_1 with probability e or L_2 with probability $1 - e$. It is easy to verify that the p-language defined earlier satisfies constraints (C1) and (C2). This operator can easily be generalized for multiple arguments. In essence, the choice operator represents a convex combination of p-languages.

We now derive an expression for the completion pdf for the composed system.
$C_1 +_e C_2 = L_1 +_e L_2 - \Lambda(L_1 +_e L_2)$
$= eL_1 - \Lambda(eL_1) + \hat{e}L_2 - \Lambda(\hat{e}L_2)$
$= eC_1 + \hat{e}C_2$

The following proposition describes property of choice with respect to the ordering.

Theorem 17.15 *Choice is a continuous operator in both of its arguments.*

Proof: We need to show that for any e,

$$K +_e (\bigsqcup_i L_i) = \bigsqcup_i (K +_e L_i)$$

This is easily verified using definitions.

∎

The **concatenation** operator denoted by $._e$ captures sequencing of two systems. Given two p-languages L_1 and L_2, and a real number e between 0 and 1, the combined system is denoted by $L_1._eL_2(s)$ for e in $[0, 1]$. Given any string t which is a prefix of s, we use s/t to denote the part of the string s left after removal of t.

Definition 17.16 $L_1._eL_2(s) = L_1(s) + e \sum_{t<s} C_1(t)L_2(s/t)$
$$= L_1(s) - eC_1(s) + e \sum_t C_1(t)L_2(s/t)$$

The above-mentioned definition has the following interpretation. The resulting system does L_1 and then on completion does L_2 with probability e. The probability that s occurs in the composed system is equal to the probability that it occurs in the first system or a part of it occurs in the first system and a nonnull part in the second. It can be shown that $\mathcal{L}$ is closed under the operation of $._e$. It is easy to check that $L_1._eL_2(\epsilon) = L_1(\epsilon) - eC_1(\epsilon) + eC_1(\epsilon)L_2(\epsilon) = 1$. Therefore, (C1) holds. We later derive an expression for $C_1._e C_2 = L_1._eL_2 - \Lambda(L_1._eL_2)$ and show that it is always positive. Hence (C2) also holds.

We define the convolution operators between two real-valued functions on A^* as follows:

$$f \circ g(s) = \sum_t f(t)g(s/t).$$

Thus, $L_1._eL_2(s)$ is defined more simply as $L_1(s) - eC_1(s) + eC_1 \circ L_2(s)$
The following proposition describes certain properties of the convolution operator.

Theorem 17.17 *(a) Convolution is associative, i.e.,*

$$f \circ (g \circ h) = (f \circ g) \circ h$$

(b) I is the identity for convolution, i.e.,

$$f \circ I = I \circ f = f$$

(c) Convolution is continuous in both arguments, i.e.

$$f \circ (\bigsqcup_i g_i) = \bigsqcup_i (f \circ g_i), (\bigsqcup_i f_i) \circ g_i = \bigsqcup_i (f \circ g_i)$$

(d) Convolution is a linear operator, i.e.,

$$f \circ (\alpha g + h) = \alpha f \circ g + f \circ h$$

(e) If $g(\epsilon) = 1$

$$\Lambda(f \circ g) = f \circ \Lambda(g) + \Lambda(f)$$

Proof: We leave (a) and (b) as an exercise. (c) We need to show that $f \circ \bigsqcup_i g_i = \bigsqcup_i f \circ g_i$. For any s,

$f \circ \bigsqcup_i g_i(s)$
$= \{\text{definition} \circ \}$
$\quad \sum_t f(t)(\bigsqcup_i g_i(s/t))$
$= \{ \text{ real analysis } \}$
$\quad \bigsqcup_i \sum_t f(t) g_i(s/t)$
$= \{\text{definition} \circ \}$
$\quad \bigsqcup_i f \circ g_i$

The continuity in the other argument is similarly proved.

(d) For any s,
$f \circ (\alpha g + h)(s)$
$= \sum_t f(t)(\alpha g + h)(s/t)$
$= \sum_t f(t)(\alpha g(s/t) + h(s/t))$
$= \sum_t f(t)\alpha g(s/t) + \sum_t f(t)h(s/t))$
$= \alpha f \circ g + f \circ h$

(e) For any s,
$\Lambda(f \circ g)$
$= \sum_a f \circ g(sa)$
$= \sum_a \sum_{t <= sa} f(t) g(sa/t)$
$= \sum_a \sum_{t \leq s} f(t) g(sa/t) + \sum_a f(sa) g(\epsilon)$
$= f \circ \Lambda(g) + \Lambda(f)$. ∎

We use $f^{(2)}$ to represent $f \circ f$. In general, we use $f^{(i)}$ to represent i times convolution of f with itself. This is well-defined because of associativity of $\circ$. We define $f^{(0)}$ to be the identity function, I. From the proof of associativity, we also note that $\sum_{s_i, 0 \leq i \leq n-1} C(s_0)C(s_1)...C(s_{n-1}) = C^{(n)}(s)$. We show the following proposition.

Theorem 17.18 *Let $\sum_s C(s) = 1$. Then, $\sum_s C^{(n)}(s) = 1$ for all n.*

Proof: We use induction on n. The proposition is clearly true for $n = 1$. Assume that it is true for $n = k$. Then, $\sum_s C^{(k+1)}(s)$
$= \sum_s C^{(k)} \circ C(s)$
$= \sum_s \sum_t C^{(k)}(t)C(s/t)$
$= \sum_u \sum_t C^{(k)}(t)C(u)$
$= \sum_u C(u) \sum_t C^{(k)}(t)$
$= 1$

We now derive the expression for completion probability for concatenation.

$C_1._eC_2 = L_1.L_2 - \Lambda(L_1.L_2)$

$= \{$ definition of $L_1.L_2\}$

$\quad L_1 + eC_1 \circ L_2 - eC_1 - \Lambda(L_1 - eC_1 + eC_1 \circ L_2)$

$= \{$ definition $C_1 = L_1 - \Lambda(L_1)\}$

$\quad C_1 + e(C_1 \circ L_2 - C_1 - \Lambda(C_1 \circ L_2) + \Lambda(C_1))$

$= \{$ property convolution $\}$

$\quad C_1 + e(C_1 \circ L_2 - C_1 - C_1 \circ \Lambda(L_2))$

$= \{$ property convolution, definition $C_2\}$

$\quad C_1(s) + eC_1 \circ C_2(s) - eC_1(s)$

$= \{$ definition $\hat{e}\}$

$\quad \hat{e}C_1(s) + eC_1 \circ C_2(s)$

We note that if $e = 0$, then the system is identical as before. On the other hand if $e = 1$, then the resulting system is obtained as a pure convolution. Since convolution is continuous, it is easy to show the following Theorem. ∎

Theorem 17.19 *Concatenation is continuous in its second argument, i.e.,*

$$K._e \bigsqcup_i L_i = \bigsqcup_i K._e L_i$$

Proof: $K._e \bigsqcup_i L_i$

$= K - eC + eC \circ \bigsqcup_i L_i$

$= \bigsqcup_i(K - eC + eC \circ L_i)$

$= \bigsqcup_i K._e L_i$

∎

However, concatenation is not even monotone in its first argument as shown by the following example. Let $K(a) = 0.2$, and $L(b) = 1.0$. Now $I \leq K$, but $I._1L$ is not comparable to $K._1L$.

We are now ready to use fixed point theory to define **recursion**. For any $K \in \mathcal{L}$, we can use $+_eK$ and $._eK$ as unary operators defined from $\mathcal{L}$ to itself. For any $X \in \mathcal{L}$, $+_eK(X) = K +_e X$, and $._eK(X) = K._eX$. As shown earlier, both of these operators are continuous in the cpo of $\mathcal{L}$. Note that we use concatenation only in the second argument as it is not continuous for the first argument. Therefore, any composition of these operators will also be continuous. We can define recursion operator denoted by $\mu X.F(x)$, where F is any function built out of the choice operator $(+)$ and the concatenation operator $(.)$. We define $\mu X.F(X) = \bigsqcup F^i(I)$. From Theorem 17.4, we get that $\bigsqcup F^i(I)$ is the least fixed point of F. In other words, $\mu X.F(X)$ satisfies the equation $X = F(X)$ and is the least such solution.

Theorem 17.20 *Let $\{X_i\}$ be a family of p-languages defined by $X_{n+1} = A + B.X_n$, where $+$ is simple pointwise addition in $\mathcal{R}$. Then, $X_n = B^n.X_0 + \sum_{i \leq n-1} B^i.A$ If $.$ is replaced by $\circ$ uniformly, then the result holds.*

Proof: Using induction on n.

∎

Example 17.21 Let us consider the p-language defined by the following equation:
$X = K +_e X$. Then $X = \bigsqcup (K+_e)^i(I)$. We define $X_n = \bigsqcup_{i \leq n} (K+_e)^i(I)$. We list first few
X_n's.
$X_0 = I$
$X_1 = K +_e I$
$X_2 = K +_e (K +_e I)$
$X_{j+1} = K +_e X_j$
$X_{j+1} = eK + \hat{e}X_j$
Thus, $X_j = (eK)^j + \sum_{i \leq n-1} \hat{e}^i eK$ (using Proposition 17.20). Then, $X_* = \lim_{j \to \infty} X_j$.
We first consider the case when $e = 1$. Then, all X_j except X_0 are K. Therefore,
$X_* = K$. When $e = 0$, then $X_* = I$. When $0 < e < 1$, the above-mentioned expression in limit reduces to
$X_* = (\Sigma_i \hat{e}^i)eK$
$= (1/(1 - \hat{e}))eK$
$= (1/e)eK = K$

Example 17.22 Consider the p-language defined by the following equation:
$X = K._e X$. If $e = 0$, then $X = K$. We now assume that $e > 0$.
Then $X = \bigsqcup (K._e)^i(I)$. We define $X_n = \bigsqcup_{i \leq n} (K._e)^i(I)$. We list first few X_n's.
$X_0 = I$
$X_1 = K._e I$
$X_2 = K._e(K._e I)$
$X_{j+1} = K._e X_j$
$X_{j+1} = K - eC + eC \circ X_j$
We use the following notation:

$$D(l, u) = \sum_{i=l}^{i=u} e^i C^{(i)}$$

$$D(j) = \sum_{i \geq j} e^i C^{(i)}$$

Thus, $X_j = e^j C^j + D(0, j - 1) \circ (K - eC)$
$= e^j C^j + D(0, j - 1) \circ K - D(1, j)$
$= D(0, j - 1) \circ K - D(1, j - 1)$
Thus, $X^* = D(0) \circ K - D(1)$
We will use this as the definition of repeated concatenation. This operator captures repetition of any system. Given any p-language L and a real number e between 0 and 1, the combined system is denoted by $L^{*e}(s)$ for e in $[0, 1]$.

Definition 17.23 $L^{*e}(s) = \sum_n e^n C^{(n)} \circ L(s) - \sum_{i \geq 1} e^i C^{(i)}(s)$
$= D(0) \circ L - D(1)$

The interpretation of the above-mentioned definition is— do L and then repeat it with probability e.

Consider a process of tossing a coin which is repeated till the result of the toss is a head. Assuming that the tail comes with probability e, this system can be modeled

as follows:
$A = \{toss\}$
$L(\epsilon) = 1, L(toss) = 1, L(s) = 0$ for other s.
Then, our system is just repeated concatenation of L. For the primitive function, completion pdf is given by $C(toss) = 1, C(s) = 0$ for other s. By using formulas for convolution, we obtain that $C^{(k)}(s) = 1$ only for $s = toss.toss.toss...k\ times$. Thus, $L^{*e}(toss^k) = e^{k-1} + e^k - e^k = e^{k-1}$ for $k \geq 1$ by Definition 17.23. This expression can be verified by calculating it directly from the problem.

17.4   PROBLEMS

17.1. Let $(X, \leq)$ be a complete lattice. A function $f : X \to X$ is said to be *disjunctive* if

$$\forall Y \subseteq X : f(\sqcup_{y \in Y} Y) = \sqcup_{y \in Y} f(y);$$

it is said to be *conjunctive* if

$$\forall Y \subseteq X : f(\sqcap_{y \in Y} Y) = \sqcap_{y \in Y} f(y);$$

it is said to be *sup-continuous* if

$$\forall \text{ increasing chain } \{y_i, i \geq 0\} \subseteq X : f(\sqcup_{i \geq 0} y_i) = \sqcup_{i \geq 0} f(y_i);$$

it is said to be *inf-continuous* if

$$\forall \text{ decreasing chain } \{y_i, i \geq 0\} \subseteq X : f(\sqcap_{i \geq 0} y_i) = \sqcap_{i \geq 0} f(y_i).$$

Prove that disjunctivity, conjunctivity, sup-continuity, and inf-continuity of f each imply monotonicity of f.

17.2. Consider the complete lattice $(X, \leq)$, where

$$X = \{a, b, c, d\}; \quad \leq\ = \{(a, b), (a, c), (b, d), (c, d), (a, d)\}.$$

Let $f : X \to X$ be defined as $f(a) = f(b) = f(c) = d$ and $f(d) = d$.
(a) Draw the Hasse diagram for the poset $(X, \leq)$.
(b) Determine whether f is disjunctive or conjunctive.

17.3. Let $(X, \leq)$ be a complete lattice and $f : X \to X$ be a function. f is said to be *increasing* if $x \leq f(x), \forall x \in X$; it is said to be *decreasing* if $f(x) \leq x, \forall x \in X$.
(a) Prove that f^* is increasing and idempotent; and f_* is decreasing, idempotent.
(b) If f is monotone (respectively, disjunctive), then show that f^* is monotone (respectively, disjunctive).
(c) If f is monotone (respectively, conjunctive), then show that f_* is monotone (respectively, conjunctive).

17.4. Let $(X, \leq)$ be a complete lattice and $f : X \to X$ be a monotone function. Show that the set of fixed points of f is also a complete lattice.

17.5. Let $(X, \leq)$ be a complete lattice and $f : X \to X$ be a monotone function. Prove that $\sup\{x \in X \mid f(x) = x\} = \sup\{x \in X \mid x \leq f(x)\}$.

17.6. Let $(X, \leq)$ be a complete lattice and $f : X \to X$ be an inf-continuous function. Prove that $f_*(\sup X)$ is the supremal fixed point of f.

17.7. Show that the convolution operator defined on p-languages is associative with p-language I as its identity.

17.8. Compute the completion probability function for repeated concatenation, i.e., compute $C^{*e} = L^{*e} - \Lambda(L^{*e})$.

17.5 BIBLIOGRAPHIC REMARKS

One of the early results on existence of fixed points of a monotone function is due to Knaster–Tarski [Tar55]. Lassez—Nguyen–Sonenberg [LNS82] provide a nice historical account of this and other fixed point theorems. The discussion of p-languages is taken from Garg [Gar92].

BIBLIOGRAPHY

[AG05] A. Agarwal and V. K. Garg. Efficient dependency tracking for relevant events in shared-memory systems. In M. K. Aguilera and J. Aspnes, editors, *Proceedings of the Twenty-Fourth Annual ACM Symposium on Principles of Distributed Computing, PODC 2005*, Las Vegas, NV, July 17-20, 2005, pages 19–28. ACM, 2005.

[AGO10] A. Agarwal, V. K. Garg, and V. A. Ogale. Modeling and analyzing periodic distributed computations. In S. Dolev, J. A. Cobb, M. J. Fischer, and M. Yung, editors, *Stabilization, Safety, and Security of Distributed Systems - 12th International Symposium, SSS 2010*, New York, NY, September 20-22, 2010. Proceedings, volume 6366 of *Lecture Notes in Computer Science*, pages 191–205. Springer, 2010.

[AV01] S. Alagar and S. Venkatesan. Techniques to tackle state explosion in global predicate detection. *IEEE Transactions on Software Engineering*, 27(8):704–714, 2001.

[Bir40] G. Birkhoff. *Lattice Theory*. Providence, RI, 1940. First edition.

[Bir48] G. Birkhoff. *Lattice Theory*. Providence, RI, 1948. Second edition.

[Bir67] G. Birkhoff. *Lattice Theory*. Providence, RI, 1967. Third edition.

[Bog93] K. P. Bogart. An obvious proof of fishburn's interval order theorem. *Discrete Mathematics*, 118(1):21–23, 1993.

[BFK+12] B. Bosek, S. Felsner, K. Kloch, T. Krawczyk, G. Matecki, and P. Micek. On-line chain partitions of orders: a survey. *Order*, 29:49–73, 2012. DOI: 10.1007/s11083-011-9197-1.

[CLM12] N. Caspard, B. Leclerc, and B. Monjardet. *Finite Ordered Sets: Concepts, Results and Uses*, volume 144. Cambridge University Press, 2012.

Introduction to Lattice Theory with Computer Science Applications, First Edition. Vijay K. Garg.
© 2015 John Wiley & Sons, Inc. Published 2015 by John Wiley & Sons, Inc.

[CG06] A. Chakraborty and V. K. Garg. On reducing the global state graph for verification of distributed computations. In *International Workshop on Microprocessor Test and Verification (MTV'06)*, Austin, TX, December 2006.

[CG95] C. Chase and V. K. Garg. On techniques and their limitations for the global predicate detection problem. In *Proceedings of the Workshop on Distributed Algorithms*, pages 303–317, France, September 1995.

[CG98] C. M. Chase and V. K. Garg. Detection of global predicates: techniques and their limitations. *Distributed Computing*, 11(4):191–201, 1998.

[CM91] R. Cooper and K. Marzullo. Consistent detection of global predicates. In *Proceedings of the Workshop on Parallel and Distributed Debuyyiny*, pages 163–173, Santa Cruz, CA, May 1991.

[CLRS01] T. H. Cormen, C. E. Leiserson, R. L. Rivest, and C. Stein. *Introduction to Algorithms*. The MIT Press and McGraw-Hill, 2001. Second edition.

[DP90] B. A. Davey and H. A. Priestley. *Introduction to Lattices and Order*. Cambridge University Press, Cambridge, UK, 1990.

[DS90] E. W. Dijkstra and C. S. Scholten. *Predicate Calculus and Program Semantics*. Springer-Verlag New York Inc., New York, 1990.

[Dil50] R. P. Dilworth. A decomposition theorem for partially ordered sets. *Annals of Mathematics*, 51:161–166, 1950.

[DM41] B. Dushnik and E. Miller. Partially ordered sets. *American Journal of Mathematics*, 63:600–610, 1941.

[Ege31] E. Egervary. On combinatorial properties of matrices. *Matematikai Lapok*, 38:16–28, 1931.

[ER03] S. Effler and F. Ruskey. A CAT algorithm for generating permutations with a fixed number of inversions. *Information Processing Letters*, 86(2), 107–112, (2003).

[FLST86] U. Faigle, L. Lovász, R. Schrader, and Gy. Turán. Searching in trees, series-parallel and interval orders. *SIAM Journal on Computing*, 15(4):1075–1084, 1986.

[Fel97] S. Felsner. On-line chain paritions of orders. *Theoretical Computer Science*, 175: 283–292, 1997.

[Fid89] C. J. Fidge. Partial orders for parallel debugging. *Proceedings of the ACM SIGPLAN/SIGOPS Workshop on Parallel and Distributed Debugging, (ACM SIGPLAN Notices)*, 24(1):183–194, 1989.

[Fis85] P. C. Fishburn. *Interval Orders and Interval Graphs*. John Wiley and Sons, 1985.

[FJN96] R. Freese, J. Jaroslav, and J. B. Nation. *Free Lattices*. American Mathematical Society, 1996.

[Ful56] D. R. Fulkerson. Note on dilworth's decomposition theorem for partially ordered sets. *Proceedings of the American Mathematical Society*, 7(4):701–702, 1956.

[Gal94] F. Galvin. A proof of dilworth's chain decomposition theorem. *American Mathematical Monthly*, 101(4):352–353, 1994.

[GR91] B. Ganter and K. Reuter. Finding all closed sets: a general approach. *Order*, 8(3):283–290, 1991.

[Gar92] V. K. Garg. An algebraic approach to modeling probabilistic discrete event systems. In *Decision and Control, 1992, Proceedings of the 31st IEEE Conference on*, pages 2348–2353. IEEE, 1992.

[Gar03] V. K. Garg. Enumerating global states of a distributed computation. In *International Conference on Parallel and Distributed Computing and Systems*, pages 134–139, November 2003.

[Gar06] V. K. Garg. Algorithmic combinatorics based on slicing posets. *Theoretical Computer Science*, 359(1-3):200–213, 2006.

[Gar12] V. K. Garg. Lattice completion algorithms for distributed computations. In *Proceedings of Principles of Distributed Systems, 16th International Conference, OPODIS 2012*, Rome, Italy, December 18-20, 2012. pages 166–180, December 2012.

[Gar13] V. K. Garg. Maximal antichain lattice algorithms for distributed computations. In D. Frey, M. Raynal, S. Sarkar, R. K. Shyamasundar, and P. Sinha, editors, *ICDCN*, volume 7730 of *Lecture Notes in Computer Science, pages 240–254. Springer, 2013*.

[Gar14] V. K. Garg. Lexical enumeration of combinatorial structures by enumerating order ideals. Technical report, University of Texas at Austin, Dept. of Electrical and Computer Engineering, Austin, TX, 2014.

[GM01] V. K. Garg and N. Mittal. On slicing a distributed computation. In *21st International Conference on Distributed Computing Systems (ICDCS' 01)*, pages 322–329, Washington - Brussels - Tokyo, April 2001. IEEE.

[GS01] V. K. Garg and C. Skawratananond. String realizers of posets with applications to distributed computing. In *20th Annual ACM Symposium on Principles of Distributed Computing (PODC-00)*, pages 72–80. ACM, August 2001.

[Grä71] G. Grätzer. *Lattice Theory*. W.H. Freeman and Company, San Francisco, CA, 1971.

[Grä03] G. Grätzer. *General Lattice Theory*. Birkhäuser, Basel, 2003.

[HM84] J.Y. Halpern and Y. Moses. Knowledge and common knowledge in a distributed environment. In *Proceedings of the ACM Symposium on Principles of Distributed Computing*, pages 50–61, Vancouver, BC, 1984.

[Hir55] T. Hiraguchi. On the dimension of orders. *Science Reports of Kanazawa University*, 4:1–20, 1955.

[HK71] J. E. Hopcroft and R. M. Karp. A $n^{5/2}$ algorithm for maximum matchings in bipartite. In *Switching and Automata Theory, 1971, 12th Annual Symposium on*, pages 122 –125, October 1971.

[IG06] S. Ikiz and V. K. Garg. Efficient incremental optimal chain partition of distributed program traces. In *ICDCS*, page 18. IEEE Computer Society, 2006.

[JRJ94] G.-V. Jourdan, J.-X. Rampon, and C. Jard. Computing on-line the lattice of maximal antichains of posets. *Order*, 11:197–210, 1994. DOI: 10.1007/BF02115811.

[Kie81] H. A. Kierstead. Recursive colorings of highly recursive graphs. *Canadian Journal of Mathematics*, 33(6):1279–1290, 1981.

[Knu98] D. E. Knuth. *Sorting and searching*, volume 3 of *The Art of Computer Programming*. Addison-Wesley, Reading, MA, Second edition, 1998.

[Koh83] K. M. Koh. On the lattice of maximum-sized antichains of a finite poset. *Algebra Universalis*, 17(1):73–86, 1983.

[Kon31] D. Konig. Graphen und matrizen. *Matematikai és Fizikai Lapok*, 38:116–119, 1931.

[Lam78] L. Lamport. Time, clocks, and the ordering of events in a distributed system. *Communications of the ACM*, 21(7):558–565, 1978.

[LNS82] J.-L. Lassez, V. L. Nguyen, and E. A. Sonenberg. Fixed point theorems and semantics: a folk tale. *Information Processing Letters*, 14(3):112–116, 1982.

[Mat89] F. Mattern. Virtual time and global states of distributed systems. In *Proceedings of the International Workshop on Parallel and Distributed Algorithms*, pages 215–226, 1989.

[Mir71] L. Mirsky. A dual of dilworth's decomposition theorem. *American Mathematical Monthly*, 78(8):876–877, 1971.

[MG01a] N. Mittal and V. K. Garg. On detecting global predicates in distributed computations. In *21st International Conference on Distributed Computing Systems (ICDCS' 01)*, pages 3–10, Washington - Brussels - Tokyo, April 2001. IEEE.

[MG01b] N. Mittal and V. K. Garg. Slicing a distributed computation: Techniques and theory. In *5th International Symposium on DIstributed Computing (DISC'01)*, October 2001.

[MG04] N. Mittal and V. K. Garg. Rectangles are better than chains for encoding partially ordered sets. Technical report, University of Texas at Austin, Dept. of Electrical and Computer Engineering, Austin, TX, September 2004.

[MSG07] N. Mittal, A. Sen, and V. K. Garg. Solving computation slicing using predicate detection. *IEEE Transactions on Parallel and Distributed Systems*, 18(12):1700–1713, 2007.

[Moh89] R. H. Mohring. Computationally tractable classes of ordered sets. *Algorithms and Order*, pages 105–192. Kluwer Academic Publishers, Dordrecht, 1989.

[NR99] L. Nourine and O. Raynaud. A fast algorithm for building lattices. *Information Processing Letters*, 71(5-6):199–204, 1999.

[NR02] L. Nourine and O. Raynaud. A fast incremental algorithm for building lattices. *Journal of Experimental & Theoretical Artificial Intelligence*, 14(2-3):217–227, 2002.

[RR79] I. Rabinovitch and I. Rival. The rank of a distributive lattice. *Discrete Mathematics*, 25(3):275–279, 1979.

[RT10] O. Raynaud and E. Thierry. The complexity of embedding orders into small products of chains. *Order*, 27:365–381, 2010.

[Rea02] N. Reading. Order dimension, strong bruhat order and lattice properties of posets. *Order*, 19:73–100, 2002.

[Reu91] K. Reuter. The jump number and the lattice of maximal antichains. *Discrete Mathematics*, 88(2â "3):289–307, 1991.

[Rom08] S. Roman. *Lattices and Ordered Sets*. Springer, 2008.

[Spi85] J. Spinrad. On comparability and permutation graphs. *SIAM Journal on Computing*, 14(3):658–670, 1985.

[SW86] D. Stanton and D. White. *Constructive Combinatorics*. Springer-Verlag, 1986.

[Ste84] G. Steiner. Single machine scheduling with precedence constraints of dimension 2. *Mathematics of Operations Research*, 9:248–259, 1984.

[Szp37] E. Szpilrajn. La dimension et la mesure. *Fundamenta Mathematicae*, 28:81–89, 1937.

[Tar55] A. Tarski. A lattice-theoretic fixed point theorem and its applications. *Pacific Journal of Mathematics*, 5:285–309, 1955.

[TG97] A. I. Tomlinson and V. K. Garg. Monitoring functions on global states of distributed programs. *Journal for Parallel and Distributed Computing, 1997. a preliminary version appeared in Proceedings of the ACM Workshop on Parallel and Distributed Debugging*, San Diego, CA, May 1993, pp.21–31.

[Tro92] W. T. Trotter. *Combinatorics and Partially Ordered Sets: Dimension Theory*. The Johns Hopkins University Press, 1992.

[vLW92] J. H. van Lint and R. M. Wilson. *A Course in Combinatorics*. Cambridge University Press, 1992.

[Wes04] D. B. West. *Order and Optimization*. 2004. pre-release version.

INDEX

Introduction to Lattice Theory with Computer Science Applications, First Edition. Vijay K. Garg.
© 2015 John Wiley & Sons, Inc. Published 2015 by John Wiley & Sons, Inc.

upper dissector, 11
upper-holdings, 9

vector clock representation, 20
vertex cover, 34

weak order, 131
well-founded, 5
width, 4

Young's lattice, 13, 124